THE SUPREME COURT BAR

Legal Elites in the

Washington Community

CONSTITUTIONALISM AND DEMOCRACY

KERMIT HALL AND DAVID O'BRIEN, EDITORS

Kevin T. McGuire
*The Supreme Court Bar: Legal Elites
in the Washington Community*

Mark Tushnet, ed.,
*The Warren Court in Historical
and Political Perspective*

THE SUPREME COURT BAR

Legal Elites in the Washington Community

KEVIN T. McGUIRE

UNIVERSITY PRESS OF VIRGINIA

Charlottesville and London

THE UNIVERSITY PRESS OF VIRGINIA

Copyright © 1993 by the Rector and Visitors
of the University of Virginia

FIRST PUBLISHED 1993

Library of Congress Cataloging-in-Publication Data

McGuire, Kevin T.
    The Supreme Court bar : legal elites in the Washington community /
Kevin T. McGuire.
        p.   cm.—(Constitutionalism and democracy)
    Includes bibliographical references and index.
    ISBN 0-8139-1449-3 (cloth)
    1. United States. Supreme Court. 2. Judicial process—United
States. 3. Lawyers—United States—Interviews. 4. Law and
politics. I. Title. II. Series.
KF8742.M34   1993
347.73'26—dc20
[347.30735]   93-3074
                                                                                CIP

PRINTED IN THE UNITED STATES OF AMERICA

FOR NANCY

CONTENTS

FIGURES AND TABLES

Figures

Tables

ACKNOWLEDGMENTS

Many people displayed extraordinary generosity in assisting with this book. The lawyers whom I interviewed freely shared their intimate knowledge of the Supreme Court with candor, good humor, and grace. These were enormously busy professionals who, despite great constraints on their time, opened their doors to me and provided a wealth of information and insight. I can scarcely imagine a more helpful set of interview subjects. Although their identities are concealed, my appreciation is not.

At various stages in the development of this project, a number of individuals contributed valuable scholarly advice. Lawrence Baum, Paul Allen Beck, and Elliot Slotnick gave me tremendous guidance from start to finish. Special thanks are extended to Gregory A. Caldeira, whose keen eye and sage counsel were always on target and unfailingly beneficial. Lee Epstein, Virginia Gray, Samuel Krislov, David M. O'Brien, W. Phillips Shively, and Frank Sorauf offered scrupulously detailed and penetrating analyses. Steven S. Smith was a patient and supportive sounding board for many of my ideas. John A. Clark was, as always, a constructive critic and an encouraging friend.

Frequently, my needs were technical in nature. Here, James Ludwig contributed his exhaustive knowledge of computer programming, and Charles E. Smith, Jr., served as a great source of assistance on issues of statistical method. In Washington, D.C., Lawrence C. Trochlil furnished inestimable support. When additional data were needed, a number of my undergraduate students cheerfully volunteered to aid in their collection.

I am indebted as well to Richard Holway, of the University Press of Virginia, for his commitment to this project, and to Pamela MacFarland Holway, who not only copyedited the manuscript with an attention to detail greater than anyone has a right to expect but suggested a wealth of substantive, stylistic, and structural improvements. I will long remain grateful for her critical intelligence, dedication, and good cheer.

Finally, I owe a good deal of my intellectual inspiration to Robert E. DiClerico, John Patrick Hagan, and John R. Williams. Sadly, the latter two must accept my gratitude posthumously.

I hope that this book reflects the many contributions of all these individuals and the extent to which I am in their debt.

THE SUPREME COURT BAR

Legal Elites in the

Washington Community

1

Introduction

Allan P. Bakke, a thirty-three-year-old NASA engineer, wanted to attend the medical school at the University of California at Davis. He had taken the Medical College Admissions Test and had scored in the top 10 percent in three areas: scientific knowledge, verbal ability, and mathematics. His academic record was sound, and he was considered to be "a very desirable applicant" following an interview by a medical college faculty member. Bakke applied in both 1973 and 1974 for admission. He was rejected both times.

The Cal-Davis medical school maintained a special admission program designed to ensure that minorities would be represented in the medical class. Under this program, sixteen of the school's one hundred first-year-class positions were designated for "economically and educationally disadvantaged" applicants, such as blacks, Hispanics, and native Americans. Applicants who applied under this program did not have to meet the minimum 2.5 grade point average otherwise considered an essential requirement for admission. As a result of applying different criteria for minorities, Cal-Davis accepted several applicants whose academic records were considerably inferior to that of Bakke, who was white.

Following his second rejection, Bakke decided to sue the university for admission to the medical school on the grounds that he had been denied a position in the entering class on account of his race. Bakke sought the assistance of a San Francisco lawyer named Reynold H. Colvin.

Counsel in Contrast

Like most attorneys, Reynold Colvin had never argued a case before the United States Supreme Court. On October 12, 1977, however, he appeared before the justices on behalf of Allan Bakke.[1] Colvin stood ready to argue that the program that denied Bakke admission as a first-year medical student violated Bakke's Fourteenth Amendment rights.

Following the arguments of the counsel for the petitioner, Archibald Cox, and Solicitor General Wade McCree, Chief Justice Warren Burger asked to hear the respondent. "Mr. Colvin," he said simply. As the lawyer approached the podium, the Court prepared to hear the case against affirmative action in what would become a landmark controversy over reverse discrimination. What the justices heard, however, was a painfully detailed recitation of the lower court record, one stubbornly reluctant to address the larger questions of public policy the Court wanted to discuss.

"It seems to me," Colvin began, "that the first thing I ought to say to this Honorable Court is that I am Allan Bakke's lawyer and Allan Bakke is my client." After presenting a brief background on the case, he proceeded to trace the course of his unsuccessful legal efforts on Bakke's behalf: "This is a question of getting Mr. Bakke into the medical school—and that's the name of the game, and we have to do that in order to be effective as lawyers and we humbly try to be effective as lawyers—[a]nd if you read the record, you will see the frantic efforts we make to get before the Court. And we tried to get before the Court on a question of injunction, on a question of andemus [*sic*], on a question of declaratory relief, each of them moving the thing forward on the calendar."

At that point, Justice William H. Rehnquist interrupted: "But no one is charging you with laches [legal neglect] here, Mr. Colvin." Rehnquist's joke brought a chorus of laughter from the courtroom. Colvin, however, doggedly pressed on, detailing the facts of the case for the justices despite repeated invitations to comment on the merits of the reverse discrimination issue. "But look at the record in the case. Look at the record in the case," Colvin persisted, as he went on to discuss measures of central tendency for the percentile scores on the Medical College Aptitude Test for various applicants to the University of California at Davis.

Justice Byron R. White, trying to move the discussion along to the heart of the case, attempted to simplify the basic issue at stake for Colvin. White asked Colvin whether "you need to go any farther than to assert . . . that he was deprived an opportunity to compete . . . because of his race. Do you need to go any farther than that? If you don't . . . you certainly are taking up a lot of your time." Colvin responded by pointing out that "there is within this record the stipulation . . . that Mr. Bakke was deprived of the opportunity to attend the University of California Medical School at Davis because of the use of the sixteen places by the special admissions program."

Finally, Justice Lewis F. Powell, Jr., broke in impatiently. "[T]he University doesn't deny or dispute the basic facts. They are perfectly clear. We are here—at least I am here—primarily to hear a constitutional argument. You have devoted twenty minutes to laboring a fact, if I may say so. I would like help, I really would, on the constitutional issues. Would you address that, please?"

In the Supreme Court, lawyers have thirty minutes to present their cases. Reynold Colvin had devoted most of those few short minutes to a recitation of the transcript of record, all of which was already available to the Court. What should have been a broad, policy-oriented discussion of the implications of affirmative action was reduced to mere description.

One alumnus of the solicitor general's office suggested that Colvin's opening statement, "I am Allan Bakke's lawyer, and Allan Bakke is my client," was potentially brilliant:

> It was such a great beginning, because it kind of reminded the Court that you couldn't decide these great issues without having actual real-life people involved—except he continued that way. . . . He couldn't be stopped. He went on blathering about what had happened in the lower court and all these things that didn't go to the nature of the really broad, overarching issue in

the case. To cede the precious argument time to somebody who really didn't have a good fix on what the issues were is a kind of a waste of that resource. (Confidential Interview; hereafter, CI)[2]

Yet Reynold Colvin was a good attorney. He had attended Boalt Hall Law School at the University of California at Berkeley and had served for several years as an assistant United States attorney before becoming a private practitioner in San Francisco. The Martindale-Hubbell national lawyer directory, which rates practitioners, had given Colvin its highest recommendation in 1970. He was not, however, a seasoned appellate practitioner with experience before the high court.[3] As the same former member of the Office of the Solicitor General noted, the Court "actually had to tell him to turn around and stop arguing to what sort of looks like a jury box. It's where the press sits. He was so used to arguing to the jury that he turned away from the Court and kept arguing sideways." The transcript of the proceedings preserves this exchange. Chief Justice Burger reminded the attorney, "Mr. Colvin, don't get too far away from the microphone, if you want to stay on the record," to which Colvin replied, "I am sorry. I sometimes think of it as a retreat."

The opposing counsel in the Bakke case was, in contrast, hardly a novice in the Supreme Court. Archibald Cox, professor of law at Harvard University and a former solicitor general of the United States appointed by President Kennedy, had numerous arguments in the Supreme Court to his credit. He appeared before the justices relaxed, conversational, and confident, "with the full assurance of a man among his peers" (Dreyfuss and Lawrence 1979, 177). Cox's argument distilled the essential issues, and his statement went straight to the heart of the California program, a desire to increase the number of minority doctors in the state. Sketching only what he felt were the crucial facts, Cox forcefully articulated for the justices the merits of the University of California's objective as it was reflected in the school's admissions program. Like Colvin, Cox had been pressed hard by the justices, but his presentation was deft nonetheless. Ultimately, the Court struck down the university's quota system but permitted such factors as race to be considered relevant to admissions.[4]

Cases in the Supreme Court often serve as vehicles for resolving social problems. In articulating their clients' interests, lawyers thus help to shape public policy. As the case of *Regents v. Bakke* dramatizes, though, there is a marked dissimilarity in the quality and effectiveness of legal representation in the Supreme Court. This in turn raises some general questions about the role of lawyers in the politics of the Court. Why, in the nation's highest court where landmark cases with far-reaching policy implications are decided, does such disparity exist, and what implications does that disparity have for how those issues are considered by the Court?

The general thesis that frames the answers to these questions is that there is an elite circle of lawyers—principal players within the Washington community—who serve as gatekeepers to the Court. Fueled by factors such as the specialization of the legal profession, the increased reliance upon Washington-based representatives for governmental advocacy, and the unique demands of litigating before the justices, these lawyers have become influential actors in the politics of the high court. These elite counsel—experienced Supreme Court practitioners, former clerks to the justices, alumni of the Office of the Solicitor General, partners in the large Washington law firms—are in constant demand among powerful and advantaged parties seeking access to the Court. These sophisticated clients, such as the wealthy, large organizations, and major corporations, retain members of this inner circle (Archibald Cox, for example) to handle their litigation in the Court; the unseasoned turn to the outer circle of advocates (Reynold Colvin, for example) for representation, those with virtually no knowledge of or experience in Supreme Court practice. Just as high-powered lobbyists are part and parcel of congressional committees and administrative agencies, the inner circle of lawyers are the gatekeepers of the Supreme Court.

Some Notes on Method

What is the relationship between the inner and outer circles of the bar and the politics of the Supreme Court? This book is directed toward developing an understanding of the Supreme Court bar and its connection to the broad range of activities associated with the Court's litigation. As many readers are undoubtedly aware, lawyers bring literally thousands of cases to the Supreme Court every year. Most of these are cases in which a party, having exhausted all other avenues of judicial redress, petitions the justices for a writ of certiorari, that is, asks the Court to review the decision of a lower appellate court. The Court, however, has broad discretion in setting its agenda, and the justices ultimately decide to consider only a tiny fraction of those filings. Once the Court agrees to decide a case on the merits, lawyers for both parties prepare written briefs for the justices and then appear before the Court in oral argument. Generally speaking, then, lawyers in the Supreme Court are active at two stages in the Court's decision making. The first is the case selection stage, when lawyers either seek or oppose review of lower court decisions. At the second stage, the justices make decisions on the merits of cases, based on briefs that have been filed and on oral arguments. In both instances, the information that reaches the Court is filtered through members of the bar, and for that reason these gatekeepers are subjects worthy of our attention.

Supreme Court Lawyers Defined

Who are these Supreme Court lawyers? It is important for the reader to understand some basic terminology that will be employed throughout the book. In general, I use the terms *Supreme Court lawyers* and *Supreme Court bar* to refer to lawyers who have been admitted to practice in the Supreme Court and who have had some occasion to participate in the Court's litigation at either the case selection stage or at the merits stage. This is a somewhat narrow definition, in that I am restricting my focus to the *active* Supreme Court bar: many attorneys are officially members of the Supreme Court bar but have never served as counsel in a Supreme Court case. Narrow or not, however, this definition embraces a wide variety of counsel, including private practitioners, state and local government attorneys, corporate counsel, and interest group litigators. The involvement of some may be limited to having sought or opposed certiorari in but a single case. Others may have had more extensive experience, arguing in some cases, serving as counsel on the merits briefs in others.

This definition has several advantages. First, it is both clear and specific. That is, it refers to an identifiable group of lawyers, active at some point in Supreme Court litigation. Second, it is of sufficient breadth to ensure coverage of the full scope of the lawyer's role. Indeed, it is imperative that our conception of a Supreme Court lawyer not be *overly* narrow, because much of what Supreme Court lawyers do often lurks beneath the surface of the more visible facets of litigation. By focusing our attention exclusively on, say, those lawyers who make oral arguments in the Court, we would exclude a fair number of attorneys whose participation in Supreme Court cases is quite significant.

Of course, there are differences among Supreme Court counsel, and our perspective on the Court's lawyers ought to take such differences into account. Perhaps the most illuminating criterion for delineating lawyers is the extent of their involvement in the Court's docket. Some Supreme Court lawyers, for example, have extensive and dramatic experience before the Court, whereas others have only the briefest of encounters. Accordingly, I distinguish between "frequent" and "infrequent" members of the bar. I often use terms such as the *elite community* and the *inner circle* to refer to the experienced lawyers; phrases such as *peripheral practitioners* and the *outer circle* are used for the remainder of the Supreme Court litigators. What distinguishes the two is that the latter participate seldom, while the former participate frequently.

The solicitor general. This analysis will be centrally concerned with the growing reliance upon specialized representatives—primarily private representatives—within the legal community in the District of Columbia. My definition of the Supreme Court bar includes one lawyer (or, more precisely, group of lawyers) who of necessity frequently appears as counsel in the Supreme Court: the solicitor general of the United States. For the most part, this lawyer is not a primary focus of my argument.

Inasmuch as the solicitor general represents the United States before the justices, he has a special working relationship with the Court (Caplan 1987; Provine 1980; Segal and Reedy 1988). On the one hand, the solicitor general is a member of the Court's bar, as are many lawyers. On the other hand, because his office has such a close connection to the Court, the solicitor general is unlike other Supreme Court advocates. To give systematic attention to the solicitor general within the context of an analysis of Supreme Court counsel is clearly an important task, but one that would demand a separate volume.

That scholars have already devoted much attention to the role of the solicitor general's office to some extent justifies the focus of this study on other Supreme Court practitioners, particularly those within the Washington community. A discussion of the Supreme Court bar, however, cannot utterly ignore some of its most significant members. When necessary, I will therefore invoke the solicitor general and his staff as points of reference, for example, in analyzing the community of Supreme Court lawyers and the nature of influence within it. In general, however, the solicitor general will remain ancillary to this inquiry.

It is, of course, the job of the solicitor general to prepare briefs for and argue in the Supreme Court. Yet those lawyers whose practice takes them to the Court only infrequently, whose primary legal work lies elsewhere, constitute the vast majority of the Court's bar. The present investigation will accordingly focus on such areas as private practice, interest groups, state government, and academia—areas where lawyers, for a variety of reasons, become practitioners in the Supreme Court, even if only on one occasion.

Data

The data I employ in this project have been drawn from four primary sources.

Survey data.   A mail survey was conducted of Supreme Court lawyers who represented both petitioners and respondents in the 1986–87 term of the Court (see Appendix 2). Seeking a cross section reflective of the attorneys active on the Court's paid docket, I drew a systematic random sample of 688 non-federal government lawyers. Of these, 327 returned the questionnaire, a response rate of roughly 48 percent. Fortunately, different groups of lawyers—private practitioners, corporate counsel, and so on—responded in virtually the same proportions in which I sampled them.[5] In light of the survey's rate of response and its apparent representativeness, I rely upon these data as the primary basis for the analysis of the Court's attorneys.

Lawyer interviews.   To provide some context for the quantitative analysis, I bring to bear a second set of data, consisting of a series of nineteen confidential interviews that were conducted with members of the Supreme Court bar. These lawyers had a variety of personal backgrounds, work environments, and experiences with the Court. Some were present or former members of the solicitor general's office; others were in private practice; a number were academics; still others had experience with the Court by virtue of working for interest groups; several were former Supreme Court law clerks. Their experience with the Court was as varied as their backgrounds. Some had been involved in only one or two Supreme Court cases; others had experience in several cases; some had several dozen to their credit.

The sample thus reflects a broad range of Supreme Court practice, but of course this group is not in any sense random or representative. The interviews tended to favor Washington-based private practitioners with considerable experience in the Supreme Court. While their perspectives were extremely valuable, they were also quite distinctive. When it is a question of characterizing the Supreme Court bar at large, I have tried to ensure that my reliance upon the insights of the Washington-based attorneys is tempered by the comments of lawyers outside of Washington who have less experience in the Court as well as by the quantitative data.

Archival data. In the analysis to follow, I also draw on an additional set of data: information on the lawyers who participated in more than one case on the merits from the 1977 through the 1982 terms of the Court. This information was collected from the *United States Reports* and *Briefs and Records of the United States Supreme Court* for the 1977 to 1982 terms and from various editions of the *Martindale-Hubbell Law Directory.* The data include the frequency and the nature of lawyers' participation in cases on the merits, as well as a number of demographic attributes such as age, legal education, and work environment.

Secondary data. I have also employed data from petitions for certiorari submitted during the 1982 term of the Court. These data were derived from the "Project on Organized Interests and the United States Supreme Court," a National Science Foundation research effort conducted principally by Gregory A. Caldeira of Ohio State University and John R. Wright of George Washington University. They include a number of variables relevant to the Court's selection of cases: disagreement among lower courts, dissent in lower courts, allegations of conflict, and the presence of amicus briefs, to name but a few. For the petitioners' counsel, I also collected additional data on their experience in the Supreme Court. I then used these data to develop a predictive model of the Court's agenda setting. Finally, from the *United States Reports* I have gathered data on the lawyers who participated in orally argued cases from the 1977 to 1982 terms of the Court. In examining the relationship between the experience of lawyers and decisions at the merits stage, I have used this information in conjunction with data drawn from the *United States Supreme Court Judicial Data Base,* Harold J. Spaeth, principal investigator.

Scope of the Study

Taken together, these data provide a powerful resource from which insights can be drawn regarding the politics of representation in the modern Supreme Court as well as its relationship to the historical bar of the Court. To that end, chapter 2 highlights the historical significance of the nineteenth-century Supreme Court bar. It focuses on the collegial nature of the early Court litigators and their relationship to the justices, tracing in addition the decline of the insular, Washington-based bar. Chapter 3 examines the elite character of the modern-day Supreme Court bar. It compares the lawyers who practice before the Court with the legal profession overall in the United States. Importantly, this chapter shows that distinct lines of stratification exist within the Court's bar, lines that draw a picture of a community of elites. These social differences translate into inequalities in representation in the Court.

Chapter 4 broadens the analysis to the legal practice of the Supreme Court bar and how it relates to litigation in the Court. The outer circle of lawyers has only fleeting encounters with Supreme Court practice; the inner circle has continuous and consistent contact. Why are some lawyers drawn into the circle of active elites while others are not? The answer lies in the common threads that run between the legal work of some lawyers and the character of litigation in the Court. By identifying some distinguishing features of Supreme Court practice, the chapter explains why corporate and appellate lawyers are the dominant members of the elite community within the Supreme Court bar.

Chapter 5 takes up the issue of when and how the inner circle and their cases are brought together. In particular, this chapter demonstrates the process whereby sophisticated litigants turn to the veteran litigators—the Supreme Court specialists—as their cases wend their way to the Court. Chapter 6 then considers this inner circle in the context of Supreme Court litigation. It examines the ostensible work of the Supreme Court lawyers: arguing before the justices, petitioning the Court, opposing review of lower court decisions. In addition, it focuses on the less visible, yet crucial, tactics of the experienced bar, such as filing amicus briefs, helping colleagues prepare certiorari petitions, and evaluating the briefs and arguments of their peers. This chapter also addresses some of the strategic politics of Supreme Court practice. Using amicus curiae briefs as an example, it discusses how the elite mobilize organized interests to help secure access to the Court's agenda.

Using professional interactions, backgrounds, and reputations, chapter 7 analyzes the social structure of the central community of expert counsel—the circle of lawyers who are most active as Supreme Court practitioners. These lawyers are fairly well integrated: many practice in Washington, and often they have served as clerks to the justices or worked in the Office of the Solicitor General. These ties are further reinforced by their continued participation in Supreme Court politics. Thus, the sociometric structure of the experienced elite is relatively closed to outsiders; the boundaries of that inner circle are not easily crossed.

As chapter 8 demonstrates, the degree of community among the elite counsel has some important implications for gaining access to the Court. This chapter examines the role of the elite in the justices' decision making as a means of characterizing the specialized bar's political significance. In particular, because of their experience with and proximity to the Court, these lawyers know how to prepare credible, intellectually sound petitions that meet the Court's informational needs while also advocating on the client's behalf. Consequently, the justices place a good deal more trust in their legal analysis and, all other things being equal, give greater weight to their briefs when determining which cases they will grant oral argument. More broadly, this analysis deals with the resurfacing of a modern-day analogue of the early Supreme Court bar: a small community of highly talented lawyers who have a significant impact on the process by which issues and ideas are represented in the United States Supreme Court.

2

The Supreme Court Lawyer

in Historical Perspective

While no judge ever profited more from argument; it is not, perhaps, diverging into the circle of exaggeration to say, that no Bar was ever more capable of aiding the mind of the Bench, than the Bar of the Supreme Court, in the time of Chief Justice Marshall.

—quoted in Charles Warren,
A History of the American Bar

Two hundred years ago, an elite community of lawyers dominated the Supreme Court. Throughout the Marshall Court, "the Supreme Court bar was a small, selective group, with the same attorneys appearing in Washington with regularity" (White 1988, 202). These eminent advocates were the principal players in the politics of the Court. As a prelude to the analysis of the contemporary community of Supreme Court practitioners, it is illuminating to consider the historical role of legal elites in the Court. Understanding these forebears and the reasons for their influence provides a sense of the institutional development of the bar and allows a more keen appreciation of its current inner circle.

The Nineteenth-Century Supreme Court Bar

In *The Washington Community, 1800–1828,* James Sterling Young places the politics of the nation's new capital in broad perspective. During the early years of the republic, he argues, the president and the Congress were the primary focus of power in Washington. The very physical facilities to which the Court was relegated reflected its lack of political prominence. To the extent that the business of the Court did arouse public interest, it seems to have been the lawyers—not the justices or the cases—who drew the greatest attention:

> The place intended for the Supreme Court on the north shore of the Tiber swamp remained unoccupied and undeveloped. Probably the expense of clearing the area, covered with brambles where it was not sunk in bogs, was considered unwarranted by the small size of the court establishment and the small volume of business handled by the judges during their brief stay in Washington each year. The court made itself inconspicuous and served justice in the basement of the Capitol. . . . The proceedings of the court attracted, on the whole, only slight attention in the capital except when lawyers of wide repute were arguing cases, and "the moment they sat down, the whole audience arose, and broke up, as if the court had adjourn'd." (Young 1966, 76)

This "unoccupied and undeveloped" quality was not unique to the Court; indeed, it was endemic to life in Washington in the early part of the nineteenth century. Recall that the capital of the young nation was not chosen from among existing cities. Rather, Washington was initially nothing more than a hundred square miles of land ceded by the Potomac states of Maryland and Virginia and consisting largely of unpleasant marshes, within which the capital community was to be established. The undeveloped city posed tremendous obstacles for the would-be traveler. As one observer ruefully remarked, "the discomforts, and dangers even, of the journeys to Washington from Boston [were] things to remember to the end of a long life."[1]

Importantly, Washington's lack of infrastructure and the absence of efficient modes of travel made propinquity the primary determinant of representation before the bench. "For these reasons," writes Charles Warren (1939, 256), "the cases before the Supreme Court were, as a rule, argued by counsel who could make the journey thither with the least difficulty; consequently the Pennsylvania, Maryland, and Virginia Bars had a practical monopoly."[2] Because travel to the District of Columbia was so problematic, the lawyers who practiced before the Court tended to hail either from Washington itself or from nearby cities such as Baltimore and Philadelphia (White 1988, 202). One account of the early federal bar notes that "[p]robably one-fifth to one-fourth of all the cases appearing in the volumes of the reporters, Henry Wheaton and Richard Peters ... were argued by Francis Scott Key, John Law, Thomas Swann, Walter Jones or Richard S. Coxe—all local counsel residing in or about Washington" (Warren 1939, 368).

Examples of the Supreme Court lawyers in the early Washington community abound. Virginia contributed outstanding litigators such as Littleton W. Tazewell, a noted admiralty lawyer, and William Wirt (White 1988, 214–29, 254–67). In private practice and as attorney general of the United States, Wirt amassed an extraordinary measure of Supreme Court advocacy, appearing between 1815 and 1835 as counsel in 170 cases.[3] "He participated in nearly all the great Marshall Court constitutional cases—*Dartmouth College, Sturges v. Crowninshield, McCulloch, Cohens, Gibbons, Ogden v. Saunders, Cherokee Nation,* and *Proprietors of the Charles River Bridge v. Proprietors of the Warren Bridge*—as well as other significant private law cases" (White 1988, 264). Wirt's successor as attorney general was a Marylander, Roger B. Taney, the future chief justice of the Supreme Court (White 1988, 290). From the Maryland bar came other lawyers who developed substantial practices before the Court: Taney's brother-in-law, Francis Scott Key, and Key's uncle, Philip Barton Key (Warren 1939, 261). Likewise, the Baltimore litigator William Pinkney had a great many appearances to his credit, arguing roughly half of the cases during the Court's 1814 term (White 1988, 245).[4]

Some before the high bench were simultaneously litigators and legislators. Daniel Webster's professional life is instructive on this point: "Webster's entry into politics, far from detracting from his legal career, facilitated it. His regular attendance in Washington made him much more accessible to the Supreme Court than the average New England lawyer" (White 1988, 274–75). Since lawyers pursuing political careers resided in Washington during congressional sessions, they were natural candidates for practice in the Supreme Court (see also Frank 1966, 93). Once again, geographical considerations shaped the nature of representation before the high bench.

During this era, oral argument—characterized by appeals to passion as well as reason—was the primary form of advocacy in the Supreme Court. White argues that,

> while the Supreme Court bar was a highly literate stratum of American society and writing a frequent form of activity for both lawyers and Justices, the oral presentation ... was still a major

form of communication in early-nineteenth-century American culture. Oratory was high art; listening to lengthy speeches was an established social and intellectual activity. . . . The effective advocate was one who could infuse his arguments with ethical appeals and who could present particular cases or applications of general principles. The oratorical mode facilitated both tasks. Rhetorical flourishes, in which the advocate made emotional appeals, were tacit reminders that law and ethics could not be separated. (White 1988, 203–4)

In *Dartmouth College v. Woodward* (1819), for example, Daniel Webster made what has become probably the most widely cited statement from a Supreme Court presentation. Arguing that his alma mater's charter, granted by King George III, constituted a contract free from government impairment, Webster addressed Chief Justice John Marshall: "Sir, you may destroy this little institution; it is weak; it is in your hands." Then, he uttered what one historian has called the sentence that "became immortal the instant it left Webster's lips": "It is sir, as I have said, a small college—and yet there are those who love it" (Alexander 1958, 64). William Wirt, another advocate who appeared regularly before the justices, was well known for his eloquence, achieving notoriety as both lawyer and author (White 1988, 254–55). Similarly, William Pinkney, whose attire and comportment during oral arguments earned him the reputation of a fop, was nonetheless an extraordinary advocate before the justices. Chief Justice Marshall once remarked that "Mr. Pinkney was the greatest man I have ever seen in a court of justice" (Warren 1939, 260; see also Ireland 1986; Shapiro 1987; White 1988, 241–54).

The distinctive skill of early advocates such as Webster, Wirt, and Pinkney can be attributed, at least in part, to the number of cases that they argued. Pinkney accumulated eighty-four appearances during his career (see Shapiro 1987; White 1988, 208). Wirt, too, had a substantial practice in the Court, appearing with comparable frequency (Warren 1939, 368), while Webster, with 168 arguments, remains virtually without peer among appellate advocates.[5] All three made arguments in *McCulloch v. Maryland* (1819) (Warren 1939, 379). Their dramatic participation in Supreme Court litigation was, moreover, not all that unusual. It merely magnified a more general tendency among the elite lawyers of the era to appear before the justices on a regular basis.

There can be little doubt that their sustained presence in the Court served to establish these elites as principals in the judicial politics of the new government. These practitioners played a vital role in both the maturation of early constitutional doctrine and the advancement of the Court's political viability. Consider the Marshall Court. Clearly, John Marshall's heady leadership as chief justice helped to develop the Supreme Court's institutional vitality. Still, as Robert McCloskey argues, in order to maintain that vitality the Court needed the support of a constituency. That responsibility largely fell on the shoulders of the Supreme Court's bar.

> An essential element of that constituency, though by no means the whole of it, was the American legal fraternity, or as it has been called in a fine phrase, "the inner republic of bench and bar." In these early days lawyers were already occupying the pivotal position in American political affairs that they have occupied ever since. And they tended to reinforce the Supreme Court, partly no doubt because they represented the affluent "haves" who would profit from the stable, nationalized structure Marshall was building, but partly too because their training had taught them to esteem the rule of law which Marshall and his associates stood for. It was not only that men like William Pinckney [*sic*] and Daniel Webster vindicated Marshallian doctrine with the magic of their oratory in formal argument before the supreme bench; they and their lesser colleagues also helped, in letters, in conversations, in appearances before lower courts, in state legislatures, and in Congress, to generate the atmosphere of consent that made Marshall's achievements possible. (McCloskey 1960, 72–73)

The members of this bar were the legal elites of the Washington community. They were part of the establishment and represented a sophisticated clientele. Moreover, these men were leaders, not only of the bar but in American politics more generally. The impact of this coterie of counsel, therefore, was pervasive, discernible in the Court but extending throughout the governing process as well.

Integrated and cohesive, the Supreme Court bar—the inner republic of bench and bar—flourished during this period. In contrast to the modern bar, the bar of the Court was then an official organization, and meetings of its membership were common, as any cursory perusal of the early reports of the Court will attest.[6] Consequently, a collegial atmosphere prevailed, not only among the lawyers but also between the bar and the justices. When Supreme Court practitioners died, the Court routinely extended its public condolences and eulogized the deceased, whereas today similar obituaries are generally reserved for the justices themselves. When Francis Scott Key passed away, for example, the United States attorney general, Hugh S. Legaré, learned of his death only moments before beginning an argument before the Court. Immediately, he informed the justices of the "very melancholy tidings" and moved that the "Court, in honour of the memory of the deceased, should stand adjourned till to-morrow." Accordingly, the Court suspended its docket for the day. When the Court reconvened the following morning, the session began with an extensive eulogy of Key, given by the attorney general. Walter Jones, another prominent Supreme Court practitioner, conveyed the resolution of regret that had been adopted by a meeting of the Supreme Court bar the previous day. The bar also dispatched a delegation from its membership to attend Key's funeral in Baltimore.[7] One historical account of the early Supreme Court noted that when two noted members of their brethren died in 1817, "it was resolved that the members of the Bar 'will wear crape on the left arm during the present Term, as a mark of respect for the illustrious talents of the deceased in professional and their eminent virtues in private life'" (Warren 1922, 474n).

Of course, not all illustrations of the social bonds among the members of the bar are so somber. Lawyers from Philadelphia who were often before the Court, for instance, found that the frequent passage to Washington served the cause of friendship quite well, as one practitioner, Peter S. DuPonceau, illustrates:

> The counsel engaged in those causes were in the habit of going together to Washington to argue their cases. . . . We hired a stage to ourselves in which we proceeded by easy journies. The Court sat then in the month of February, so that we had to travel in the depth of winter through bad roads in no very comfortable way. Nevertheless, as soon as we were out of the city, and felt the flush of air, we were like school boys in the playground on a holiday.
>
> Flashes of wit shot their corruscations on all sides; puns of the genuine Philadelphia stamp were handed about, old college stories were revived, songs were sung—in short it might have

been taken for anything but the grave counsellors of the celebrated Bar of Philadelphia. (Quoted in Warren 1939, 256)

Within the capital, the pattern of professional propinquity continued. As James Sterling Young has observed, "Members of the different branches of government chose to situate themselves close to the respective centers of power with which they were affiliated, seeking their primary associations in extra-official life among their fellow branch members" (1966, 68). Thus, the lawyers and the justices shared living quarters in the boardinghouses that functioned as social centers for the early Washington government community (Krislov 1965, 53). When Thomas A. Emmet traveled to the capital to argue *Gibbons v. Ogden*, for instance, he shared living quarters with a fellow New York litigator, Charles Glidden Haines, who was then before the Court to argue in the case of *Ogden v. Saunders* (White 1988, 213). In these boardinghouses, interpersonal bonds were both established and strengthened.[8] Other historical evidence suggests the existence of social ties between the Supreme Court bar and the federal government more generally. Commenting on the social habits of the Washington elite, for example, one observer noted that "the dinner-giving system has increased very much. . . . The Court and Bar dine today with the President" (quoted in Warren 1926, 472). Witness also the strong friendship between the prominent counsel Francis Scott Key and Chief Justice John Marshall (Delaplaine 1937, 407).

Even in the twilight years of the Supreme Court bar, the close association between bench and bar remained evident. When after twenty-eight years on the Court, Justice Samuel Nelson resigned in December of 1872, the Supreme Court bar convened and extended a letter of "deep regret," expressing both the bar's sadness at Nelson's resignation and admiration for his contributions to the Court. A month later, from his home in Cooperstown, New York, Nelson posted this response:

> *Gentlemen:*
> Your favor of the 14 ult., inclosing a letter of one hundred and twenty-one distinguished members of the bar of the Supreme Court of the United States relating to my resignation of the office of Associate Justice of that court, has been received.
> I am deeply grateful for the too favorable opinion expressed in my judicial services, and of personal regard and friendship. So general a concurrence of eminent members of the bar, who have

personally witnessed the administration of justice in the court, and who, themselves, largely participated in it, in the expression of a favorable opinion of myself, as a humble member of it, cannot but affect me most sensibly and gratefully. Most of the names are familiar to me, and many of them I recognize as intimate associates and friends; and each and all of them have my earnest prayer that their useful lives may be long and happy.

You, gentlemen, have my hearty thanks for the kind and friendly manner in which you have communicated this ever to be remembered tribute of my professional brethren.

I am, with great respect and regard, your friend,

S. Nelson[9]

The relatively modest social distance between lawyers and justices—their close professional and personal association—was particularly important in that it helped to institutionalize these practitioners as the gatekeepers for the Supreme Court. In consequence of their frequent appearances before the Court, "the seeds of doctrines, and the authorities on which they rested, were planted in Justices' minds by counsel. Decisions evolved when those ideas were combined in discussions at the boardinghouse with views held by the Justices themselves" (White 1988, 291).

Such an integrated organization of attorneys, however, was not long sustained. Travel to Washington improved following the War of 1812, and lawyers from beyond the banks of the Potomac River began to appear regularly before the Court.[10] As the capital became increasingly accessible, Supreme Court practice became an attractive proposition for those who, in the absence of faster, more effective modes of transport, might not have chosen to make the journey to the District of Columbia. A good illustration is contained in Martin Van Buren's invitation to Benjamin F. Butler, the attorney general of New York, to become President Andrew Jackson's attorney general. Trying to convince his former law partner to accept the post, the vice president reasoned:

You can enter upon the business of the Supreme Court of U.S. . . . . [and] attend the higher courts at N. York and Albany. All previous Atty. Genls. who desired it have done so in respect to their own States.

To the former place you will next season be able to go in 15 hours, and to the latter in a day and a night. What then is there

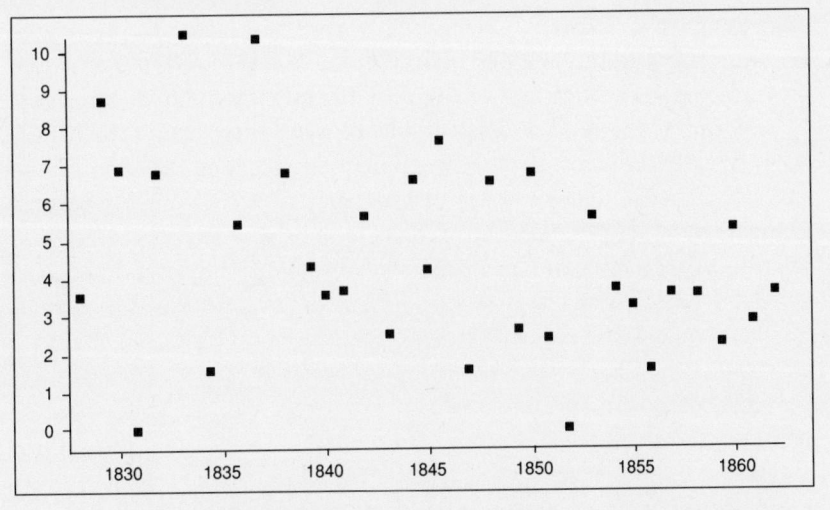

FIGURE 2.1. Percentage of Supreme Court bar admissions from Washington, D.C., 1828–62. Data for 1835 were not available. (*Source: United States Reports*)

to prevent you from [accepting]? Nothing, that I can see. . . . The only exception need be, your visits to N. York during the sittings of the Court, when you can take your family with you, without stopping between this and N.Y—especially when the railroad, the making of which is now under full operation, is completed. (Quoted in Butler 1942, 12)

Modernization therefore had the effect of widening the circle of attorneys to such an extent that an insular bar no longer existed (Frank 1958, 93–94; White 1988, 202; see also Warren 1939, 276). Figure 2.1 shows the declining proportion of admissions to the bar by Washington counsel in the antebellum Supreme Court. During the waning years of the Marshall Court, residents of the federal city accounted for as much as 10 percent of the annual admissions to the Supreme Court bar. Subsequent years, however, witnessed a steady decline in Washington-based practitioners. This trend suggests that when cases came before the justices, rather than refer their business to Washington counsel, lawyers simply sought admission to the Court's bar so that they themselves could represent their clients before the high bench.

Despite the decrease during these years, Washington continued to contribute more lawyers per capita to the Supreme Court bar than any other geographic location. During the early 1800s, over 2,200 new law-yers were admitted to practice in the Court. Of that number, the largest proportions were from New York and Pennsylvania (28 percent and 10 percent, respectively), whereas Washington lawyers constituted roughly 5 percent of new admissions. The capital, however, was sparsely populated and not yet a major legal center (White 1988, 202). Controlling for population, one discovers that New York lawyers were admitted to practice in the Court at the rate of one for every 5,000 people. Pennsylvania's lawyer-to-population ratio during that period was one lawyer per 10,000. Washington, by comparison, boasted ap-proximately one Supreme Court counsel for every 500 persons.[11]

Notwithstanding Washington's generally disproportionate share of newcomers to the bar, the postbellum Court marked the end of the integrated Supreme Court bar. By this time, the insular group of prom-inent attorneys practicing law in and around the nation's capital had been supplanted by a larger, more fluid set of Supreme Court prac-titioners. As will become evident, recent years have witnessed a resur-gence in the social integration of the Court's bar. Although clearly a "Supreme Court bar" in the historical sense no longer exists, there is nonetheless a community of experienced lawyers with strong social ties that can appropriately be considered its modern analogue. Before examining this elite circle systematically, I will sketch its membership and discuss some of the reasons for its development.

The Modern Supreme Court Bar

The address of the United States Supreme Court is One First Street, NE. Today, only a short distance from that site, one can again observe what was true during the Marshall Court: prominent appellate advo-cates—legal elites in the Washington community—locating their prac-tices in close proximity to the Court. Who are these lawyers? They are former members of the solicitor general's staff who now utilize their enormous Supreme Court expertise in private practice. They are for-mer clerks to the justices who have seen the Court from the inside. They are well-educated, talented litigators who work in some of the nation's largest, most prestigious law firms and who represent a so-phisticated clientele in the Court. They are counsel to any number of organized interests that have established offices throughout the neigh-boring streets of the capital community and that use appellate litigation to further their policy goals. These lawyers position cases in lower courts for possible appeals. They file briefs at the agenda stage and argue cases on the merits. They strategize with amici curiae and consult with less experienced counsel. They are, in sum, central actors in the politics of the Supreme Court. Such is the nature of the new "inner republic." Why has the discrete Supreme Court bar reappeared? Changes in the way interests are represented in government, as well as the stratification within the legal profession, appear to have brought about the return of identifiable Supreme Court practitioners.

The Rise of Washington Representation

The 1960s were witness to an enormous surge in the number of groups in the nation's capital (Berry 1989; Schlozman and Tierney 1986; Walker 1983). Seeking to advance their concerns in the arena of public policy, organized interest groups established themselves within the Washington community in great numbers. Among the more effective resources available to give voice to such interests were lawyers. Articulate, skilled at writing and research, lawyers were natural candidates for pressure politics (Schlozman and Tierney 1986, 99).

Lawyer-lobbyists were a valued commodity, as is evident from the growth of new law firms in the capital as well as the increased number of branch offices established in Washington by firms from across the country. In the decade between 1978 and 1988, as the nation's large law firms expanded, Washington was, far and away, the most popular location for a branch office (Bellows 1988–89). Indeed, between 1972 and 1983 the Washington bar more than tripled in size (Berry 1989, 25–27). A great wealth of legal expertise thus became concentrated in the District of Columbia. Significantly, a great many of these lawyers were active in practices that involved federal government relations (Goulden 1972).

Legal Stratification

At the same time that the Washington legal community was expanding, the legal profession in general was undergoing specialization (see Abel 1989, 202–7). In fact, for some time now lawyers have divided their labor by focusing their expertise (Heinz and Laumann 1982). Without question, the specialization of the Washington firms reflects the central importance of the federal government for their practices.

Perhaps the best example of the relationship between specialized law practice and the interests served by Washington representation is the concentration of administrative lawyers in the capital. Corporations seeking expert counsel to negotiate the maze of administrative hearings and regulations turn over and over again to the Washington firms for help. These firms enjoy such a wealth of expertise on federal policy making in part because many of their lawyers previously worked in the national government (Berry 1989, 91–92). This experience translates into access. Clearly, one of the primary reasons these members of the Washington community are so highly sought after is that they have the entree that other lawyers do not (Schlozman and Tierney 1986, 100).

Why should the desire of large organizations for specialized legal assistance be restricted to administrative lawyers? After all, corporations and other organizations have a variety of legal needs, and often those needs extend to the Supreme Court. As in any other case, litigants (if they are able) are likely to look for the most suitable and skilled lawyers available, and the lawyers they are apt to seek are often in Washington. In the context of representation in the federal government more generally, Berry has called attention to the growing role of Washington law firms in pressure politics: "[T]he success of so many new firms and the rapid growth of some old ones indicate that they too have participated in the rapid growth of Washington lobbying. Smaller 'boutique' firms compete by offering specializations, while the larger firms are successfully cashing in on the lobbying boom by broadening the array of services they provide" (1989, 27). As these law firms have become a more attractive resource in other arenas of policy making— congressional committees and administrative agencies, for example— judicial representation from the Washington firms has been sought with comparable alacrity. The data in Figure 2.2 illustrate this trend. Reflecting the percentage of petitions for review filed by law firms in Chicago, New York, and Washington, they suggest that, as the ranks of professional representatives began to swell in the nation's capital, so too did the reliance of litigants upon Washington-based Supreme Court counsel.[12] In 1940, only 1 percent of appeals and petitions for certiorari were filed by law firms in Washington. In the years that followed, however, the Washington law firms were increasingly a source for representation in the Court, participating in roughly 5 percent of the Court's cases in 1955. The capital's share of the private bar continued to grow, reaching 10 percent by the mid-1980s. In only twenty-

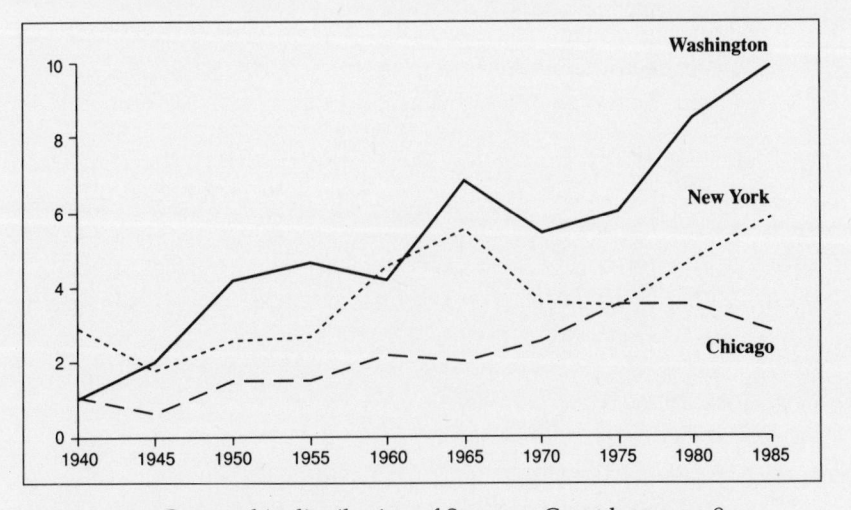

FIGURE 2.2. Geographic distribution of Supreme Court bar, 1940–85. (*Source: United States Law Week*)

five years, the proportion of petitions brought to the Court by law firms in the District of Columbia increased tenfold. Although Washington does have its competitors—Chicago and New York, both of which also command successively greater proportions of the Court's docket—their rates of increase are modest by comparison, and their absolute percentages remain well below Washington's. In fact, the percentage of petitions filed by Washington law firms in 1985 was greater than that of New York and Chicago combined. (By contrast, their collective share of the national bar was more than twice that of the capital.) Notwithstanding fluctuations over time, the increased frequency with which Washington counsel are before the Supreme Court strikingly parallels the more general trend in recent decades toward the use of Washington-based representatives for governmental advocacy. As one well-known lawyer in a large Washington firm commented:

> It used to be, back in the days when all of us thought of ourselves as generalists rather than specialists in one very narrow field, that if you were to acquire a reputation as a good appellate advocate, other lawyers would bring cases to you, and you'd have many opportunities. Today, Supreme Court advocacy is becoming

something of a narrow specialty in and of itself. Most lawyers don't even bother to read the Supreme Court's decisions. Some of us read them on a regular basis. (CI)

What is especially noteworthy is that the expanded use of Washington firms has taken place during a time in which the number of filings in the Court has escalated rather dramatically. Other things being equal, as the number of cases increases, one might expect any city's contribution to the bar to remain relatively stable. Instead, as the Court's docket expanded from the 1970s to the mid-1980s, litigants also relied upon Washington-based counsel more and more. In short, more cases were being brought to the Court, and more of those cases were brought by lawyers in the capital. Thus, the District of Columbia— specifically, that city's law firms—is the place where litigants come in search of the "Supreme Court lawyers," the elite circle of lawyers who have first-hand knowledge of the Court's proceedings. Who are these practitioners who comprise the Washington community?

The Elite Community: A Case in Point

On July 1, 1991, four Washington lawyers announced the formation of Klein, Farr, Smith & Taranto. Situated at the edge of Rock Creek, just on the eastern side of Georgetown, the Washington firm advertised that it would "emphasize Supreme Court and Appellate Practice."[13] The emergence of this firm—as much as any other—signals the return of the Supreme Court practitioners.

That the four name partners—Joel I. Klein, H. Bartow Farr III, Paul M. Smith, and Richard G. Taranto—formed a law firm that focused specifically on Supreme Court litigation was scarcely surprising, given their mutual backgrounds and experiences. All four had impressive academic credentials. Klein earned a degree from Columbia University before moving on to the Harvard Law School, where he served on the *Harvard Law Review*. Farr, a Princeton graduate, served as the editor-in-chief of the law review at Arizona State University. Smith held the top editorial post for the law journal at his alma mater, Yale University. Taranto, too, had been educated at Yale and served as an editor for the *Yale Law Journal*.

Even more noteworthy, all had been among the select group of bright, young attorneys chosen to serve as clerks to the justices of the United States Supreme Court. Both Klein and Smith served in the chambers of Justice Lewis F. Powell, Jr.; Farr was a clerk to Justice William H. Rehnquist; Taranto held a clerkship in Justice Sandra Day O'Connor's office.

And their Supreme Court cachet did not end there. Bartow Farr's direct experience with Supreme Court litigation, for instance, extended beyond his tenure as a clerk. Following his clerkship, he took a position at the Justice Department, where he served in the Office of the Solicitor General from 1976 to 1978. As an assistant to the solicitor general, Farr had the opportunity to handle a great volume of appellate litigation, helping prepare Supreme Court briefs on behalf of the United States and arguing before the justices on a sustained basis. Likewise, during Charles Fried's tenure as solicitor general, Richard Taranto had also served as a member of that office.

These lawyers had previously worked together at Onek, Klein & Farr, a Washington boutique firm that dissolved over disagreements about firm expansion but that was well regarded for its Supreme Court talent. Indeed, there were far more former Supreme Court clerks interested in joining their ranks than the firm could accommodate. Now, in its new incarnation, the firm would focus its attention on continuing to carve out a distinctive Supreme Court practice (Kerlow 1991).

The firm of Klein, Farr, Smith & Taranto is representative of the community of lawyers increasingly involved in Supreme Court litigation: former clerks to the justices who know the inner workings of the Court, alumni of the solicitor general's office boasting Supreme Court appearances in the double digits, Washington-based attorneys who work in close proximity to One First Street, NE. Litigants in the Supreme Court seek out these lawyers for much the same reason that individuals, interest groups, and organizations pursue Washington representation: to gain *access* to the federal government (see Schlozman and Tierney 1986, 100). In the case of the Supreme Court, access might come in the form of securing a position on the justices' plenary agenda. As Farr himself has suggested, "Somebody who's good can help move a case up in a pile of petitions" (Wermiel 1989, B3).

Of course, relying upon any single example as a means of characterizing the elite community tends to conceal important variations within that group. Indeed, those variations will be explored throughout this book. Nonetheless, the basic division is clear. Close to the Court stand the experienced and influential gatekeepers, that small inner circle of elites tied to the Washington community. Beyond them exists the larger outer circle of relatively inexperienced litigators, the fluid cast of counselors who remain outside of the power politics of the Supreme Court.

3

An Elite Set of Litigators

 The modern Supreme Court lawyer does not closely resemble his counterpart of the nineteenth century. Although these lawyers have assumed the gatekeeping role of their latter-day brethren, the current bar of the high court is quite different from the bar that existed in the dawning days of the republic. Many early litigators, for instance, were members of Congress serving in Washington during legislative sessions. Today, it would be quite unusual for a senator or member of Congress to appear at the podium to argue a case—although members of Congress do, on occasion, participate in Court litigation as amici curiae. In the 1800s, when formal legal training did not exist, attorneys studied law either on their own or under the tutelage of practicing advocates (Neubauer 1991, 104–5; Vago 1991, 251–53; Warren 1939). In contrast, a good many modern Supreme Court lawyers have been trained at the nation's elite law schools. Furthermore, virtually all of the Supreme Court counsel in the nineteenth century were male. In short, historical comparisons reveal a similarity in function but not in form. Still, like their antecedents, the lawyers of the modern Supreme Court remain an elite set of political actors. Why?

In part, the transformation of the Supreme Court bar reflects changes in the legal profession at large. Legal education has been formalized and is now open to a wide range of students; admission to practice is regulated; the bar in general is increasingly more specialized and stratified (see Abel 1989; Vago 1991). More than anything else, though, the stratification of the bar accounts for the distinctive character of the Court's counsel. At the broadest level, this stratification has resulted in the formation of two major groups—lawyers from lower socioeconomic backgrounds who serve individual clients and smaller economic interests, and lawyers from more privileged backgrounds who represent large organizations and wealthy corporate interests (Heinz and Laumann 1982).

These social lines within the bar have a direct bearing upon the nature and quality of legal representation generally and thus affect judicial outcomes. Those who occupy the positions of occupational prestige represent the wealthy and powerful and, like many elites, are advantaged in judicial politics (see Galanter 1974). The consequences of this stratification are exemplified, even magnified, among the litigators who practice in the Supreme Court. In order to grasp the direction and magnitude of their influence as gatekeepers to the Court, one must compare them to their peers in the legal profession, to see what distinguishes those who become active Supreme Court practitioners from those who do not.

Attributes of the Supreme Court Bar

The typical Supreme Court lawyer is a forty-five-year-old, Harvard-educated private practitioner, based in New York, Washington, or Chicago. He specializes in appellate litigation and has at least a half dozen Supreme Court cases to his credit. He is a liberal white Protestant, with strong attachment to the Democratic party. Of course, such a general sketch cannot capture the complexity of the full picture, as the following examination of the Supreme Court bar will reveal.[1]

Size. The number of lawyers in the United States is fast approaching one million (Abel 1989). In 1985, the American Bar Foundation estimated that there was one lawyer for every 360 persons (Curran et al. 1986, 3). That same year, there were over twenty-five hundred paid petitions for review in the United States Supreme Court.[2] Thus, the average attorney had virtually no chance of serving as counsel in one of these cases. Looking at the number of those petitions that the Court granted review and subsequently gave plenary treatment, one finds that a very small number of lawyers—roughly one in two thousand—made an oral argument in the Court's 1985 term. Of course, a sizable portion of the Court's calendar in any term is commanded by members of the solicitor general's office, the roughly two dozen federal government lawyers who appear on behalf of the United States. In consequence of the solicitor general's dominance, the already minuscule likelihood of participation shrinks even further.

The official "Bar of the Supreme Court," which consists of those attorneys who have been admitted to practice before the Court, is quite large but of unknown numbers. Since 1925, roughly 134,000 lawyers have been admitted to the bar, with an additional 5,000 attorneys joining the ranks each year (Stern, Gressman, and Shapiro 1986, 731). Unfortunately, though, the Court does not purge its rolls. Thus, the size of its actual current membership cannot be established, although it is unquestionably smaller than these figures suggest. Attrition has certainly diminished the numbers. Moreover, the active bar—the subject of our investigation—is only a subset of the official bar, many of whom seek membership as a mark of professional status.[3] Moreover, regardless of the formal bar's size, the likelihood of serving as counsel, even at the case selection stage, remains minimal at best. In any given term, therefore, only a small segment of the legal community participates in Supreme Court litigation.

Employment setting. Part of the reason why the Court's counsel tend to be an elite group is that many occupy positions that command considerable social, political, and economic resources. This concentration of legal power is significant, because so much of the practice in the Supreme Court thereby becomes a function of where and for whom one works. Some legal positions inevitably lead to litigation in the Court, the most obvious and notable example being an appointment in the solicitor general's office. Other employment settings, however, are also conducive to interactions with the Court, such as positions that are by design directed toward appellate practice.[4]

The litigators who are engaged in the Court's docket are differentiated much in the manner of the general population of the bar, as is clear from table 3.1. This table compares the employment settings of Supreme Court lawyers and the American bar. Private practitioners

TABLE 3.1. Employment setting of Supreme Court bar and national bar

Type of employment	Supreme Court bar (%)	National bar (%)
Private practice	75.0	70.2
State and local government	16.6	5.0
Organized interests	2.5	0.8
Academic	1.8	1.1
Legal aid/public defender	1.5	1.2
Corporate counsel	1.2	9.7
Other	1.2	12.1

Sources: Curran et al. 1986 for the national bar; 1990 survey data for the Supreme Court bar ($N = 325$).

Note: "Other" includes, for example, lawyers who serve in the judiciary, attorneys in the federal government, and lawyers who are retired or otherwise inactive. In some instances, here and elsewhere, percentages may not total 100 because of rounding.

dominate the bar among both groups. A closer look at the Court's attorneys shows that of the 75 percent who practice law privately, 18 percent are solo practitioners while the remaining 82 percent work in a law firm. On the one hand, these figures correspond to the relative decline in solo attorneys nationally in favor of employment with a firm (Abel 1989, 178–84). On the other hand, despite the general trend away from solo practice, some 49 percent of private attorneys continue to operate in a solo setting (Curran 1986, 27–30). In comparison to the private American bar in toto, therefore, the average Supreme Court practitioner is nearly three times more likely to enjoy the comparatively prestigious status of employment with a law firm.

It is here, in the law firms, that one finds many of the Court's active litigators. Attorneys who work in firms—especially large firms—are more likely to serve clients whose business activities make them candidates for litigation in the high court. As one lawyer in a large Washington firm put it,

> If you're an appellate lawyer for a big corporation or another major litigant, sooner or later, you're going to end up in the Supreme Court. And if you continue to be Burlington Northern's appellate

lawyer, every time Burlington Northern goes to the Supreme Court, you're going to go, too. (CI)

Some 5 percent of all lawyers are employed in state and local government, but at the level of the Supreme Court the proportion of counsel who work in state government is more than three times the national average. Since state and local agencies are so often involved in the issues that dominate the justices' agenda—criminal and constitutional cases, for example—it is not surprising to find that over 15 percent of Supreme Court attorneys represent state governments.

Private practice and service to state and local government together provide employment for the vast majority of lawyers, at both the Supreme Court and the national level. A small but significant minority of lawyers, however, work in the service of organized interests.[5] This general category encompasses a varied set of associations, including "such groups as unions, trade or professional associations . . . or other special- or common-interest organizations, including law reform or legal advocacy groups" (Curran et al. 1985, 594).

Organized interests are among the most active participants in Supreme Court litigation (see, for example, Caldeira and Wright 1990a; Casper 1972; O'Connor and Epstein 1982), and among such organizations one is likely to find some of the Court's most notable practitioners. Laurence Gold of the AFL-CIO, Jack Greenberg of the NAACP Legal Defense Fund, Alan Morrison of the Public Citizen Litigation Group, and Burt Neuborne of the American Civil Liberties Union, to name but a few, are routinely singled out by other lawyers for their distinctive skills in Supreme Court litigation. One former interest group attorney, now in private practice, offered this comment on the composition of the Court's bar:

> You take, certainly, Justice [Thurgood] Marshall, Jack Greenberg, and now Julius Chambers, who are involved in so many cases because they work for the Legal Defense Fund. [Their] cases do get up there. If you work for the American Civil Liberties Union, you've got the same thing. (CI)

Still, whether one focuses on the Court's bar or the distribution of lawyers nationally, the attorneys who work for organized interests do not constitute a large portion of the legal universe.

Members of the legal professoriate often appear in Supreme Court litigation, sometimes in the Court's most visible cases. Laurence Tribe of Harvard University, the scholar whose mammoth constitutional law text is a staple of many law schools, is probably the most renowned academic lawyer. One of his more recent appearances was in *Bowers v. Hardwick*, the 1986 controversy over a Georgia sodomy law, a case that Tribe agreed to argue on behalf of the ACLU. Early in 1992, in *Cipollone v. Liggett Group, Inc.*, he took on the powerful tobacco companies before the justices, arguing that warning labels do not insulate cigarette manufacturers from liability suits.[6] Likewise, Charles Alan Wright of the University of Texas at Austin appeared before the justices in *San Antonio v. Rodriguez*, a prominent case that involved a challenge to the financing of public schools in Texas (Irons 1990). Other notable academics with varying degrees of Supreme Court experience include Alan Dershowitz of Harvard University, Michael Gottesman of Georgetown University, and Eugene Gressman of Seton Hall University.

Together, these legal scholars form but a small portion of the Court's bar. Nationally, their numbers are slightly less. There may, however, be a qualitative difference between the academics who litigate in the Court and those who do not. Abel notes that "[a]lthough law teachers are increasingly differentiated from practitioners, most still are not scholars. . . . A study of publications by tenured faculty in the early 1980s revealed that 44 percent had published nothing in the last three years, and the median number of publications was only one" (1989, 174). In contrast, the academic lawyers in the Supreme Court bar, more often than not, are associated with the nation's better law programs. Many have national reputations, both as scholars and as appellate advocates.

Gideon v. Wainwright (1963) established the right of criminal defendants to legal counsel, and along with the growing concern the Supreme Court showed for the accused came an acceleration in the number of agencies designed to provide legal assistance to those incapable of paying for such services (Abel 1989, 131–32). Thus, to the extent that consumers of legal aid services have cases that raise constitutional questions, their counsel will appear in Supreme Court litigation. Such participation, proportionally speaking, is not insignificant. As Susan Lawrence (1990) has demonstrated, the Legal Service Program has developed sophisticated litigation strategies in the Supreme Court. The savvy litigators within that organization have not only provided the poor with an effective voice in the Court but also have contributed to the development of several areas of the law.

One kind of lawyer clearly underrepresented in the Supreme Court is the corporate in-house counsel, one of the most prestigious positions within the profession (see Heinz and Laumann 1982). Roughly 10 percent of all lawyers serve as in-house counsel, but their representation in the Court is the smallest for any category of lawyer. Moreover, the field of corporate law has shown enormous growth in comparison to the public sector (Abel 1989, 168). If the bar of the Supreme Court is, on balance, a select group of advocates relative to the national bar, why then would there be nearly ten times as many corporate lawyers nationally than one finds in the Supreme Court?

Perhaps the most significant reason has to do with the nature of corporate practice. Office work is endemic to the enterprise of corporate representation; house counsel seldom appear in court, and their work is generally not directed toward litigation (Heinz and Laumann 1982, 59–83). In other words, few corporate counsel are called upon to litigate in *any* court; accordingly, one might expect to find few on the docket of the nation's most significant tribunal.

Another reason for the relative scarcity of corporate lawyers among the Supreme Court bar has to do with legal specialization, a topic to which I will turn in the next chapter. Briefly, corporations are among the most likely to seek specialists when they find themselves involved in Supreme Court cases. Business interests, of course, do litigate in the Court, but under such circumstances large corporations often turn to lawyers who have had the greatest experience before the justices. Such lawyers overwhelmingly reside in private practice.

Age.　Rising to the top in politics or business takes time, and lawyers in the Court are not exempt from this rule. With age come experience and expertise, both scarce resources in the Supreme Court. One would thus expect the Court's bar to be a more seasoned group, superior in professional maturity. How old are the Court's lawyers? Table 3.2 shows the composition by age of both the American bar and bar of the Court. Somewhat surprisingly, the median age of the Court's bar is only slightly higher than that of the overall lawyer population. A closer look at the data, however, reveals more significant differences.

Some 30 percent of all attorneys are under the age of thirty-five. By

TABLE 3.2. Age distribution of Supreme Court bar and national bar

Age	Supreme Court bar (%)	National bar (%)
Less than 35	11.2	30.4
35 to 44	49.2	31.9
45 to 64	33.6	25.9
65 and over	5.9	11.7
Median age	42 years	40 years

Sources: Curran et al. 1986 for the national bar; 1990 survey data for the Supreme Court bar ($N = 321$).

comparison, the proportion of Supreme Court advocates within that age cohort is just slightly over one third the national figure. Further, more than 80 percent of the Court's bar falls between the ages of thirty-five and sixty-four, with nearly half of all Supreme Court lawyers aged between thirty-five and forty-four. Thus, the Supreme Court bar is dominated by those who have reached a level of professional maturity and who are in the prime years of their legal careers.

This is not the case for American lawyers in general. In recent years, one national transformation within the profession has been the general lowering of age and collective legal experience. Half of all practicing lawyers have been admitted to the bar since 1967; consequently, American lawyers are younger today than they were a generation ago (Curran 1986, 23–25). On balance, then, the bar of the Court tends to be older than its national counterpart. Statistically, the distribution of age for Supreme Court lawyers is relatively normal. In comparison, the distribution for lawyers nationally shows a stronger concentration among the younger age groups.

Gender. As with many elites, Supreme Court practitioners are overwhelmingly male. Few women have entered the ranks of attorneys active in litigation before the Court: only 7.3 percent of the Supreme Court bar is female. By contrast, the proportion of women within the national bar is 13.1 percent (Curran et al. 1986), nearly twice the percentage of female lawyers in the Court. Still, both figures are modest compared to the number of women in the American population as a whole.

Recent years, however, have witnessed an influx of women into the ·

legal profession (Curran 1986). Prior to the mid-1980s, the distribution of the sexes among practicing lawyers was virtually identical to the present gender distribution of the Supreme Court bar. In other words, in terms of gender, the present collection of Supreme Court litigators is a representative cross section of American lawyers a decade ago. One might speculate, then, that as these young female lawyers become established in the profession and gain practical legal experience, they will tend to enter the ranks of the Court's counsel in greater numbers. If the hiring practices of the nation's larger law firms are indicative of a trend toward greater diversity within the legal profession, then women (and racial minorities) will surely have growing representation among the Court's lawyers. As Robert L. Nelson has noted, "All major firms have highly organized recruiting and summer internship programs. This has contributed to greater heterogeneity in the ethnic and law school backgrounds of the newer partners and associates" (1981, 131). Granted, Nelson goes on to point out that "[t]he proportions of minorities in large firms is probably less than their proportion in the profession as a whole" but adds that "[t]he large firms I interviewed have hired a significant proportion of women in recent years" (1981, 131n).

To a certain extent, women have already achieved a visible presence. Several of the Court's more notable practitioners are women, and the solicitor general's office has admitted women in increasing numbers. In 1982, for example, three of the eighteen members of the solicitor general's office were women.[7] At the state level, one encounters the names Judith Gordon and Rita Eppler, who appear on behalf of New York and Ohio, respectively, while Janet Benshoof has represented the ACLU before the justices over the past several terms. Benshoof's appearances in connection with a pair of controversies concerning the regulation of abortion garnered particular attention from Court watchers (see, for example, Mauro 1989a), and she now heads the Center for Reproductive Law and Policy, an abortion-rights legal team that splintered from the ACLU's national organization (Margolick 1992). Indeed, one might suspect that the Court's ongoing willingness to consider women's issues—abortion, the effect of the industrial workplace on reproduction, and so on—will result in an increased reliance upon female litigators. Although there are no longitudinal data on the gender of Supreme Court lawyers, the disparity between its current membership and lawyers nationally might well dissipate over the next few years (see Nelson 1981, 131).

City of practice. Baltimore, Philadelphia, and Washington no longer have the primary claim to the bar of the Court. In any given term, petitions will come to the Court bearing the names of attorneys from across the country. Still, like their elite predecessors, the majority of the Supreme Court's lawyers continue to practice in only a few major metropolitan centers.

Surveying the geographic distribution of the bar is worthwhile, primarily because there are such marked differences in the types of lawyers found from one location to the next (see, for example, Carlin 1962; Handler 1967; Heinz and Laumann 1982; Landon 1985). Data on the geographic distribution of the Supreme Court bar can be found in table 3.3. This table lists the cities that contain the largest numbers of Supreme Court lawyers and compares each city's percentage of the Court's bar to its percentage of the total population of American lawyers. These figures indicate that half of the active Supreme Court bar can be found within a relatively small number of metropolitan areas, with three centers of business, law, and commerce heading the list. Taken together, New York, Washington, and Chicago lawyers constitute nearly one quarter of all Supreme Court counsel. Although these cities have been the subject of legal scholarship (Heinz and Laumann 1982; Nelson et al. 1988; Smigel 1964), the relationship of their lawyers to the Supreme Court has not received attention.

In part, the dominance of these three cities at the bar is a function of the Court's docket. Many large businesses and industries have their headquarters in these locations. Likewise, a multitude of organized interests—many of which are frequent litigators before the Court (see O'Connor and Epstein 1989)—are based there. The Court's policy agenda alone, however, cannot account for this geographic concentration of the Court's attorneys.

Another reason that these cities boast such a large share of the Court's bar is related to the demographics of the bar nationally. Indeed, these three cities also contain the largest proportion of the total population of lawyers. Consider the availability of legal services within those cities: twenty of the nation's thirty largest law firms have their principal offices in either New York, Washington, or Chicago (see Nel-

TABLE 3.3. Principal urban locations for Supreme Court bar and national bar

City	Supreme Court bar (%)	National bar (%)	Difference (%)
New York	8.3	7.3	1.0
Washington	8.2	5.7	2.5
Chicago	6.6	4.8	1.8
Los Angeles	3.3	4.6	−1.3
San Francisco	3.3	2.8	0.5
Philadelphia	2.5	1.4	1.1
Dallas	1.8	1.5	0.3
Pittsburgh	1.8	1.0	0.8
Detroit	1.5	1.9	−0.4
Houston	1.5	1.7	−0.2
Miami	1.5	1.2	0.3
St. Louis	1.3	0.9	0.4
Atlanta	1.1	1.3	−0.2
Kansas City	1.0	0.8	0.2
Montgomery	1.0	0.1	0.9
Phoenix	1.0	0.7	0.3
Baltimore	0.9	1.2	−0.3
Minneapolis	0.9	1.3	−0.4
Austin	0.8	0.4	0.4
Lexington	0.6	0.2	0.4
San Diego	0.6	0.9	−0.3
Boston	0.5	2.4	−1.9

Sources: Curran et al. 1986 for the national bar; 1990 survey data for the Supreme Court bar ($N = 785$).

son 1981). Moreover, it is increasingly common for law firms outside of Washington to establish a satellite office in the capital.[8] For example, O'Melveny & Myers, the nation's ninth largest law firm, is based in Los Angeles but maintains a prominent Washington office, in which one of the Court's most active and well-respected advocates, William T. Coleman, Jr., is employed.

Perhaps most important, the data in table 3.3 hint at the dominance of the elite Washington community within the bar of the Court. Washington has more lawyers per capita than any other American city and thus a disproportionate share of the national bar (Curran et al. 1985).[9]

Interestingly, the capital's share of the Supreme Court bar is not just greater than its share of all lawyers, but dramatically so—almost 50 percent more than its already rich representation of counsel. Although in an absolute sense the Washington bar does not dominate the Supreme Court, the nation's capital stands out as the city making the largest possible contribution to the Supreme Court bar. More generally, a modest linear relationship exists between how far a city is from Washington and its share of Supreme Court lawyers. Statistically, the correlation between the cities' proportional differences—Supreme Court bar percentage minus national bar percentage—and distance from the capital city is -.32. In other words, the closer a city is to Washington, the greater its share of the Supreme Court's bar, even when one controls for its contribution to the bar nationally.[10]

Legal education.   Quality of education is one of the factors that distinguishes those who are elevated in the social hierarchy (Mills 1956). Thus, it is useful to survey the law schools from which the Court's counsel have graduated, especially since a lawyer's legal training can have a considerable effect on his career path (see, for example, Abel 1989; Smigel 1964; Stover 1981–82). Heinz and Laumann (1982), for instance, found that attorneys trained at elite law schools went on to enter the most prestigious jobs.

In order to examine legal education within the Court's bar, I assigned the various law schools which its members have attended to one of five categories—distinguished, strong, good, average, and below average—corresponding to each law school's national prestige ranking.[11] The results are presented in table 3.4. The "distinguished" law schools stand out as most likely to produce members of the Supreme Court bar. Indeed, the elite law schools have educated a third of the Court's attorneys, with law schools such as Harvard, Michigan, Yale, and Chicago serving as the chief training grounds for those who go on to practice in the Supreme Court. Taking into account the law schools considered "strong" and "good" as well, one finds that 70 percent of the Court's lawyers attended an above average law school. These numbers suggest that the Supreme Court bar is populated with well-trained practitioners. This in turn raises the question of precisely which law schools future Supreme Court lawyers attended most frequently. This information is presented in table 3.5.

Given the variety and quality of legal education in the nation's capi-

TABLE 3.4. Legal education of Supreme Court bar and national bar

Ranking of law school	Supreme Court bar (%)	National bar (%)
Distinguished	32.4	12.9
Strong	18.5	18.0
Good	18.5	19.0
Average	13.9	19.1
Below average	16.7	31.0

Sources: The Official Guide to U.S. Law Schools 1990–91 for the national bar; 1990 survey data for the Supreme Court bar (N = 324).

Note: Law school attendance is not included in the *Lawyer Statistical Report.* The *Martindale-Hubbell Law Directory* does note where lawyers received their degrees, but coding such a mammoth set of volumes would be an impractical task. I have opted instead to present the proportion of first-year, full-time students enrolled as of fall 1989 in the 175 American Bar Association-approved law schools. Obviously, law school attendance and law school graduation are quite different, to say nothing of bar examination success rates. However, these figures do suggest, in broad terms, the proportion of lawyers who are likely to fall into these ranking categories at a given time.

tal, one might speculate that many members of the Court's bar are Washington-trained. In fact, fully 5 percent of Supreme Court lawyers graduated from one of four law schools within the federal city—American, Catholic, George Washington, and Georgetown. Overall, 5 percent may seem a modest contribution, but then only 2 percent of American law schools are located in that city. As table 3.5 shows, however, the Washington schools do not share equally in their training of Supreme Court lawyers. In fact, only one—George Washington—is among the most frequently attended law schools. Perhaps predictably, Harvard produces the most Supreme Court lawyers. Of the remaining thirteen schools on the list, seven are, like Harvard, in the "distinguished" category: Michigan, Texas, Virginia, NYU, Berkeley, Pennsylvania, and Yale. Only one—Alabama—is "average"; the other five are classified as either "strong" or "good."

Obviously, success at a prestigious educational institution often translates into professional success (see, for example, Heinz and Laumann 1982). Examining the graduates of these schools in terms of their employment settings, one discovers that on average 73 percent practice in the generally more lucrative setting of a law firm. As one might expect, prestigious legal training leads to a fruitful practice and, given

TABLE 3.5. Principal law schools attended by Supreme Court lawyers (in percent)

Harvard University	8.6
University of Michigan	5.2
University of Texas at Austin	3.4
University of Alabama	2.5
George Washington University	2.2
University of Virginia	2.2
New York University	1.9
University of California at Berkeley	1.9
University of Florida	1.5
University of Illinois	1.5
University of Notre Dame	1.5
University of Pennsylvania	1.5
St. Louis University	1.5
Yale University	1.5

Source: 1990 survey data ($N = 324$).

that the Court's bar is dominated by firm practitioners, for some to Supreme Court experience.

In comparison to the legal education of lawyers nationally, the Supreme Court bar has more graduates of the best law schools. The majority of lawyers in both groups—about 51 percent of Supreme Court lawyers and 56 percent of lawyers nationally—obtained their legal training at a school that falls into one of the middle categories, the average to strong law schools. At the extremes, however, the differences become quite distinct: 32 percent of the Court's lawyers were trained at distinguished law schools, while nationally these institutions train roughly two and a half times fewer advocates. Likewise, nearly one third of the nation's lawyers are trained at below average institutions, almost twice the proportion at the Supreme Court level. When I turn to the Court's inner circle of practitioners (chapter 7), it will become apparent that distinguished legal education is even more restricted in compass.

Race. Among those who hold positions of influence in the United States, minorities are clearly underrepresented. Not surprisingly, then, as an elite stratum of the legal population, the Supreme Court bar consists almost entirely of whites—98 percent in fact. That so few minorities practice before the Court must be, in part, a reflection of their small numbers in the bar at large (see *Statistical Abstract of the United States* 1990, 1991). Although traditionally underrepresented groups, such as blacks and Hispanics, have begun to increase in number within the overall population of lawyers (Abel 1989, 99–108), a similar trend cannot be detected among Supreme Court practitioners. Hispanics, for example, constitute over 8 percent of the United States population but only 2 percent of the national bar and less than 1 percent of the Supreme Court bar.

Blacks have made the greatest gains among minorities, yet they still account for but 2 percent of all lawyers. Among Supreme Court counsel, they appear in a slightly smaller proportion, roughly 1 percent. Of course, their numbers within the Supreme Court bar are clearly not commensurate with their influence. Several black lawyers have distinguished themselves as Supreme Court practitioners, many playing prominent roles in civil rights litigation (see Kluger 1975). Recent notables include former Solicitor General Wade H. McCree and William T. Coleman, Jr., secretary of transportation under President Ford and widely regarded as one of the Court's most skillful advocates (Greenya 1987). Of course, Justice Thurgood Marshall was an active advocate prior to coming to the Court. During the 1960s his service on behalf of the NAACP Legal Defense Fund as well as his tenure as solicitor general brought him numerous opportunities to brief and argue cases for the Court.

What does the future hold? Although the legal profession has disproportionately few minority members, many large firms have become more aggressive in recruiting minorities (Nelson 1981). As minorities gain more of a foothold in the American bar, their position within the smaller segment of Supreme Court lawyers may eventually strengthen.

Religion.   From the standpoint of religious faith, there is considerable evidence that the influential members of American society are not representative of the United States population as a whole (Alba and Moore 1982; Dye 1990; Mills 1956). Lawyers certainly do not mirror the American population on this score (see Abel 1989), and the difference is equally glaring for the bar of the Supreme Court. It is therefore instructive to consider how the Supreme Court bar compares not only to the overall population of lawyers but also to the American people in general. Table 3.6 presents the denominational preferences of the

TABLE 3.6. Religious affiliation of Supreme Court bar, national bar, and U.S. population

Religion	Supreme Court bar (%)	National bar (%)	U.S. population (%)
Catholic	24	29	28
Jewish	23	12	2
Protestant	34	53	57
Other	4	6	4
None	15	—	9

Sources: Auerbach 1984 for the national bar; *Statistical Abstract of the United States* 1990 for the U.S. population; 1990 survey data for the Supreme Court bar ($N = 313$).

Note: "Other" and "None" categories are combined for the national bar. Figures for the national bar are taken from a sample of students in ABA-approved law schools in 1975 (see Auerbach 1984). These percentages can thus be viewed as roughly representative of the experienced, middle-aged lawyers in practice some fifteen years later.

Supreme Court bar, a sample of the American bar, and the United States population.

Like most Americans, the majority of American lawyers are Protestants. Further, the proportion of Catholics in the two groups is virtually identical. Among Supreme Court lawyers in particular, however, religious faith is much more evenly distributed than it is among the population overall. Protestants still outnumber members of other faiths but to a significantly smaller degree. Only about a third of Supreme Court lawyers are Protestant, in striking contrast to both American lawyers as a whole and the population generally, where Protestant religions garner well over half the faithful. Catholics, though, account for a relatively comparable portion of all three groups.

It is the Jewish members of the bar who afford the greatest contrast. Six times as many lawyers are Jewish than are Americans generally. Still, Jews comprise barely one tenth of all lawyers. At the level of the Supreme Court, however, this figure jumps to almost one quarter. Why the disparity? The most likely explanation serves indirectly to reinforce the image of the Supreme Court bar as an elite subset of attorneys.

As I noted earlier, relative to the bar as a whole, the Supreme Court bar claims a disproportionate number of outstanding legal minds, products of the nation's elite law programs. In fact, distinguished law schools stood out as the greatest contributors to the pool of Supreme Court practitioners. Significantly, a majority of the Jewish members of the Supreme Court bar (51 percent) attended the nation's most prestigious law schools. In comparison, only 27 percent of non-Jewish Supreme Court practitioners can boast an elite legal education. The disproportionate Jewish share of the Court's bar, therefore, presumably stems from superior legal training. This finding is consistent with previous research on the nexus between legal education and religious preference (Auerbach 1984).

In the survey, lawyers were given the option to indicate other denominational preferences. Only a few, however, did so. Beyond the three major religious categories, the only notable distinction of the Supreme Court bar is its substantial number of atheists. This probably reflects the cosmopolitan nature of the respondents: the more elite the sample, the more atheism one would expect to encounter. Although the percentage of Supreme Court lawyers who consider themselves atheists is larger than that observed for the American population, this proportion is more or less congruent with the findings in other studies of the bar. In the context of the urban bar, Heinz and Laumann (1982) reported a similar share for atheism among Chicago practitioners. Nonetheless, it is fair to characterize the bar of the Court as one would the bar in general: largely affiliated with traditional religions.

Political beliefs.　　Socioeconomic status correlates strongly with political attitudes. Social elites generally have more education and higher incomes and tend to hold more conservative views than the balance of the population (see, for example, Nie, Verba, and Petrocik 1979, 213–17). Our expectation might therefore be that the bar of the Court would be skewed in favor of conservative Republicans. After all, lawyers are among the highest wage earners in America, and existing survey research indicates that such a social cohort would strongly identify with the Republican party. The data in table 3.7, however, tell a different tale.

Broadly speaking, the Supreme Court's lawyers are considerably more pro-Democratic than the American people as a whole. Nearly one half the Court's bar identify either weakly or strongly with the Democratic party in comparison to roughly one third of the population nationally. Among Republicans, the variation is comparable, the ratio between these two groups being roughly equivalent to the Democratic differential. Thus, the Supreme Court bar, far from being dominated

TABLE 3.7. Political affiliation of Supreme Court bar, national bar, and U.S. population

Political party	Supreme Court bar (%)	National bar (%)	U.S. population (%)
Democratic	47	37	35
Republican	21	54	28

Sources: American Bar Association Journal 1983 for the national bar; Stanley and Niemi 1990 for the U.S. population; 1990 survey data for the Supreme Court bar ($N = 309$).

by Republicans, evinces a much greater attachment to the politics of the left than does the American population generally.

How do Supreme Court lawyers stack up against the legal profession as a whole? Interestingly, the liberal bias manifests itself even more meaningfully when the Court's counsel are gauged against their brethren. As has been noted, lawyers are apt to be conservative; thus, it occasions no surprise to discover that the proportion of Republicans in the legal profession is nearly double that in the population overall. Strikingly, however, despite their sizable preponderance within the bar generally, Republicans within the Court's bar are relatively meager in number. In fact, the ratio between GOP counsel in the two groups is better than two-to-one in favor of the national bar. In contrast, the Democrats' share of the Court's bar—nearly one half of all Supreme Court counsel—is almost 25 percent greater than their proportion in the legal profession at large.

There are several possible reasons for the liberal dominance. Liberal attorneys typically have been interested in using litigation as a means of law reform and thus, all other things being equal, are more likely to become involved in the myriad policy disputes that find their way to the Court. In contrast, lawyers who are only infrequently involved directly in *any* litigation—corporate house counsel, for example—may be inherently sympathetic to business and hence more conservative. Then again, it might be that liberal lawyers responded to my survey with greater alacrity than conservative ones. Regardless of the interpretations one might bring to bear to these data, however, the results do demonstrate that the political preferences of Supreme Court lawyers differ markedly not only from those of the American population but also from those of their peers within the legal profession.

Conclusion

Lawyers are an elite group in American society, and those who litigate before the Supreme Court are even further elevated in the social hierarchy. Given the contours of the Supreme Court bar that have emerged in this chapter, it is plain that Supreme Court lawyers are not a representative sample of the American legal profession. On the contrary, these lawyers are an elite within an elite. Fully one third of the Court's counsel were educated at the nation's most distinguished law schools, and the great majority of them have sought employment in urban law firms, primarily in Washington, New York, and Chicago. Moreover, Supreme Court lawyers are older and have practiced longer than most lawyers in the United States.

This stratification has important implications for our understanding of the politics of litigation in the Supreme Court. The modern bar of the Supreme Court has a discrete identity as a legal elite, and its experienced practitioners are the primary power brokers in Supreme Court politics. Issues that make their way through the judicial hierarchy as far as the Supreme Court are likely to be socially and/or politically significant. As chapter 8 will explore in greater detail, the nature of the lawyers who argue these issues is equally crucial.

Of course, in some respects, the Supreme Court bar is similar (at least demographically speaking) to the overall legal profession. Both groups consist largely of white males; a majority in each group are private practitioners; in both instances, substantial numbers work in urban locations. In subsequent chapters, when the analysis turns to the inner circle of the bar—the repeat players who have regular and active involvement in Supreme Court litigation[12]—the influence of this community of lawyers on Supreme Court decision making will emerge even more clearly.

4

The Boundaries of the Bar

Law Practice and

Supreme Court Practice

In the early years of the Marshall Court, a great proportion of the Court's docket consisted of cases involving questions of maritime law. Indeed, controversies over piracy, prizes, ships, and cargo were the prevailing concerns in the federal courts. The large number of admiralty cases during this period stimulated the growth of the early Supreme Court bar, many of whose members were maritime specialists (see White 1988, 201–2). Perhaps the best example is William Pinkney, one of the leaders of the bar in the Washington community during the early nineteenth century. A renowned Baltimore attorney, Pinkney was probably the leading admiralty expert among those who litigated in the Court. "Pinkney's career before the Supreme Court, which spanned the period from 1812 to 1822, was the golden age of prize law. Ninety-three reported cases concerning maritime captures were decided in this period. . . . Pinkney argued in slightly over one-third of the ninety-three cases, many of which resulted in landmark decisions" (Ireland 1986, 95). Another nineteenth-century Supreme Court specialist, Jeremiah Sullivan Black, maintained a considerable Supreme Court practice in disputes over western land claims. Between 1861 and 1865, his expertise was sought no less than a dozen times in land disputes before the Court; he was victorious in virtually all of those cases (Brigance 1934, 141).

In contrast, some lawyers—the great historical orators—excelled in cases involving broader questions, such as the scope of governmental power. As a Supreme Court advocate, Daniel Webster is no doubt best remembered for his participation in constitutional cases, such as *McCulloch v. Maryland, Dartmouth College v. Woodward,* and *Gibbons v. Ogden.* Webster's gift as an attorney (and his skill in constitutional litigation) lay not in his command of specific fields of the law but rather in his ability to deliver articulate and compelling oratory (White 1988, 275–76). Policy and principle were the order of the day, and on these grounds Webster could dominate.

These historical examples illustrate the connection between a lawyer's practice and his work as a litigator in the Supreme Court. Naturally, distinguished lawyers like Pinkney and Black were engaged in Supreme Court practice because they showed genuine skill as appellate advocates. Still, no doubt they were valued, in no small part, because of their expertise in the substantive fields of the law that were frequently on the Court's agenda. In contrast, accomplished Supreme Court attorneys such as Webster were sought out again and again because their skills in advocacy were so well-suited to the forum in which they appeared. Today, as then, the nature of the work that lawyers perform is manifest in their Supreme Court practice. After all, lawyers are selected on the basis of their perceived strengths and the appropriateness of their expertise to the needs of their clients.

In this chapter, I will attempt to unlock the dynamics of the bar of the Supreme Court. Are some lawyers drawn into a circle of active advocates while others are not? If so, why do those lawyers become frequent litigators in the Court? Is it their substantive expertise, or is it their skill as appellate counsel? To the extent that the bar is stratified, what are the consequences of its stratification? To answer these questions, one must first consider the character of Supreme Court practice and the degree to which it can be distinguished from other appellate practice.

Why Is Supreme Court Practice Unique?

The Supreme Court is the nation's highest court, and as such it speaks with finality. Since the Court occupies a special position in the judicial system, practicing before the justices differs from other kinds of appellate work. That three of the Court's most notable advocates have written a mammoth volume on Supreme Court practice is testimony to the Court's distinctive status (see Stern, Gressman, and Shapiro 1986). It also raises the issue of how the members of the Court's bar themselves view the litigation experience.

When asked what distinguishes Supreme Court practice—that is, how does it differ from other types of appellate practice—lawyers tend to mention a variety of characteristics. Some advocates, for example, focused on the excitement of litigating before the Supreme Court. "Well, obviously, at first, it's just the drama of it," noted one veteran. Another seasoned advocate pointed to "the imperial majesty of your surroundings," while one novice, with but a single case to his credit, likened his Supreme Court experience to "walking into a buzz saw." Naturally, generalizing about the uniqueness of the Court on the evidence of the impressions of lawyers who have practiced there can be a knotty intellectual problem, since the various lenses through which different lawyers view the Court may produce conflicting perspectives. The Supreme Court may seem much like a United States court of appeals to one lawyer. Another attorney may feel that appearing before the Supreme Court demands the same set of skills required for arguing in a state supreme court. Still another might see Supreme Court litigation as something quite apart from all other appellate practice. These qualitative assessments may depend upon the experiences that a given lawyer brings to the Court. Still, in general the lawyers whom I interviewed tended to highlight certain procedural and substantive differences associated with Supreme Court practice.

Procedural Differences

Discretionary review. Since the Judiciary Act of 1925, which established the Court's certiorari or discretionary jurisdiction, the Supreme Court has been free to select virtually its entire plenary docket.[1] Over time, Congress has also afforded the justices considerably greater leeway in their selection of cases, to the point where very few cases now require mandatory review.[2] The justices grant review to only a modest portion of the cases on their discretionary docket. In recent terms, the Court has selected between 150 and 180 of the nearly 5,000 petitions it annually receives (see O'Brien 1990, 218–20).

Courts of appeals, in contrast, do not have a discretionary review process. The unsuccessful party from a dispute in a lower court is entitled to an appeal in the circuit as a matter of right (Stern 1981, 18–22; also Martineau 1983, 9–14; Tigar 1987, 12–15). An alumnus of the solicitor general's office, now in private practice, offered this perspective:

> The first major difference is that there is a process which does not involve primarily the merits of the legal issue, but other questions, like the *importance* of the legal issue. It's a highly specialized and relatively unique process that goes on to get in the doors of the Supreme Court. (CI)

Similarly, a lawyer in a large Washington firm, also a former associate of the solicitor general's office, commented:

> The biggest difference between the Supreme Court and the court of appeals is the certiorari process. The court of appeals cases go up by a matter of right. You don't have to go through the discretionary review. So the filings that you put to the Court at that level are fundamentally different from anything you'll do in any other court, unless it's a state court where they have certiorari. But basically that is a unique filing, and there is a unique set of skills that goes into figuring out the best way to pitch a case, to attract the Court's attention. (CI)

Indeed, the issue of discretionary review is significant for petitioners and respondents alike.

> Well, the key difference has to do with the pre-grant stage. . . . That's the very major difference: that you have to learn how to write cert petitions and oppositions, both of which are very important. And those are very different from typical appeals briefs. (CI)[3]

In short, the circuit courts *have* to hear appeals; the Supreme Court does not. In any legal action, it is incumbent upon the lawyer to argue the substantive issues of his or her case. At the level of the Supreme Court, however, there is an additional complication in that the lawyer must first argue the case's "review worthiness" (or "nonreview worthiness")—something that many lawyers immediately point to as a distinctive characteristic of Supreme Court practice.

Oral argument. Judges, lawyers, and scholars have long commented on the importance of oral argument in the Supreme Court.[4]

In interviews, Supreme Court lawyers suggested several reasons why arguing before the justices is different from appearing before other tribunals. The two most frequently singled out were the size of the Court and the time allotted for oral presentations. As one public interest lawyer put it, there are notable differences at the oral argument stage, "not the least of which is that there are nine justices, [whereas] most appeals courts have only three . . . and how incredibly short the time is up there and how they really stick to the half hour" (CI). Another litigator, a Washington private practitioner, explained:

> Time is so limited in the presentation of the oral argument. It's extremely important that you realize that you can't present your full case in your argument. You need to focus on the things that you think are either troubling the Court or are most likely to appeal to the Court. You can prepare as much as you like and have in mind exactly what you want to say but be cut off by questions and have your whole timetable destroyed. (CI)

A lawyer in the solicitor general's office offered a similar opinion:

> The time is limited. You have to have a clear concept of what it is that makes a difference to how your case should come out and make your points about that, rather than fritter away your time on things that ultimately don't matter. (CI)

The combination of nine justices and the short amount of time available can be especially daunting to the advocate, particularly if he or she is caught in a rapid fire of questions from the bench (Shapiro 1984, 553). One Washington practitioner nicely captured the difficulties involved in presenting an argument briefly before such a large court:

> The most fascinating part about it is [that] in the compass of a half an hour with nine people there throwing questions at you— although usually there are only three or four really active questioners—you have to rearrange your argument. But you may have eight or nine points you want to make in your thirty minutes, and the first question you get is on point seven, and they want to know about point seven, although you haven't gotten to it yet. You can never say, "Wait till I get to it." You have to rearrange your whole argument. (CI)[5]

Many lawyers perceive the amount of time the Court allocates for oral argument to be all too brief, especially because a nine-member panel increases the likelihood of numerous questions. As one of the Court's eminent practitioners points out, oral argument before the Court takes place in "an atmosphere in which severe time constraints and rough-and-tumble questioning are the order of the day" (Shapiro 1984, 553). Thus, even a seasoned appellate advocate may find advocacy in the Court unusual and intimidating—although for their part the justices seem quite satisfied.[6]

Substantive Differences

Policy considerations.   Without question, the most distinctive feature of Supreme Court practice in the eyes of the bar is the Court's willingness to consider the ramifications of its decisions for public policy. Lawyers volunteered, over and over again, that advocates in the Supreme Court must weigh the political, social, and economic consequences of a case, not simply its legal significance. Consider, for example, these views:

> The Supreme Court is much more like a legislative body than most lower courts are. Most lower courts adhere more closely to the fiction that they are just sort of looking up the law and applying it. The justices care as much about the policy implications of what they do—what kind of society it's going to produce—as they do about the technical, legal merits of what they do. So, when you're arguing at the Supreme Court level, it is not enough to say, "Well, here is what this line of cases said, and this is what you ought to do." You've got to come up with a *reason* for that, a good reason, a socially useful reason. It may be separation of powers or the importance of clear rules in contracts or whatever, but you've got to have a reason. You can't just say, "That's the law, and that's the way it is." (CI)

> There's no point trying to interpret the Supreme Court to itself, because they know perfectly well what they meant, and they're not going to listen to any argument that they really meant something else. The justices are not interested really in what lower courts have held, except to the extent that the decisions are directly related to the case. But, they are not interested in a string

of citations about what other courts have decided. They are more interested in policy. (CI)

You really have to persuade the Court that it wants to come to the result that you want it to take, not that there's some rule that can be derived from precedents that compels that result. And while certainly lower courts differ within the federal system, it's much more true that if you can persuade a court of appeals that a couple of Supreme Court cases taken together really compel a result, then they'll pretty much do what they perceive that this precedent requires them to do. The Supreme Court writes those precedents and can rewrite them, and it can reinterpret what it has said, if it is persuaded that it is wrong. So, in that sense, it is more creative and policy-oriented than arguments in the lower courts, which tend to be conducted, at least in the federal system, in a more precedent-bound setting. (CI)

One lawyer—an experienced advocate in the Court, both in and out of the federal government—offered probably the best summation of this unique quality of Supreme Court practice:

I think the simplest way to put it is, in the courts of appeals you're basically talking about what the law *is*. In the Supreme Court, you're talking about what the law *ought* to be. It's much more policy-oriented, much more inclined to go beyond the narrow confines of a particular case to talk about how this decision would impact on the development of the law generally. (CI)

The notion that the Court is free to consider the broad implications of its decisions is certainly not new. Constitutional history clearly demonstrates that the justices have always viewed precedents as open to challenge. As Justice William Douglas argued, "The place of *stare decisis* in constitutional law is . . . tenuous. A judge looking at a constitutional decision may have compulsions to revere past history and accept what was once written. But he remembers above all else that it is the Constitution which he swore to support and defend, not the gloss which his predecessors may have put on it" (Douglas 1949, 523). The Court is generally interested in significant issues of public policy. Rule 10 of the Court's rules sets out the few formal criteria for the selection of cases, one of which is the significance of the issue in a case and its need for resolution.[7] Policy implications are just as crucial, if not more so, at the merits stage than at the case selection stage. Thus, a lawyer preparing briefs or oral arguments for the Court faces a rather special task:

> Policy—and I don't mean this in the sense of legislative policy, but I mean in the sense of thinking about the ramifications of the decision for the legal system—is much more important. So you would write a brief quite differently for the Supreme Court from the way you write it for the court of appeals. (CI)

Not all lawyers recognize that the practical effects of the Court's decisions greatly concern the justices, and "[m]any lawyers approach oral argument in the Supreme Court as they would oral argument in, say, the state supreme court of Arkansas" (CI). This puts a premium on an advocate's ability not only to make a logical argument that compels a particular result in a case but also to articulate the costs and benefits of that result with regard to public policy. As one lawyer put it, the justices "are interested in very practical reasons why they should decide your way and in all of the horrors that would occur if they didn't" (CI).

In order to assess the potential implications of decisions, the Court at times makes use of hypothetical questions in oral argument in an effort to see beyond the immediate factual situation. By setting up such hypothetical situations, "the Court is testing the outer reaches both of what the advocate is asking it to declare and of what the Court may, in fact, have to decide" (Prettyman 1984, 556). One experienced member of the Court's bar observed that the novice in the Supreme Court often is unprepared to field hypothetical questions from the justices:

> I'm astonished how many people argue before the Court who are not prepared to answer even the simplest hypothetical. . . . A good example is the argument the other day in the check point case [*Michigan v. Sitz*] where they stopped people to test for alcohol, and O'Connor, for example, was asking, "Well, if you had a section of Detroit that was extremely drug-ridden and dangerous, could you stop people to check, you know, identification and so forth?" And I was surprised to read that . . . the government [lawyer] really seemed to have not anticipated that question. (CI)

Along with the increased sensitivity to social policy comes a decreased reliance on precedent as a guide for the lawyer's argument.

Obviously, some justices feel more bound by precedent than others. Regardless of the specific dispositions of the justices, though, an attorney must also face the issue of the Court's interpretation of precedent. The problem of determining the value that the Court attaches to precedent as well as the substantive meaning of that precedent further distinguishes Supreme Court cases from other appellate litigation. As one lawyer told me:

> It's hard to tell the Supreme Court what it meant last term in the XYZ case, when they're all sitting there, and they all participated and wrote it. . . . You've got to tell them what they *should* have meant or they should do now that they didn't clarify. . . . They're not bound by precedent in the same way that lower courts are, and they don't give a damn if ten circuits have gone one way. If they think that's wrong, they'll just do it—end of discussion. (CI)

Several of the Court's leading practitioners have likewise noted that an argument before the justices "should attempt to convince the Court as a matter of reason and principle. . . . Supreme Court justices cast a skeptical eye on contentions that they are bound to reach a certain result because of prior decisions. . . . They may ultimately base their decision on the prior authorities, but they are more likely to do so if they are persuaded that the decision is right as a matter of principle. If it is not so persuaded, the Court will generally find little difficulty in distinguishing—or even ignoring—the earlier authorities" (Stern, Gressman, and Shapiro 1986, 602). In short, precedent, while not without value, can be readily sacrificed before larger issues of public policy at the level of the Supreme Court.

Quality of the Court.　In making comparisons between the Supreme Court and other appellate courts, lawyers often discuss the disparity between the legal minds serving on the bench. One lawyer noted that, for the Court, "there are higher standards generally [and] the Court is very able. Well, lower courts are, too, but not all" (CI). Conceivably, one might argue that, given the often poor representation by counsel in the Court, the quality of the justices stands out in comparison. Yet even the most seasoned of Supreme Court advocates will readily acknowledge the justices' superior intellect:

> I've argued six or seven cases in the Supreme Court, and I've been counsel in about two hundred, [and] there are nine justices

> up there [who] are all pretty smart. . . . In most appellate courts
> . . . you rarely get [judges] who are as smart and can be as en-
> gaged as these. (CI)

Another lawyer with whom I spoke was even more blunt in discrimi-
nating between the Supreme Court and, in this instance, the federal
circuit bench:

> The quality of the work [in the Supreme Court] is exquisitely
> good, whereas the quality of the work that comes out from . . .
> the circuits is really an uneven mix. I mean, some of the judges
> are excellent . . . but for the most part, they're hacks, really disap-
> pointing, some of the garbage that they put out. (CI)

Supreme Court lawyers are therefore practicing before a qualitatively
different court from any other they are likely to encounter. Not only
must Supreme Court counsel face the additional complications of discretionary review and the need to be versed in political as well as legal
discourse, but they must also come to terms with these differences
under more sophisticated and critical judicial scrutiny.

These substantive and procedural differences highlight the singular
nature of Supreme Court practice. Regardless of the nature and extent
of their experience with the justices, lawyers routinely pointed to these
characteristics as setting the Supreme Court apart from other tribunals.
Of course, the uniqueness of the Supreme Court ought not to be overestimated. Several lawyers offered assessments such as this one:

> It's different in some respects, but in most respects it's just like
> any other appellate court. You're arguing to a unique court, and
> it's the same nine justices who hear every case, unlike in most
> lower courts. Their decisions are final. They may be more con-
> cerned about the policy implications of what they're doing than
> lower courts are. But it's not that much different from arguing to
> a court of appeals, I would think, at least at the merits stage. (CI)

If there is much that distinguishes Supreme Court practice, what, if
anything, characterizes the law practice of Supreme Court lawyers—
in terms of clients, allocation of resources, and substantive specialization—and how does their legal work relate to practice in the Court?
To frame that discussion, let us first briefly consider the structure of
the legal profession generally.

The Work of the Supreme Court Lawyer

How does the legal practice of the Supreme Court lawyers compare with that of the profession overall? We have seen that, from a demographic perspective, the Supreme Court bar is not representative of the bar as a whole, but what about from a professional perspective? Such comparisons between the two groups can be illuminated by the legal profession's rather clear demarcations.

Generally, the national bar can be thought of as consisting of two separate hemispheres, the two groups divided primarily on the basis of the clients which they serve. The lawyers in one group—the corporate or organizational hemisphere—come from more affluent backgrounds, are better educated, work in large law firms or big organizations such as corporations or government, represent fewer clients, litigate less frequently, are more specialized, and command more professional prestige. The lawyers in the other group—the personal or individual hemisphere—come from less affluent backgrounds, are less well educated, work in smaller firms or in solo practice, represent more clients, litigate more frequently, have more generalized practices, and are held in lower occupational esteem (Heinz and Laumann 1982; see also Baum 1990, 74). Of course, scholars have differentiated lawyers in a number of ways—by client, field of specialization, and work environment, among others (see, for example, Abel 1989; Carlin 1962; Handler 1967; Heinz and Laumann 1982; Landon 1985; Nelson 1981; S. Olson 1984; Sarat and Felstiner 1986). But the common thread that weaves this scholarship together is the recognition that substantial professional stratification exists within the bar.

How do these studies relate to our understanding of the Supreme Court lawyers? Is the division between corporate and individual representation pertinent to Supreme Court lawyers, or would some alternative criterion provide us with a better picture of the Court's counsel? Does the structure of the profession look the same for the Supreme Court bar as it does for the bar in toto, or are there systematic differences between the two? It is obvious that the Supreme Court bar is involved in litigation; what is less clear is the extent of its experience in litigation.

A good way to begin our investigation of the law practice of the Court's lawyers is to consider their clients, fields of specialization, and the amount and type of litigation they perform. Table 4.1 provides data

TABLE 4.1. Clients, fields of specialization, and time spent in litigation for Supreme Court lawyers

	All Supreme Court lawyers (%)	Solo practice (%)	Law firm (%)	State and local government (%)
Clients				
Major corporations	24.2	2.2	36.4	0.1
Small businesses	13.0	16.4	17.6	0.1
Blue-collar workers	9.8	23.5	9.0	1.5
Professionals	9.5	12.5	11.7	1.1
Clerical workers	3.4	7.6	3.6	0.0
Unemployed	3.3	5.5	2.5	1.5
Labor unions	2.3	3.4	1.6	0.0
Criminal defendants	1.6	3.0	1.1	1.9
Political activists	1.4	4.4	0.7	0.0
Students	0.6	1.2	0.4	0.0
Field of specialization				
Appellate litigation	30.6	37.2	21.4	53.7
Criminal law	20.2	37.2	9.5	40.7
Civil rights and liberties	16.2	23.3	13.4	14.8

Labor law	14.5	11.6	15.9	1.1
Personal injury law	13.8	23.3	15.9	5.6
Administrative law	9.8	14.0	7.0	22.2
Municipal law	5.8	4.7	7.0	16.7
Commercial law	4.0	2.0	4.0	0.0
Patent law	3.7	4.7	5.0	0.0
Constitutional law	3.3	0.0	0.0	0.0
Type of litigation				
State trial courts	24.8	36.1	27.0	17.5
Federal trial courts	23.2	18.6	27.0	11.8
State appellate courts	12.0	12.7	8.6	25.6
Administrative proceedings	10.1	7.3	12.6	5.3
Federal appellate courts	9.3	10.2	8.1	8.3
N	327	43	201	54

Source: 1990 survey data.

Note: The fields of specialization do not reflect all the possible areas of lawyer expertise, only those most frequently mentioned in the survey either by the lawyers as a whole or by a specific group of attorneys. For the text of the questions on which the above percentages are based, see Appendix 2.

on these issues for Supreme Court lawyers both as a group and within specific employment settings.

Clients.   As we have noted, the legal profession can be divided into two hemispheres, on the basis of the clients served—corporations versus individuals. As table 4.1 illustrates, Supreme Court lawyers are primarily counsel to business interests, serving only modest segments of the community of individuals, whose financial stakes are smaller by comparison. For example, major corporations constitute approximately one quarter of the average Supreme Court lawyer's clients. In comparison, less wealthy clients—such as blue-collar workers, sales and clerical personnel, and the unemployed—lag behind in their share of the bar's client base. This distribution of clientele should not be surprising, given the social composition of the bar. In a group dominated by law firm lawyers, one would expect a heavy concentration of corporate clients.

In examining clients in the context of employment setting, one notices a consistency in professional stratification between the Supreme Court litigators and the American bar at large. The solo practitioner, for example, draws his clientele from a variety of sources. Blue-collar workers, small businesses, and professionals constitute his most frequent employers; major corporations are at the bottom of his client list. Attorneys who work in a firm stand in stark contrast; their principal client source is the large corporation. These divisions correspond to what is known about the legal profession from other sources: large corporate interests seek law firm representation, while solo attorneys devote their efforts primarily to a variety of individuals.[8]

Given these divisions, it could be argued that the Supreme Court's bar parallels the population of American lawyers, at least in the context of clientele. But a closer look does reveal some interesting differences. Let us take law firms, for example. Corporate clients constitute 36 percent of the business of Supreme Court lawyers who work in law firms. Yet among all firms, the average percentage of corporate receipts is only slightly more than 6 percent.[9] If one examines only the largest American law firms—those whose annual receipts are in excess of $1 million—this figure rises considerably, to 16.6 percent, although that is still less than half the corporate share of the Supreme Court lawyers. In other words, the firms in which Supreme Court lawyers are employed appear to be twice as likely to represent major corporations than many of the nation's biggest firms. One should also bear in mind that representing major corporations generally entails high prestige and income for lawyers in comparison to, say, criminal work, the financial and psychological rewards for which are substantially smaller.

At the same time, when it comes to clients who are less likely to contribute to the economic vitality of the practice, the difference between the two groups largely vanishes. With respect to the law firm's share of criminal work, for example, the two groups are quite similar. Supreme Court lawyers who practice in law firms report that criminal defendants constitute an average of 1.1 percent of their client list. The nation's largest firms report a roughly comparable figure of 0.6 percent, while the average for all national firms is virtually identical to that for Supreme Court firms. Moreover, the clients of the Supreme Court lawyers in private practice are more or less similar to the clients that private lawyers serve generally.

One should not, then, try to argue that a thoroughgoing difference exists between Supreme Court lawyers and lawyers nationally in terms of clientele. What is striking, however, is the extent to which the law firms that employ Supreme Court lawyers have cornered the market in corporate representation. As one current member of the solicitor general's office noted:

> It's gotten to the point now where, at least the major corporations that want somebody in the Supreme Court, probably have a list of ten people to go to. I think the average lawyer is not going to be called. (CI)

Specialization.　What can fields of legal specialization tell us about the practice of Supreme Court lawyers? Some 93 percent of the Supreme Court bar specializes in some field of the law; their most frequent fields of focus are presented in table 4.1.

For the bar of the Supreme Court, the practice of the law marches in step with the substantive agenda of the Court. Consider, for a moment, the areas of policy that are most frequently of concern to the justices. During the 1980s civil liberties cases, focusing on issues such as freedom of expression and the procedural rights of the accused, made up some 51 percent of the Court's plenary docket, while a substantial share of the docket dealt with the government regulation of the economy, including labor-management relations, antitrust, securities, and environmental law (see Baum 1989, 166–67). Criminal law, civil liberties, and labor law continue to dominate the substantive work of the Court, and indeed it is these areas of the law that Supreme Court practitioners mention most frequently as their fields of special concern. In addition, lawyers who specialize in administrative and municipal law are likely to be involved in a fair amount of economic regulatory litigation. Thus, one suspects that legal representation in the Supreme Court is, at least in part, a function of legal specialization. Patent cases will be handled by patent lawyers, civil liberties cases by civil liberties lawyers, and so on.

Of course, it is quite possible that the preferred fields of specialization among Supreme Court lawyers may simply reflect trends within the larger legal population. In their study of the Chicago bar, for example, Heinz and Laumann (1982) found that 15 percent of lawyers specialized in personal injury, virtually identical to the proportion of the Court's lawyers that does so. The same could also be said for antitrust, commercial, and patent law. Notwithstanding these similarities, certain differences—particularly those pertaining to the most frequent areas of specialization—are too large to be considered a product of chance. The percentage of the Supreme Court counsel specializing in labor law, for example, is fully five times the proportion that Heinz and Laumann report. There are nearly three times more criminal law specialists among Supreme Court lawyers, while the ratio of civil liberties lawyers between the two groups is eight to one in favor of the Court's bar. In short, legal specialization among Supreme Court lawyers is in some ways a function of the Court's agenda; it does not simply reflect the preferences of the American bar as a whole.

The most common area of expertise among the Supreme Court bar is, however, a procedural rather than a substantive field of the law: appellate litigation. Nearly one third of the Court's bar lists appellate practice as an area of professional emphasis. In fact, the number of lawyers who specialize in this area is more than 50 percent greater than the number for the next most popular field of practice, criminal law. The emphasis on appellate expertise is not only sensible but also crucial for Supreme Court lawyers, because it allows them to span a variety of substantive areas. One practitioner in a large Washington firm offered a perfect illustration of this point:

You just have to have an incredible breadth of knowledge in the law. If you're going to practice in the Court, you're not going to see the same legal issues routinely. So that on any given day, at least for me, I have matters as diverse as statutory interpretation of a criminal statute, a question of the constitutionality of a probationary arrangement, problems with section 2 of the antitrust law, and a host of preemption questions of one sort or another, and the supremacy clause. That's just to name a few of the cases we have right now. (CI)

Data confirm that Supreme Court lawyers who have appellate experience are likely not only to have additional specialties but also to have a greater number of specialties. The correlation between appellate practice and the total number of lawyer specialties is .53. Civil liberties lawyers also have more areas of interest ($r = .49$). In contrast stand the highly specialized lawyers who practice in areas such as patent law. The correlation between patent law and total fields of interest is less than .01. The degree of interest in appellate litigation varies with the employment setting of Supreme Court lawyers as well. Among solo practitioners, 37 percent report a special interest in appellate litigation, whereas only 21 percent of the practitioners who work in law firms are appellate lawyers. Some 54 percent of state and local government counsel, however, are appellate lawyers. Such differences probably reflect the influence of increased specialization among firm lawyers generally as well as the specialized litigation offices in many state governments (see Epstein and O'Connor 1988; Heinz and Laumann 1982). But regardless of how or where they practice, Supreme Court lawyers report this procedural specialization most frequently.

Time spent in litigation.   It is certainly clear that, among lawyers generally, some litigate more often than others (Heinz and Laumann 1982). But what of the Supreme Court bar? Where and how often do these lawyers litigate? As table 4.1 reveals, Supreme Court lawyers are, on the whole, fairly litigious. Roughly 79 percent of the average Supreme Court practitioner's time is spent preparing for and appearing in court. Lawyers divide that time fairly evenly between state and federal trial courts, which together consume nearly half of the bar's litigation efforts. In fact, given that the time spent in administrative proceedings is probably more pertinent to trial rather than appellate litigation, this figure should probably be higher. In contrast, the combined totals for appellate work do not equal even one half the amount of time devoted to trial practice.

Nonetheless, Supreme Court lawyers spend almost a quarter of their time in the nation's appellate courts. Moreover, when involved in appellate litigation, lawyers will appear in federal, as opposed to state, appellate courts roughly 44 percent of the time. Solo practitioners, as most lawyers in the individual hemisphere, spend a great deal of their time—roughly 80 percent—in the courtroom. What is particularly interesting is the extent of litigation activity among law firm practitioners and state and local government counsel, two groups who should, other things being equal, litigate less frequently. And yet litigation accounts for over 60 percent of the work that both groups do, which is a very sizable share.

A structural interpretation.   How do these various attributes of the Supreme Court lawyers' practice fit together? Is there a logical coherence to their work, and, if so, what form does it assume? These questions can be addressed through the use of factor analysis, a multidimensional scaling technique that, utilizing similarities data, analyzes correlations.[10] Through a simultaneous comparison of the various characteristics of lawyers, one may be able to arrive at a more comprehensive understanding of the practice of Supreme Court lawyers. This analysis is similar to the work of Heinz and Laumann on the hemispheres of the legal profession (despite the fact that these authors used a different multidimensional scaling technique, one based on dissimilarities data). Consequently, any structural patterns that might emerge for Supreme Court lawyers can be compared against our knowledge of the American bar as a whole.

One of the best ways to convey the overall results of this factor analysis is to plot the coordinates of the factor loadings of the lawyer variables in a dimensional space, as has been done in figure 4.1, one dimension, or factor, appearing on the horizontal axis, the other on the vertical. This provides us with an informative blueprint of the Supreme Court lawyers' practice. How do the Court's counsel compare to the legal profession in general?

A close inspection of the relative placement of the lawyer variables suggests reasonable interpretations of both dimensions. The horizontal factor closely resembles the distinction between the two hemispheres of the profession. Moving from left to right, one sees a transition from corporate to individual interests.[11] Lawyers representing major corporate clients, patent attorneys, and those who litigate in the administra-

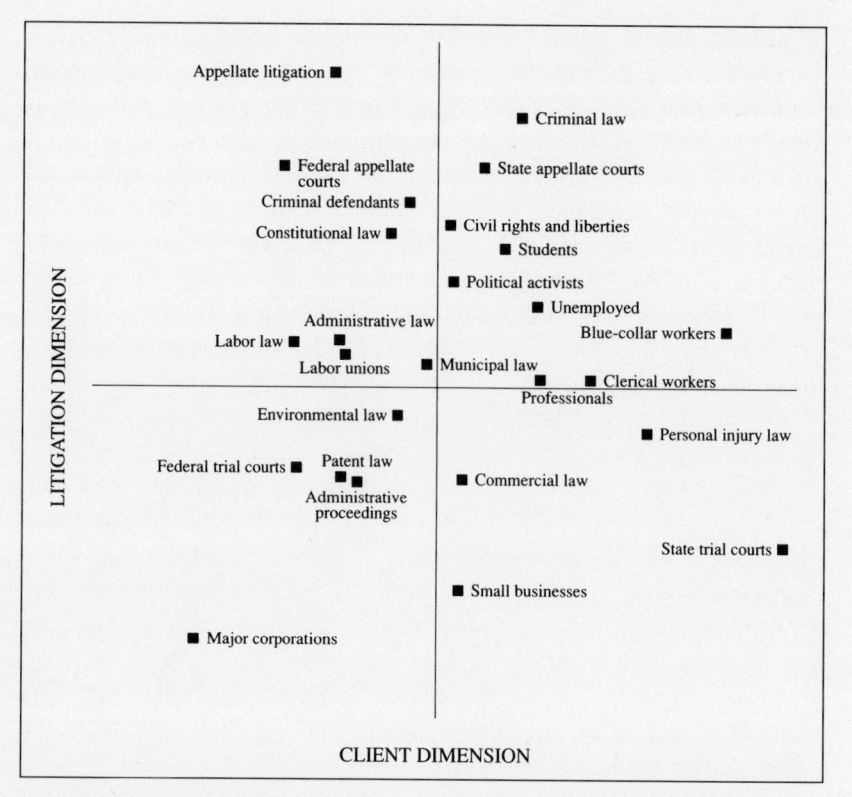

FIGURE 4.1. Dimensional analysis of Supreme Court lawyers: Clients, specialization, and time spent in litigation. For the factor loadings used to generate this diagram, see Appendix 1.

tive setting, for instance, appear on the lower left of the space. In contrast, personal injury lawyers, as well as counsel to the unemployed and to blue-collar workers, are placed to the right.

The vertical dimension appears to reflect the differences between appellate and trial litigation. Lawyer characteristics associated with trial work cluster at the bottom of the figure; those qualities connected with appellate work can be found in the upper portion of the figure. Accordingly, appellate specialists, constitutional and civil liberties lawyers, and the litigators who frequent the federal and state appellate courts are located at the top of the dimensional space, while commercial specialists, counsel to small businesses, and attorneys who appear in federal and state trial courts find themselves at the opposite end of the dimension. Heinz and Laumann, of course, draw a distinction between office work and litigation, whereas for the Supreme Court lawyers I posit a distinction between types of litigation. To put it another way: for the members of the Court's bar, the question is not *whether* they litigate but *where* they litigate. As has been noted, Supreme Court lawyers have an unusually high degree of courtroom experience. Thus, the office versus litigation dimension, while by no means irrelevant, has somewhat less importance for this group. That the appellate / trial factor is so evident, even within the existing structure of the corporate / individual factor, is testimony not only to the power of the two hemispheres thesis but also to the structure of the legal practice of the Supreme Court bar.

The Inner and Outer Circles

I have argued that an increased reliance upon the Washington community for representation before the federal government, together with the specialization of the legal profession, has served as an impetus for the return of a Supreme Court bar. Thus far, however, I have not systematically investigated why some lawyers are drawn into the elite, experienced community of Supreme Court practitioners—those who have regular contact with the Court—while other lawyers remain on the periphery of the Supreme Court. For the Supreme Court lawyers themselves, the importance of the two dimensions of legal practice— litigation and clientele—in shaping the boundaries of the Supreme Court bar is to some extent self-evident. When I asked Supreme Court lawyers why some of their peers had more experience in the Court than others, they frequently offered an explanation in terms of the kind of legal work one performs. This lawyer's response perhaps best typifies their common sentiment:

> Because of the type of practice they have. I do a great deal of appellate litigation, which obviously means that the chances of one of my cases ending up in the Supreme Court are much greater than someone who does predominantly district court trial work. Plus, just the nature of the issues that you're dealing with; someone, for example, who practices, say, in one area in the field of civil rights. Just by its nature, those cases were being taken

[to the Supreme Court]. Now, someone who's dealing in abortion rights, for example, is much more likely [to have Supreme Court experience] than the typical lawyer. (CI)

She and other lawyers saw Supreme Court practice in large part as a function of a variety of characteristics associated with appellate litigation. Certain substantive specializations, such as civil rights, are located at the appellate end of the litigation dimension, as is the procedural specialty of appellate practice itself. In addition, some employment settings appear especially closely linked with the domain of appeals work. In this regard, interest group work was probably the most frequently cited example.

I got a lot of my initial Supreme Court experience working with the ACLU. Alan Morrison [of the Public Citizen Litigation Group] has gotten a lot of his Supreme Court experience because of where he works. You know, the kinds of issues that Public Citizen and a lot of the environmental groups and the consumer groups he's involved with [tend to] litigate. . . . You just happen to work in places that litigate matters that go to the Supreme Court. (CI)

If the comments of the Court's lawyers themselves suggest anything, it is that those whose practice characteristics cluster within the appellate field are more likely to be active members of the Supreme Court bar.

The reflections of these lawyers comport well with the two-dimensional interpretation of the Supreme Court's lawyers. Moreover, they provide some clues as to the relationship between those dimensions and the degree of participation in Court litigation. Who, then, are the lawyers who litigate in the Court most frequently, and what distinguishes them from those whose practice in the Court is more sporadic?

The practice characteristics from the factor analysis can be usefully employed to illuminate the boundaries of the bar. All other things being equal, one wants to know the degree to which each characteristic is associated with experience litigating in the Court. As part of the survey, lawyers were asked to indicate the number of cases they had handled in the Supreme Court at the case selection stage—as counsel for the petitioner / appellant or the respondent / appellee—as well as the number of appearances they had made before the justices as counsel for either side. By calculating the partial correlation between each characteristic and the volume of experience in the Court, then, one can assess the relative differences between the various counsel and reach some conclusions about which lawyers are consistently the most active and steady practitioners before the justices.

Two sets of partials have been calculated, one for the stage of case selection and one for decisions on the merits.[12] In the first set are the correlations between the practice characteristics employed in the factor analysis and the number of cases in which a lawyer participated as counsel for the petitioner / appellant or the respondent / appellee at the agenda stage. The second set of partials are the correlations between those same practice characteristics and the number of times a lawyer argued on behalf of the petitioner / appellant or the respondent / appellee, that is, his or her number of previous appearances before the Court on the merits. Thus, there are two correlations for each variable. These data were used to create figure 4.2.

The figure conveys, quite vividly, several features of the bar's structure. First, these data reveal that participation at the agenda and merits stages are related. That is, lawyers who have a strong association with Supreme Court practice at the one stage generally participate to a comparable degree in the other. More important, the figure illustrates the stratification of the Court's bar. Indeed, it reveals, in no uncertain terms, which types of lawyers are likely to be members of the active, elite community and which attorneys are likely to remain relative outsiders. In the lower left of the figure is one cluster of practitioners, virtually all of them negatively correlated with Supreme Court practice at both the agenda and merits stages. In the upper right of the figure, another group of counsel appears. What binds them together is their generally positive association with active participation at both stages of the Court's decision making. What is one to make of these two distinct groups? What sets one apart from the other, and what implications might our interpretations have for how interests are represented in the Court? Let us consider these questions in relation to the two dimensions of the Supreme Court bar's practice.

The Litigation Dimension

One way of assessing the relevance of legal practice to Supreme Court practice is to compare the overall role of trial and appellate characteristics. In making such an assessment, one cannot escape a significant

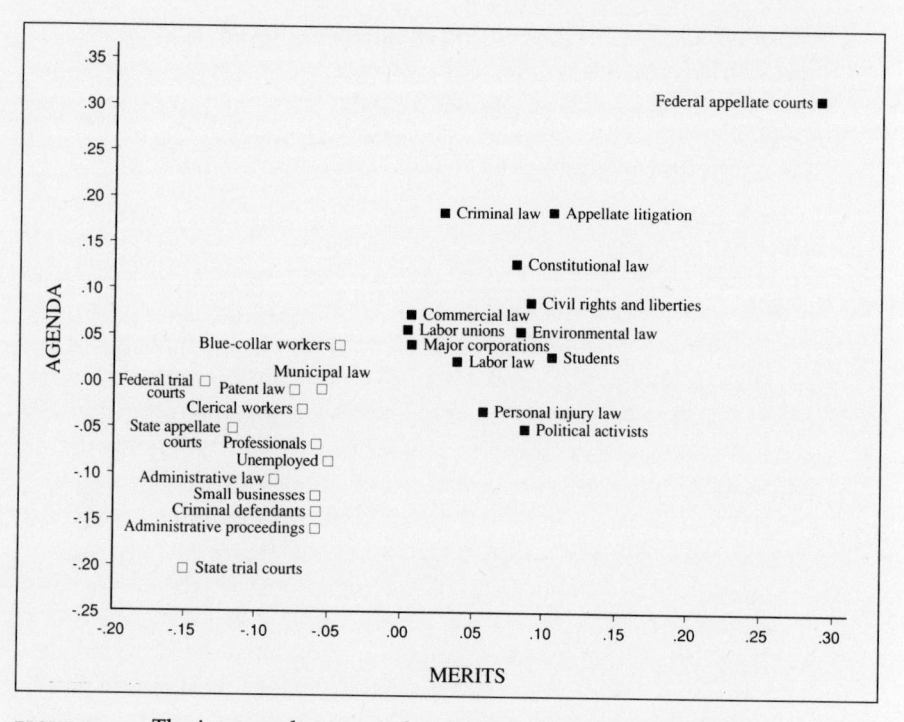

FIGURE 4.2. The inner and outer circles: Partial correlations of Supreme Court lawyers with litigation experience at the agenda and merits stages

fact: the centrality of appellate work for Supreme Court practice. Constitutional and civil liberties lawyers, criminal counsel, appellate specialists and federal appellate litigators—all of whom clustered high on the litigation dimension—are among the most active of Supreme Court litigators. Whether at the petition stage or at the merits stage, appellate lawyers are likely to be drawn into the group of experienced Supreme Court counsel. Why?

Earlier in this chapter, I argued that Supreme Court practice was unique in a number of respects, not the least of which derived from the need to address the wisdom of public policy as embodied in legal doctrine. Appellate lawyers are, as a matter of principle, called upon to litigate issues of law, not fact. Thus, their skills and their approach to litigation make them attractive candidates for Supreme Court work. Far and away, the lawyers who litigate in federal appellate courts are sought out most consistently to handle cases at the next highest level—the Supreme Court. This relationship seems natural, as one advocate explained:

> Fundamentally, I don't think Supreme Court practice is different from other appellate practice. It's more formalized than the Fifth Circuit, for example. The time constraints are more strict, and there's a consciousness that whatever is decided at that level is final. But as far as the fundamental basis of the way in which one argues a case on appeal, I think it's pretty much the same. (CI)

The patterning of appellate lawyer characteristics that emerges in figure 4.1 served to reinforce this point. On close inspection, one notices several of the most active Supreme Court lawyers—constitutional law and civil liberties specialists, as well as those who are counsel to students, activists, and criminal defendants—cluster together in a nearly circular fashion. This cluster, while admittedly tenuous, is nonetheless suggestive for the interpretation of figure 4.2, inasmuch as this cohort of the active group of Supreme Court practitioners has as its common denominator the tendency to deal with legal abstractions and the policy implications of litigation. One member of the solicitor general's staff, reflecting on his job, illustrated the relevance of this fact for practice in the Court:

> In a lot of cases, you're involved in making law that's broadly applicable. And I think the litigation tends to be more academic, in some ways, as opposed to the kind of fact-specific stuff that a lot of lawyers do. That's one of the things that attracted me to it. I have a kind of academic bent myself. So I like this. There's a little bit more looking at logic, first principles in the Supreme Court than there is in lower courts. So you need to be able to reason and really explain, from a common sense view and a broad legal perspective, why your position makes sense. (CI)

In contrast, many of the lawyer characteristics found on the trial end of the litigation dimension are negatively associated with Supreme Court practice. At both the state and federal levels, trial lawyers are relatively inactive members of the Supreme Court bar. Likewise, those who are counsel to small businesses, professionals, and sales clients are part of the peripheral group of practitioners in the Court. Rarely does the work of such lawyers involve dealing with policy abstractions and the rationale of legal principles. If anything, just the opposite is the case, given that many of these lawyers specialize in highly technical fields, such as intellectual property. Patent experts, for example, do not appear before the justices with any regularity.

Part of the reason why the lawyers on the trial end of the litigation dimension have fewer Supreme Court cases has to do with the nature of trial representation. As one lawyer in the solicitor general's office explained:

> Lawyers have to learn to get away from facts a little bit, because the Supreme Court is interested in the implications of its decisions, not just the facts of particular cases. You see a lot of advocates who have worked on cases at the trial level where the main idea was to hammer the facts at the court, and they have a hard time in the Supreme Court deviating from their own factual pattern. (CI)

The bar is well aware that the abilities valued in a trial lawyer have less relevance for Supreme Court practice. In the succinct words of one Washington attorney, "Supreme Court work just calls for different skills than trial work" (CI). When I asked lawyers to name the most effective Supreme Court counsel, rarely were trial attorneys singled out; rather, they focused almost exclusively on those whose most notable work is done on appeal. Even the most successful trial lawyers tend not to be Supreme Court lawyers. The *National Law Journal* has, since 1985, profiled the nation's top trial litigators (see Fisk 1990). Of the forty-five advocates that the journal has selected, only two—Floyd Abrams and the late Edward Bennett Williams—were mentioned as distinguished Supreme Court lawyers.

Of course, not all lawyers who do appeals work are extensively involved in Supreme Court practice. Litigators who practice in state appellate courts and those who represent criminal defendants are two notable examples. Although they practice in the appellate setting, they are not a part of the group that consistently handles litigation in the Court. This may, in part, be a function of the quality of argument expected of such lawyers, as an alumnus of the solicitor general's office suggested:

> There are relatively poor standards of lawyering among lawyers for indigent defendants, and, in fact, a lot of the state cases are not very well argued on the state side either. (CI)

To the extent that trial counsel do have contact with the Court, it is infrequent and sporadic whereas appellate litigators appear quite regularly before the justices, at both the agenda and merits stages. What implications does this difference have for the structure of the Supreme Court bar?

Since we are comparing the practice of lawyers *within* the bar of the Court, these results mean that appellate practice is concentrated among a smaller number of Supreme Court lawyers.[13] The appellate lawyers have, on balance, more cases in the Court than do trial lawyers and thus constitute a more elite stratum. The Supreme Court practice of appellate lawyers is consistent and integrated; these are the practitioners whose counsel will be sought time and time again. In contrast, the trial lawyers constitute the fleeting component of the Court's bar whose work before the Court reflects a more or less incidental contact with a different kind of practice, one very much unlike their own. Thus, Supreme Court work for the trial counsel is dispersed among a wider array of advocates.

In general, then, the Court's bar consists of two distinct groups: a smaller inner circle of appellate practitioners and a larger outer circle of trial lawyers. Indeed, the lines that demarcate the two groups are relatively clear. Given the unique nature of Supreme Court practice, these results make a good deal of sense. One would be surprised to learn that a constantly changing cast of appellate lawyers petition the Court or argue before the justices while a small number of trial lawyers were consistently sought for litigation. The litigation dimension thus reveals a great deal about the structure of the bar. It does not, however, provide a complete account of the patterns of litigation in the Supreme Court.

The Client Dimension

The distinction that Heinz and Laumann draw between institutional and individual representation affords one of the most powerful approaches to describing the contours of the legal profession, and its relevance for the Supreme Court lawyers has already been illustrated. Here, the central concern is the relationship between these two hemispheres and the nature of legal participation in the Court.

Once again, figure 4.2 is instructive. It illustrates that lawyers who serve large institutional interests are part of the active cohort of counsel, while those whose practice is oriented toward smaller individual interests remain on the periphery. Lawyers who serve major corporations or represent labor unions are more often before the Court than, say, counsel to small businesses or to blue-collar workers. Commercial lawyers, whose clients come to them when large sums of money are at stake, are also part of the active elite, as are environmental litigators, who, regardless of which side they represent in a dispute, must deal with policies that may be national in scope. After all, many cases wind up before the Supreme Court precisely because they involve issues crucial to major financial interests or organized groups, such as labor unions: the regulation of economic activity, controversies over statutory construction, or cases that arise from the review of agency rulings.[14] In addition, given the prestige attached to corporate work, such practice tends to attract a higher calibre of legal talent.[15] There can be no doubt, then, that the lawyers who represent large aggregations of interests—and thus broad matters of public policy—are members of the inner circle of litigators.

Moving from left to right across the horizontal client dimension in figure 4.1, one next encounters the cluster of patent lawyers, administrative practitioners, and litigators who work in the federal trial courts. Despite their proximity to the corporate lawyers, one would be hard-pressed to make the case that counsel such as these are active in Supreme Court practice. The reason is clear—they are not organizational lawyers. Rather, they represent a more narrow range of concerns or practice in venues whose professional propinquity to the Supreme Court is rather distant. Thus, they are members of the outer circle.

How do the lawyers on the noncorporate side of the client dimension compare? As a glance at the variables on the right in figure 4.1 reveals, a number of characteristics—including small business clients, state trial court work, personal injury specialization, as well as representation of the unemployed, blue-collar workers, professionals, and sales personnel—cluster on the side of solo practice. With the sole exception of specialists in personal injury, these lawyers are part of the more fluid set of advocates who belong to the outer circle, and not surprisingly, given that lawyers in the individual hemisphere are less likely than their corporate colleagues to become involved in the type of litigation that makes its way to the Supreme Court. More often than not, solo practice is relatively structured, routine, and at times even bureaucratic (Carlin 1962; Heinz and Laumann 1982). Lawyers who normally represent small businesses or the unemployed or who litigate in state trial courts will rarely be called upon to argue the far-reaching public policy ramifications of judicial decisions. A former attorney of the solicitor general's office offered this rather dismal view of the performance of such lawyers in the Court:

> A lot of that work is pretty bad. I think a couple of things happen, one of which is that it's such an exciting experience to have a case in the Supreme Court, people tend not to want to let loose of it. They don't want to say to the client, "I'm not competent to take your case." Indeed, I suppose in the worst-case scenario, they don't know they're not competent because they don't really understand what it would mean to be competent. I think you get a lot of people who should have let someone else take the case over, either because of their own ego or just a naive failure to understand what's involved in the case. (CI)

To the extent that lawyers in this group are involved in litigation before the Court, then, they tend to be less conversant with the language that the justices speak.

With respect to the client dimension in figure 4.1, it is worth observing that most of the characteristics on the left side are related to national issues while those variables on the right are more closely associated with state and local issues. Trial and appellate litigation at the federal level are located on the corporate side, for instance, whereas litigation in both kinds of state courts falls within the noncorporate sector. To be sure, issues that make their way onto the Court's docket frequently arise in state courts, but state courts themselves are called upon to resolve questions of state law, which might or might not involve issues of national concern. It is in the federal judicial system where questions of nationwide significance are handled as a matter of course. On balance, the lawyers who work in the state courts—at either the trial or appellate level—thus remain at the outer boundaries of the bar.

The structural interpretation of the practice of these lawyers sheds further light on the social organization of the Supreme Court bar. Corporate and organizational work is dominated by the small group of active elite, whereas individual representation is dispersed throughout the larger segment of "one-shotters." As one expects, members of the inner circle of the Supreme Court bar occupy the more prestigious positions within the profession. The well-educated lawyers in the large, visible firms that represent major corporate interests will be the Supreme Court counsel who are retained consistently. These are the lawyers whose talents are the most sought after and who can therefore cultivate a Supreme Court practice. Alternatively, the solo practitioners, serving legal consumers of lower socioeconomic status, remain outside the elite community.

This division of counsel into the inner and outer circles has fundamental implications for the representation of interests in the Court. To the extent that there is a core group—small, stable, integrated, discrete—who handle Supreme Court litigation frequently, then members of this inner circle have an advantage in seeking access to the Court's agenda. Representation by this group of repeat players redounds to the benefit of those who employ them, as Galanter has explained (1974, 98–103). In the words of one scholar, "The advantages Galanter describes which are relevant to case selection are: expertise, ready access to specialists, enjoyment of economies of scale, low start-up costs for any particular case, credibility, the ability to play the odds, the ability to play for beneficial structural changes as well as immediate gains, and the ability to discern which outcomes will make the most tangible differences" (Provine 1980, 91).

The lawyers in the inner circle, having written briefs for and argued in the Court many times, are mindful of how to structure their arguments so as to satisfy the justices' concerns and expectations. Moreover, they can evaluate cases, distinguishing between strong and weak candidates for review. In short, the experienced elite are specialists, familiar with Supreme Court practice. Unlike the outer circle, whose task is complicated by the distinctive nature of litigating in the Court, the elite can focus their efforts primarily on securing access to the Court's agenda. In turn, the inner circle's regular contact with the justices establishes its members as credible, effective litigators.

Conclusion

Practicing law in the Supreme Court of the United States places special demands on a lawyer, and some members of the bar are more apt to meet those demands than others. The lawyer who serves institutional and organizational interests or whose practice involves appellate litigation is called more consistently to the Court. The advocate with a parochial client base and trial-oriented practice, however, remains at a fair professional distance from the marble palace.

The bar of the Court, then, is stratified, with the litigation and client dimensions demarcating the two major strata: the elite inner circle, whose members return to the high court again and again, and the larger outer circle of lawyers with only marginal involvement in the Court's docket. The appellate lawyers and the counsel to the wealthy, who do significant and sustained Supreme Court work, are the strong holds of the elite. Trial lawyers, solo practitioners, and the attorneys who serve more modest financial interests are the outsiders. Their exposure to the business of the Court is largely unsystematic. When they do participate in Supreme Court litigation, their responsibilities may dictate that they cross over and interact with the elite; they do not, however, remain among them.

Of the two dimensions, that of litigation appears to hold greater promise for differentiating between these two groups, perhaps because of the special requisites of Supreme Court practice. As a former member of the solicitor general's office pointed out, versatility is indispensable:

> You cannot hold yourself out as a [Supreme Court] practitioner without the ability to kind of dance through a fairly diverse set of legal issues. And that's not a talent that everybody has. A lot of people get good because they focus on one thing, learn it very well, and stick with it. But that's not a luxury Supreme Court lawyers can afford. (CI)

Often, the lawyers who litigate frequently before the Court have abilities that allow them to span the range of legal issues while also serving the specific demands of individual cases and clients. In contrast, the lawyers who specialize in trial practice—those who do not routinely deal with abstractions or broad policy questions—tend not to have active Supreme Court practices.

This division between the inner and outer circles has ramifications for the litigants who depend upon lawyers to act as intermediaries, to represent their interests effectively before the justices, and to gain access to the Court's plenary agenda. It is no accident, then, that the lawyers within the inner circle are counsel to the rich and powerful litigants. A small group of elites who have developed expertise and credibility through their consistent participation in Supreme Court politics can exploit their talents and resources for their clientele. The members of the inner circle—the organizational and appellate practitioners—are the insiders of judicial politics. As was the case among their forebears, the institutional litigators (the William Pinkneys) and the appellate counsel (the Daniel Websters) constitute the pool of experienced talent from which sophisticated consumers of legal services prefer to draw their representation. Like Pinkney and Webster, the lawyers in this inner circle are gatekeepers to the Supreme Court.

5

Activating the Elite

Timing is important in politics, and effective political actors use it to their advantage. Knowing when conditions are ripe for action—for legislation, for bureaucratic reorganization, for budgetary reform, for lobbying a congressional staffer—can have a considerable impact on political outcomes. For example, commenting on congressional pressure politics, Berry argues that "[u]sually the substantive decisions that Congress makes on questions of public policy are made either prior to formal committee deliberations or during the 'markup' of a bill by committee members. Trying to change legislation on the floor of either house through amendments is a chancy strategy. Says one corporate lobbyist, 'You have to start at the bottom. You have to start at the subcommittee level. . . . If you wait until it gets to the floor, your efforts will work very seldom'" (1989, 140–41).

Timing—getting the right lawyer at the right moment—is no less critical in Supreme Court litigation. Securing a member of the inner circle to handle an appeal or to seek review in the Court affords a crucial advantage to a litigant, since such lawyers have the ability both to assess the odds of success and to tailor arguments so as to maximize those odds (see Galanter 1974; also Provine 1980, 45). In contrast, staying the course with a lawyer from the outer circle may cost the litigant his access to the Court. Understanding when and how the inner circle becomes involved in Supreme Court litigation, therefore, is one of the keys to unlocking the pattern of its influence.

As I have argued, the experienced Supreme Court litigators serve as gatekeepers, as primary filters through which pass a wide range of issues and concerns that the justices annually face. These lawyers draft petitions and oppositions at the agenda stage. They prepare briefs on the merits. Although ostensibly filed by organized interests, amicus briefs are also the product of their craftsmanship. In short, they determine whether and how issues get through to the justices. Once one sees how the systematic participation of the elite lawyers compares to the random involvement of the outer circle, one begins to appreciate how the experienced counsel's control of a case and its agenda cannot but have far-reaching implications for decisions the Court makes about its own agenda. Indeed, the elites of the Supreme Court bar have deep roots in the Court's decision making. In this chapter, I examine the ways in which advantages accumulate for the experienced counsel by exploring when and how lawyers become involved in Supreme Court litigation.

Opportunities for Influence

If litigants want to gain access to the Supreme Court, it is helpful to exploit the talents of the inner circle of the bar as soon after a trial decision as possible. The vagaries of individual cases, however, complicate this principle. Experienced Supreme Court counsel are well aware that attorneys become involved at different stages, depending upon the nature of their practice, and that there are systematic ways in which this involvement comes about. Of course, some lawyers see their participation in Supreme Court litigation as random—as "episodic" or "not very regularized." These are the sentiments of the outer circle of practitioners.

Most lawyers who end up arguing before the Court have been involved in a case from the earliest stages of litigation. To a large degree, this is because few cases are seen from the outset as candidates for the Supreme Court. Consequently, many private lawyers are swept into the Court on the tide of the broad policy issues raised by their cases. Table 5.1 shows the proportion of Supreme Court lawyers initially becoming

TABLE 5.1. Initial stage of lawyer involvement (in percent)

Administrative proceeding	13.2
Trial court	54.5
Appellate court	23.7
Supreme Court agenda	6.8
Supreme Court merits	1.8

Source: 1990 survey data ($N = 325$).

Note: The figures include all lawyers who participated at the agenda stage in the 1986–87 term, whether as counsel for petitioners or respondents. If the table is reproduced to include only those lawyers whose cases were decided on the merits, however, the percentages are quite similar. In other words, the stage of initial involvement does not differ significantly between the agenda and merits lawyers. The same applies to table 5.2.

involved at each stage of the litigation process. These data reveal that some two-thirds of these lawyers are involved early in the process, usually at the trial level or in an administrative proceeding. Thus, the average Supreme Court attorney is likely to have handled a case virtually since its inception. For the most part, the Supreme Court lawyers themselves confirm this impression. One alumnus of the solicitor general's office, now in private practice, commented:

> It seems to me that, in most of the cases, the lawyers have handled it from the trial court on. It's not like they've gone out and gotten new lawyers. (CI)

Still, a substantial proportion of lawyers—roughly one quarter—did not come on board until after a trial court decision. Indeed, somewhat less frequently did lawyers mention their initial involvement as having occurred following the trial stage. The relative scantness of this testimony lends credence to the data in table 5.1, which indicate that a smaller percentage of advocates first participate on appeal. Nonetheless, a good many lawyers are sought first as counsel on appeal, as this practitioner suggests:

> I've been involved in a number of cases where we were seeking certiorari or resisting certiorari, as the case may be. In most of those cases, I think I had been involved at least at the appellate level. (CI)

TABLE 5.2. Initial stage of lawyer involvement by employment setting

Employment setting	Administrative proceeding (%)	Trial (%)	Appeal (%)	Supreme Court agenda (%)	Supreme Court merits (%)	N
Solo practitioner	20.5	53.8	23.1	2.6	0.0	39
Law firm	13.6	61.4	18.5	4.9	1.6	184
State and local government	5.9	33.3	49.0	9.8	2.0	51

Source: 1990 survey data.

Likewise, a former litigator for the federal government, now working in a large Washington firm, sees the same basic pattern in both government work and private practice, namely, that the appeals lawyer shepherds the case through to the Court:

> When I was with the Federal Communications Commission doing appellate litigation, if one of the cases that I was handling ended up before the Supreme Court, I continued to handle it. In private practice, I would say that it's very much the same situation, for the most part. I think it's the attorney who handled the case in the court of appeals who simply takes the case in the Supreme Court. (CI)

But whether the Supreme Court practitioners enter litigation at the trial or the appeals stage, one thing is clear: very few lawyers first become involved at the level of the Supreme Court. Only about 7 percent make their initial contribution at the stage of case selection, and even fewer—less than 2 percent—are first asked to provide their skills solely at the merits stage. What characteristics distinguish the lawyers involved at the early stages from those who become involved only later in the litigation? Since the two dimensions of legal practice proved helpful for an understanding of the structure of the Supreme Court bar, perhaps these same two dimensions—litigation and clientele— can be used to explain why lawyers are activated when they are.

Types of lawyer. First, in order to consider the possible effects of employment setting, I have assembled the data presented in table 5.2.[1] Among private practitioners, the evidence again points to the trial and administrative phases as the most frequent points of entry into the litigation process. About 75 percent of both solo and firm counsel became involved at the trial stage. Yet at the Supreme Court level there are some differences. Nearly twice as many firm lawyers were sought at the agenda stage than were solo practitioners. Moreover, in no instance was a solo attorney brought on board at the merits. The fact nonetheless remains that private lawyers are generally engaged early in the process.

Among state and local government counsel, however, the situation changes. Well over 50 percent of these lawyers do not become involved until after a trial court decision, a considerably higher percentage than the proportion of private counsel in that category. In part, this reflects the common division of labor among state counsel, as many state governments maintain special offices to handle appellate litigation, which effectively serve much the same function as the solicitor general does at the federal level (see Epstein and O'Connor 1988).[2] Not all states, however, maintain such offices (see, for example, Baum 1986, 68).[3] Quite apart from this specialization, state attorneys general and their assistants often find it attractive to assume responsibility for their cases once they have found their way to the Court. Political motivations, therefore, might account for their later entry, as this lawyer observed:

> If you get an attorney general of a state who has a big case in the Supreme Court, politically he's not going to let anybody argue that case, other than himself or somebody in his office. If you want to lose an election, all you need to say is that you're such a lousy lawyer that you can't defend your state. (CI)

Clearly, the trial versus appellate dimension has some relevance for our account of when lawyers are engaged in Supreme Court litigation. Those who share appellate practice characteristics (for example, those who litigate in state appellate courts) are involved on appeal, while those with trial attributes (such as solo practitioners) are involved at the earliest stages of litigation.

Characteristics of practice.   Another way to examine the relationship between the two dimensions of legal practice and the issue of when lawyers first become active in a case is to consider some of the professional attributes of the lawyers who become involved at different stages in litigation. Table 5.3 shows the principal clients and areas of

TABLE 5.3. Clients, fields of specialization, and time spent in litigation by stage of initial involvement

	Administrative Proceeding (%)	Trial (%)	Appeal (%)	Supreme Court agenda (%)	Supreme Court merits (%)	Total mean
Clients						
Small businesses	22.6	15.1	7.5	6.2	5.0	13.5
Major corporations	24.8	26.8	18.1	24.7	67.5	24.8
Professionals	13.5	10.3	9.3	5.2	0.0	10.0
Blue-collar workers	8.3	11.3	7.4	6.8	0.0	9.5
Clerical workers	5.6	3.9	2.2	0.5	0.0	3.4
Procedural specialties						
Appellate litigation	18.9	21.9	50.7	47.4	50.0	30.7
Administrative law	32.4	8.1	9.6	0.0	0.0	10.9
Substantive specialties						
Criminal law	2.7	11.9	38.4	42.1	25.0	19.5
Patent law	8.1	5.6	0.0	0.0	0.0	4.1
Courts						
Administrative proceedings	30.5	7.0	7.9	8.2	0.0	10.1
State trial courts	13.3	30.6	21.8	17.2	5.0	25.0
State appellate courts	4.7	9.1	22.9	13.2	12.5	12.3
Federal trial courts	14.7	27.0	20.2	20.6	41.3	23.5
Federal appellate courts	6.6	8.1	13.5	12.9	21.3	9.8

Source: 1990 survey data (N = 293).

specialization, as well as the amount of time spent in the various courts, for those Supreme Court lawyers entering litigation at each of the five stages. What can these figures tell us? Let us look first at the question of clientele.

In table 5.3 I have calculated the mean percentage of clients for the five largest sources of legal business given in table 4.1. A clear contrast emerges between the types of clientele, one which corresponds to the two hemispheres of the legal profession. The average percentages of noncorporate clients decline steadily as the litigation progresses. The mean percentages for corporate clients are relatively steady by comparison, and even show a sharp increase among those attorneys who were not activated until the merits stage. Apart from in-house counsel, the lawyers who serve the interests of large corporations are generally found in the large law firms. It is no coincidence that this is also where one is likely to find experienced Supreme Court lawyers. One attorney for a large Chicago-based firm, who obviously recognized that two hemispheres exist in the legal profession, explained why his office would attract largely corporate clients in Supreme Court cases:

> You have to distinguish between individual and corporate clients, because the individual is not likely to be a very sophisticated consumer of legal services. In that case, the decision of how to handle a case in the Supreme Court is likely to be made by the person's lawyer. When dealing with a corporate case, you have in-house counsel who are managing the lawyers. They may be perfectly satisfied with the representation they received below, but they're quite sophisticated consumers of legal services, and they realize that when they've got an important case in the Supreme Court, they ought to get somebody who knows what they're doing there. (CI)

In other words, those who can afford to change their legal representation later in the litigation process will probably do so, if it is seen as prudent.

By contrast, the less stable client base of noncorporate lawyers is reflected by their much earlier involvement in the litigation process. The average percentage of small business, professional, blue-collar, and clerical clients is greatest for those lawyers who are first involved at the trial or administrative stages, whereas those who become active at the merits stage almost never represent such clients. These findings help to reinforce the argument that those lawyers who usually represent individuals—the larger outer circle of the Supreme Court bar—will be called upon to provide services at the trial level. Since such lawyers generally lack extensive appellate skills or experience, they are not natural candidates to be called in for a case on appeal or at the Supreme Court level. It is quite possible, moreover, that some of these lawyers' clients would prefer to switch to a more experienced appellate advocate as the case progresses, but few who hire a solo practitioner can afford to make a change on appeal (if they can afford an appeal at all). Clearly, such lawyers are involved at the level of the Supreme Court, but their introduction to the litigation will likely have taken place much earlier, as the general decline in the mean percentages for noncorporate clients in table 5.3 bears out.

Second, there is the issue of legal specialization. The specific areas of the law to which lawyers address themselves and the point at which lawyers first become involved in litigation are almost certainly connected, but in what ways? Arguably, specialization may play one of two roles in determining when lawyers become involved in cases, one procedural, the other substantive. That is, given a group of lawyers who specialize in a particular component of the litigation process itself, one might expect to see those lawyers concentrated in that stage of the litigation process most proximate to their area of expertise. Similarly, there may be substantive areas of the law that have a greater applicability at a particular phase of litigation. For each of these possibilities, let us take two examples to illustrate the potential set of relationships.

In table 5.3, I have calculated the proportion of lawyers at each stage who specialize in appellate litigation, as well as administrative, criminal, and patent law. The data for the appellate and administrative specialties can be used to evaluate the procedural role of legal expertise, while those for criminal and patent law pertain to the substantive role.

With regard to procedural specialties, an expertise in appellate practice is far more common among the lawyers who enter late into the process of litigation. Fewer than one quarter of those advocates whose initial involvement in a case was at the trial stage were appellate specialists. That proportion more than doubles at the appeals stage, however, as well as the Court's agenda and merits stages. The other procedural emphasis, administrative law, tells a different tale. Not surprisingly, an administrative focus distinguishes about a third of the lawyers whose Supreme Court work began at the administrative level. The proportion of such specialists decreases about fourfold at both the levels of trial and appeal, and none of the lawyers who became active at the level of the Supreme Court had such expertise.[4]

In the two substantive examples, similar patterns emerge. Criminal law is more likely to be a specialization of those lawyers who are involved later, rather than earlier, in the process. Only about 12 percent of trial lawyers have an interest in criminal law, but the proportion of lawyers with this specialty is considerably larger at all the successive stages. This may be a function of the stratified state government bar. States' trial attorneys may be functioning as generalists, and their criminal cases may be handed over to specialists on appeal. Indeed, a good many states have now institutionalized their Supreme Court practice by creating offices specifically designed to handle their litigation in the high court (Epstein and O'Connor 1988). This interpretation might also explain why the number of criminal law specialists who embark on a case at the merits level is considerably lower than the comparable figures at the appellate level and the Court's stage of case selection. Presumably, many state criminal lawyers are called upon to handle appeals and to oppose Supreme Court review, but their participation may well end there, as the state is often quite successful in opposing review of criminal cases. Although the numbers are less dramatic for patent lawyers, patent attorneys do appear to enter the process more or less exclusively at the earliest stages, as one might expect. Once in the Supreme Court, litigants simply do not turn suddenly to a sophisticated patent expert to argue the public policy ramifications of a potential decision.

It is no accident that appellate litigation and criminal law have greater applicability to the later stages of Supreme Court cases, given that both of these specialties ranked high on the appellate end of the litigation dimension. By the same token, an interest in administrative or patent law—both of which fell at the trial end of the litigation factor—tends to be more prevalent among the lawyers who are engaged at the trial level. One Court practitioner, who has been engaged primarily on the strength of his appellate expertise, put it this way:

I still read all the Supreme Court cases, and therefore I know what the Court has done in the past. I do think that makes a difference, in comparison to a guy who maybe has a tax case, and all he does is read tax cases. (CI)

As the previous chapter illustrated, appellate lawyers are concentrated within the inner circle, while trial counsel remain at the outer boundaries of the bar.

Still another way to consider the potential influence of the litigation dimension is to examine specific experience in the courtroom. After all, if some attorneys spend the majority of their time in state trial courts, it is a safe bet that these lawyers will be involved early in the process of litigation. Likewise, lawyers who perform primarily federal appellate work will probably not appear at least until an appeal is filed in one of the courts of appeals. To test these assumptions, I have also calculated the average percentage of time lawyers spend in various courtroom settings at each stage of the litigation process.

Clearly, the type of court in which lawyers spend the bulk of their time is related to when they are activated in the process of Supreme Court litigation, and often in rather predictable ways. On average, lawyers who spend their time in administrative courts become involved at the administrative level. State trial court lawyers are activated at the trial stage, while state appellate counsel are not brought on until there is an appeal. Among federal practitioners, similar patterns emerge. Attorneys who are called into action after an initial trial spend more time in federal appellate courts than does the average Supreme Court lawyer. Similarly, those who participate first at the fact-finding stage spend a larger proportion of their time in the federal trial setting. Interestingly enough, however, lawyers who were not mobilized until the merits stage have the highest average of federal trial court work. Since most opportunities to litigate in the federal system occur at the trial level, it might be that the high concentration of lawyers with substantial experience in the federal trial setting who are sought to handle a case on the merits simply reflects the litigants' desire to secure counsel with a working knowledge of the federal courts. In any event, lawyers who spend more time in the federal courts are most likely to be engaged at a later stage.

Supreme Court experience. When lawyers become involved seems to be reasonably clearly related to both the litigation and client dimensions of practice. The results fit well not only with existing legal scholarship but also with the sentiments of the Supreme Court lawyers themselves. The analysis thus far, however, raises a broader—and in some sense a more fundamental—issue: Is there something about the specific qualities we have identified that ties them together and determines when lawyers become involved in Supreme Court litigation? The answer is yes. The common thread is the degree of prior experience in the Court. That is, if one looks at what differentiates lawyers who are involved at each stage in the litigation process, one finds that attorneys who are mobilized later share one basic characteristic, namely, membership in the inner circle of the Supreme Court bar. Some lawyers—those in larger law firms who represent corporate clients or those with expertise in appellate litigation, for example—are typically members of the experienced elite. In contrast, those whose involvement in Supreme Court cases begins in the earlier stages—say, solo practitioners who represent the noncorporate clients or state trial lawyers—belong to the outer circle of counsel who have little or no prior contact with the Court.

Would one expect Supreme Court litigants to consider experience when choosing legal representation? The answer seems obvious, as it did to this lawyer:

> With certain clients, of course. It would be irrational not to, if you lost a case in the court of appeals, wanted to take it to the Supreme Court, and were looking around for a new lawyer. It would be bizarre not to take into account how much experience the lawyers had in litigating in the Supreme Court. (CI)

Although the political significance of representation by an expert member of a specialized Supreme Court bar will be addressed later, it is useful at this point to consider the potential relationship between a lawyer's degree of experience in the Court and the stage at which he or she becomes involved in litigation.

This relationship can be examined through an analysis of the probability that a lawyer will become involved at a particular stage, given changes in his or her experience and success as a member of the Court's bar. Probit analysis provides us with a means of calculating these probabilities, which can then be used further to clarify the issue of when lawyers are activated. The data presented in tables 5.4 and 5.5, reflecting simple bivariate estimates in which experience and suc-

TABLE 5.4. Effect of experience on stage at which Supreme Court lawyers are activated

	Trial	Appeal	Supreme Court agenda	Supreme Court merits
Agenda experience				
0	.79	.18	.05	.01
25	.67	.24	.07	.01
50	.54	.30	.09	.04
75	.41	.38	.12	.10
100	.28	.46	.16	.21
Merits experience				
0	.72	.23	.04	.01
5	.54	.25	.12	.04
10	.35	.26	.27	.10
15	.19	.28	.48	.23
20	.09	.30	.69	.41

Source: 1990 survey data.

Note: Agenda experience refers to the number of previous cases in which a lawyer has either sought or opposed review of a lower court decision in the Supreme Court. Merits experience refers to the number of previous cases in which a lawyer has made oral arguments before the Court. For the probit equations on which the above probabilities are based, see Appendix 1.

cess serve as predictors for each stage, provide a general overview of the relationship in question.[5]

Turning first to table 5.4, one sees that experience in the Court has a dramatic effect on when lawyers become attached to cases. Lawyers with no prior experience with the business of the Court are virtually certain to have served as counsel beginning at the trial stage. Members of the outer circle simply are not sought either to obtain review or to brief and argue a case on the merits. After all, legal representation is costly, and "clients don't want to pay for your initiation" (CI). In contrast, the veteran Court advocates have a much greater probability of being activated later in the process. One lawyer, whose firm obviously does a good deal of Supreme Court work, illustrated this point perfectly:

Of the twenty-five cases that we've briefed and argued in the last six years, I think only one of them was a case where [the firm] represented one of the parties at the trial level. And I think that in only one or two of them did we have any involvement in the court of appeals stage. (CI)

Not all litigants, however, choose to turn to experienced counsel. Many do not have the money or the knowledge required to seek out expert assistance. One current member of the solicitor general's staff made this observation:

Many clients are relatively unsophisticated about who is a good lawyer. They don't really have any way of knowing who is the person to do the job for them in the Supreme Court. (CI)

Of course, some consumers of legal services do appreciate the importance of experience and are willing to bear the costs associated with it. Said another lawyer employed at a major firm:

A lawyer might represent clients that understand the value of Supreme Court practice and are happy to pay people to take things there. I represent several organizations that understand that. A lot of groups are just not that sophisticated. (CI)

Nonetheless, in broad terms, one can see that those making decisions about the appropriateness of counsel at various stages of litigation do so in ways one would expect. If a client decides to seek new counsel later in litigation, he or she will probably turn to those who have appeared before the Court on previous occasions. The most apparent feature of this relationship is that agenda and merits experience are seen as most useful when exploited early in the litigation process. That is, familiarity with the Court's process of case selection has its greatest relevance at the appellate stage, while experience in oral argument is most applicable to the Court's agenda stage.

There is other evidence to support the conclusion that lawyers with considerable Supreme Court experience are often tapped at the appeals stage to lend their expertise. In his study of church-state litigation, for example, Sorauf (1976) found that Leo Pfeffer, an attorney for the American Jewish Congress, had considerable involvement at the appellate stage in a number of the Court's cases involving religion.

Likewise, in *INS v. Chadha* (1983), Alan Morrison, head of the Public Citizen Litigation Group, did not assume responsibility for the case until the appellate stage (see Craig 1988). Lawyers who have handled the largest number of cases at the agenda stage have nearly a 50 percent chance of being called in at the appeals stage. Similarly, lawyers with experience in oral argument are likely to be asked to prepare certiorari petitions (or oppositions). A lawyer with fifteen previous arguments, for example, has roughly a .50 probability of being activated after an appeal; the probability increases to .70 for a lawyer with twenty appearances before the Court.

Of course, experience also has some effect on whether lawyers are engaged at the merits stage. In his analysis of lawyers of the Warren Court, Casper (1972) found that, more than any other category of litigation, civil rights cases were likely to be argued by a specialized appellate bar brought in to argue at the merits stage. Which lawyers are brought on board after the justices agree to hear a case? The experienced lawyers, particularly those who have argued earlier cases in the high court. If a lawyer has as many as fifteen arguments to his credit, the odds are roughly one in four that he will be sought at the merits. With twenty arguments, a lawyer has better than a 40 percent chance of being engaged at the merits.

For a lawyer with no previous arguments to be activated this late in the litigation is therefore quite atypical. Reflecting on how he came to be asked to prepare a brief on the merits and argue before the justices, even though he had no prior experience in the Supreme Court, one lawyer commented that "this has got to be the strangest one of all, that they brought in outside counsel who had never argued before" (CI). Oddly enough, he was selected as counsel only after the litigant had interviewed several Washington firms that possessed ample Supreme Court talent.

As table 5.5 reveals, an analysis of the rates of success yields results that, if somewhat less striking, are still relatively consistent with the above tendency for litigants to turn to the experienced elite later in the process. Granted, when experience and success are compared, the more conspicuous Supreme Court lawyers appear to have the edge over the more successful when it comes to the selection of counsel. One appellate practitioner, employed at a firm boasting a relatively large pool of Supreme Court practitioners, told me that:

TABLE 5.5. Effect of success on stage at which Supreme Court lawyers are activated

	Trial	Appeal	Supreme Court agenda	Supreme Court merits
Agenda success				
0%	.71	.21	.07	.01
25%	.70	.22	.07	.01
50%	.68	.24	.07	.01
75%	.67	.25	.06	.02
100%	.66	.27	.06	.03
Merits success				
0%	.71	.22	.05	.01
25%	.64	.25	.07	.02
50%	.57	.27	.11	.03
75%	.49	.30	.16	.03
100%	.42	.33	.21	.04

Source: 1990 survey data.
Note: The figures in the first column refer to the proportion of previous Supreme Court cases in which a lawyer was successful at the agenda stage or at the merits stage. For the probit equations on which the probabilities are based, see Appendix 1.

> For us, the Supreme Court practice has been very successful, I think. It's a high visibility practice, which is helpful for the firm. (CI)

Consistent with the data on the effects of experience, the effect of merits success seems to be greatest for those lawyers who are sought to lend their services at the case selection stage, as the change in probabilities for merits success demonstrates. Proportionally, the change is greatest for those lawyers activated at the case selection stage, the probabilities ranging from .05 to .21. In contrast, the change for those who are called in on appeal is much more confined, running from a minimum of .22 to a maximum of .33, while the effect of merits success on those who are first involved at the merits is negligible, the probability merely inching up from .01 to .04. These data suggest that at the point when a case makes it all the way to the Court, many litigants then decide to turn to visible and effective members of the Supreme

Court bar—those who have previously argued successfully before the Court—either to seek or to oppose review. The comments of one alumnus of the solicitor general's office, now in private practice, support this interpretation:

> I suppose there are two paradigm situations, if you're talking about private litigation. The first is that the lawyer has a case that starts off at the trial court, and, when it gets to the court of appeals or the state supreme court, an important decision is made that is worthy of Supreme Court review, and certiorari is sought and granted, and the lawyer finds himself or herself in the Supreme Court. Now the second pattern is that you have a case that's litigated in the lower courts that's important to a client—the client could be a big company, a wealthy individual, but it could also be an organization—and somebody with influence on the party comes along and says, "This case is important to you; you ought to have a Supreme Court specialist handle it." And the art of getting the Supreme Court to review a case is a somewhat special artist thing. So they bring in Supreme Court counsel. Now, that may be true even though very competent counsel has handled the case in the lower courts. But when they get to the Supreme Court, some clients feel that there are lawyers who have a lot of experience with the Supreme Court and that they ought to use them. (CI)

Overall, both Supreme Court experience and success have their greatest effect after the initial trial court decision. When a case reaches the appeals stage, or when it has reached the Court, the lawyers who are brought in as new advocates are likely to have proven themselves effective litigators before the justices; that is, they are likely to be members of the inner circle of the bar. Nowhere were these results better validated than in the comments of one of the most respected members of the Supreme Court bar:

> My cases come in a number of ways. They can come after a trial and before the court of appeals, in a case where a party thinks it's sufficiently important that they need special counsel or where a party believes that the case may go the Supreme Court or that the other party may try to take the case to the Supreme Court. So, in that instance, I would become involved in arguing in the

court of appeals or advising at that level, to make sure that the issues are preserved for Supreme Court review. Secondly, they might come after a court of appeals or a state supreme court decision, seeking me either to obtain Supreme Court review or to keep somebody else from getting Supreme Court review. And thirdly, they can come after the Supreme Court agrees to hear a case, where suddenly a party will seek outside counsel, either because they believe it's necessary or because there are two parties on their side, and they can't come to an agreement as to which one is going to argue. (CI)

This is as perceptive an assessment as one could hope to hear. The inner circle is sought after a trial court decision. Given their appellate expertise and Supreme Court experience, these lawyers are in a position to develop the direction of the case—to amplify certain questions, to downplay others, to evaluate the significance of a case, to navigate the often choppy waters of the stream of appellate litigation that runs to the Supreme Court. Organizational and institutional litigants are in the best position to recognize the potential influence of these lawyers and to afford to retain one of the experienced elite. Understanding why the elite are activated at the appellate level is, however, only half the story. The question of how that process works has yet to be addressed.

Investing in Expertise

What brings members of the elite and their cases together? Often, lawyers work on retainer, representing longtime clients, while others have cases referred to them by their fellow litigators. Still others work for organized interests, their clients being channeled to them through the respective organizations. Each of these considerations can be important (Casper 1972). However, since previous experience in the Supreme Court is so strongly related to the selection of lawyers, it is also likely that lawyers may be chosen because of their professional reputations. Professional reputations, of course, come in many types. One attorney may have a reputation as an effective labor lawyer; another may be known for civil liberties work. But Supreme Court experience itself may garner a lawyer a reputation, as the impact of previous Supreme Court experience on when lawyers are activated suggests.

TABLE 5.6. Basis for selection reported by Supreme Court lawyers

Employment setting	Prior client (%)	Reputation (%)	Peer referral (%)	Group referral (%)	Request of friend (%)	N
All lawyers	74.0	16.8	12.8	1.8	1.5	327
Solo practitioner	65.0	25.0	22.5	0.0	7.5	40
Law firm	73.9	16.3	14.1	1.1	0.5	184
State and local government	86.0	7.8	2.0	3.9	0.0	51

Source: 1990 survey data.
Note: Percentages may not total 100, since some lawyers may have more than one reason for being selected.

What patterns of selection prevail, then, with regard to members of the Supreme Court bar, particularly those within the inner circle?

For the most part, lawyers report having represented their Supreme Court clients in other contexts, as is evident in table 5.6. This table gives the criteria for lawyer selection for all Supreme Court litigators, as well as for the three largest categories of counsel. About three-fourths of the Supreme Court bar come to the Court having already represented their clients elsewhere, something which also holds true for each of the segments of the bar, whether private practitioners or state and local government counsel.

Among private attorneys, Supreme Court lawyers employed by a firm are more likely to have represented their clients previously than are solo practitioners. Although not all clients will retain the same firm in any given case, many legal consumers do maintain consistent ties with certain law firms.

> Obviously, if the client had come to one of the big firms in the country—there must be thirty of them, truly national firms—then I think the client would probably stay with that lawyer, all the way up to the Supreme Court. (CI)

Corporate interests, for example—traditional consumers of law firm services—are normally represented by large firms on an ongoing basis (Smigel 1964; Vago 1991). An established client base is particularly crucial to the bigger law firms (Nelson 1981), and corporate representation is among the most important staple sources of legal business for firms generally and Supreme Court firm attorneys specifically (Galanter and Palay 1991; see also chapter 4). Sustained representation by firm counsel is particularly prevalent among the Supreme Court bar, with three out of four law firm practitioners having already represented their clients elsewhere.

In contrast, solo practitioners are the least likely to have represented their clients in another context. These lawyers generally do not have formal mechanisms for expanding their practice. Often, their clients are referred to them through family connections or civic and religious groups or even on the recommendation of a friend (Carlin 1962). This produces a general mix of clients. Some of these may opt for litigation, and, of those who do so, a small number may eventually seek (or oppose) review in the Supreme Court—although, when it comes to state cases, a fair number of clients may be quick to exhaust the available remedies and thus find themselves knocking on the doors of the Supreme Court, given the absence of intermediate appellate courts in about one quarter of the states (Baum 1986, 44). As the data in table 5.6 confirm, there is no regular pattern to the ways in which cases come to the solo practitioner. Once again, the client dimension appears to differentiate lawyers, the corporate client being represented on a relatively regular basis, whereas the representation of individual clients is more ad hoc.

Of all attorneys, however, state and local government counsel are the ones most likely to represent their respective clients on an ongoing basis. Little needs to be said on this score, since the reason is fairly obvious. Lawyers who represent state governments in the Supreme Court are generally duly designated representatives, such as attorneys general. In some instances, though, states do bring in private Supreme Court counsel for assistance. For instance, in *Missouri v. Jenkins* (1990), an alumnus of the solicitor general's office, H. Bartow Farr III, represented the state of Missouri (see Mauro 1989b). In addition, state and local litigators occasionally have cases referred to them by groups of which they are members.

A significant minority of Supreme Court lawyers, about 17 percent, report that they were chosen because of their professional reputation. Given this criterion, lawyers of high educational, social, and professional prestige are likely to be preferred. One measure of an attorney's reputation is, of course, the cost of legal services, and indeed lawyers with reputations as Supreme Court experts are not cheap. In 1983, for example, one prominent Supreme Court specialist was charging some clients as much as $525 per hour (Lauter 1987).

Referrals from fellow lawyers can play an important role in establishing lawyer-client relationships (Carlin 1962). In the context of Supreme Court litigation, Casper (1972) found that peer referral was fairly frequently responsible for the involvement of at least some Court practitioners. Increasingly, when lawyers refer business to their colleagues, the referral often takes place between lawyers who have mutual legal interests. As Heinz and Laumann argue, "Patent lawyers, for example, may maintain close ties with counsel for corporations likely to invent patentable products, and lawyers specializing in commercial litigation may seek connections with office lawyers who represent commercial enterprises" (1982, 60). Thus, in the Supreme Court, a corporate house counsel who rarely litigates probably will coordinate legal work, performing an administrative as opposed to a litigious function. Often, he will "decide what work to send outside and where to send it" (Abel 1989, 170). Galanter and Palay describe this process: "Rather than choose a law firm to marry for life, corporate counsel now increasingly choose particular lawyers or firms for specific projects. . . . In choosing an outside attorney for a specific task, a corporation without able and experienced in-house counsel will need to look for simple, familiar signals of quality and capacity, such as the size or reputation of the law firm. But where the client possesses an expert purchaser of legal services, the expert can delve more deeply into the quality of prospective outside attorneys" (1991, 113–14). It is not accidental that there are so few active members of the Supreme Court bar who are in-house counsel. Indeed, it should be plain that in the Supreme Court their role is one of locating counsel, rather than serving as counsel.

Policy knowledge v. process knowledge.   What other considerations might influence clients in their selection of counsel? If a party believes that its case may eventually go to the Supreme Court, two basic motivations come into play when that party selects a lawyer. First, lawyers can be chosen because of their reputations as skilled appellate counsel, that is, because of their familiarity with the Supreme Court process. These are the modern Daniel Websters. Second, lawyers—the modern William Pinkneys—may possess an especially thorough knowledge of a particular policy area critical to the client's case.

Indeed, substantive expertise alone can lead to Supreme Court work, as one law firm practitioner attested:

> I guess I've actually argued two cases before the Supreme Court, one of which grew out of nothing to do with my being in Washington but instead grew out of the fact that I had first had a similar case involving the same basic issue which I had won in the court of claims. (CI)

Clients look for lawyers with such policy knowledge, particularly successful ones, when selecting counsel. When corporate house counsel begin considering appellate representation, for instance, success in a substantive legal area may be the primary reason for choosing a given attorney.

> They look for experience with the kind of issue that their case raises. If you've won another case very close to their issue, that's a very good recommendation. It makes sense to the client. It also make sense to the client's general counsel, who may be making the recommendation about who to hire to argue the case. It's good for the CEO or the stockholders to know that. (CI)

Command of policy alone does not, however, always guarantee that a lawyer will be a viable candidate for Supreme Court work. As I have noted, appellate experts have a flexibility that allows them to specialize in a number of specific fields of the law. Such a combination is particularly impressive to the non-Supreme Court lawyer, who may refer business to an appellate advocate who shares his substantive interests. As one lawyer, who maintains an active involvement in associations of trial lawyers, noted:

> A lot of the Supreme Court work that I've handled in the last two or three years has been based on referral to me by plaintiffs' trial lawyers in antitrust cases. I've had seven antitrust cases in the Supreme Court in the last year—argued one and successfully opposed cert in the other six. Those were all referrals from plaintiffs' trial lawyers. So, I cultivate the plaintiffs' trial bar. . . . You know, I sort of keep visible among trial lawyers. That's a major source of Supreme Court referrals for me. (CI)

To some degree, then, both clients and fellow lawyers are aware of the command of process and policy that certain litigators possess. Such

TABLE 5.7. Lawyers reporting peer referral or legal reputation as basis for selection (in percent)

Level of involvement	Referral	Reputation
Administrative proceeding	2.3	11.6
Trial	10.7	15.8
Appeal	20.8	14.3
Supreme Court agenda	22.7	31.8
Supreme Court merits	16.7	66.7

Source: 1990 survey data ($N = 325$).

talents can, moreover, prove particularly valuable in securing Supreme Court work, especially at the later stages of litigation. Let us compare the importance of both professional reputation and peer referral for the lawyers activated at each stage. On this basis, one may be able to make some preliminary inferences about the relative significance of policy and process expertise.

In the survey, I asked lawyers to indicate how they became involved in their cases from the 1986 term, giving the respondents several options from which to choose (see Appendix 2). These options, which were not mutually exclusive, included referrals from another lawyer and professional reputation. Table 5.7 separates lawyers by the stage of their initial involvement and shows the proportion of lawyers who reported peer referral or professional reputation as a criterion for selection at each stage.

Reputations grow increasingly more important as the litigation process progresses. Nearly 70 percent of the lawyers who were mobilized at the merits stage, for instance, saw their professional reputation as a significant reason why they were chosen as counsel. It is very likely that these lawyers are experts on process, as opposed to policy, and can thus represent any party in the Court with more or less equal competence.

> There are people who are very different and very effective. Obviously, people like Larry Tribe are very skilled lawyers. He represented Pennzoil as well as the guy in *Bowers v. Hardwick*. Those are two wide spectrums of clients. (CI)

(Tribe was counsel on the petition for review in *Pennzoil v. Texaco* [1987], whereas he became involved only at the merits stage in *Bowers v. Hardwick* [1986].) An alumnus of the solicitor general's office also illustrated this point quite nicely:

> In a case I worked on last fall, the folks that came to me had many millions of dollars involved in their case. The lawyers thought they understood the case real well; they just wanted to make sure that they were correctly positioning it vis-à-vis the Supreme Court. This case involved in-house counsel plus at least two specialized counsel that had been involved in the litigation below. (CI)

When one considers those lawyers whose cases were referred to them by a colleague, the results tell a similar tale. Of the lawyers who became active at the trial stage, only 11 percent became involved because of a referral by a fellow litigator, but among the lawyers who were mobilized subsequent to a trial, the proportion is markedly greater. Naturally, this may reflect a recognition of policy expertise, but it probably suggests an appreciation of practical appellate experience as well.

> It's more likely that, in cases coming up from the circuits or state supreme courts, the attorneys may find that they know people in Washington who are known for having argued cases before the Court, or even in a particular policy area, and then search out to see if that lawyer is available. In a case that I had on behalf of the state of Maryland, there was a confluence of things that resulted in my being asked by the state to argue it. One was I had been involved in the area of state authority over wildlife for a number of years on behalf of a group of fifty states. So, I was known to Maryland, and they asked me to come and help out in the trial court. Then, when it went to the Supreme Court, their attorney, who just hadn't been on his feet that much, asked me to take it over, which I did with great pleasure. (CI)

In table 5.8, I address the comparative importance of expertise on policy and process. Using probit analysis, I have measured the effects of several of the most common fields of legal specialization and the time spent in various litigation settings on how lawyers are chosen by clients. In general terms, these data suggest that procedural expertise

TABLE 5.8. Effect of legal specialization and litigation experience on selection of lawyers

	Reputation	Peer referral
Specialization		
Appellate litigation	.22	.20
Administrative law	.12	.08
Criminal law	.17	.14
Civil liberties	.17	.12
Labor law	.08	.05
Litigation experience		
Administrative proceedings	.05	.01
State trial courts	.24	.22
State appellate courts	.08	.11
Federal trial courts	.11	.07
Federal appellate courts	.59	.28

Source: 1990 survey data ($N = 294$).

Note: The probabilities, which are based on probit estimates, reflect the independent effect of each factor on the two selection criteria. Because time spent in litigation setting is a continuous variable, I have multiplied each of the litigation coefficients by 100%. For the full equations for both the reputation and the referral models, see Appendix 1.

is of greater significance. Appellate practitioners and those lawyers who litigate in federal courts of appeals have the greatest likelihood of being selected because of their professional reputation. (These, it should be noted, are the lawyers of the elite community within the Supreme Court bar.) Similarly, when a lawyer refers a case to a colleague, he or she may do so on the basis of firsthand knowledge of that lawyer's appellate expertise, as one former associate of the solicitor general's office illustrated:

> I've only argued four cases in the Supreme Court since I came into private practice, and one of them was on a referral from the solicitor general's office. (CI)

On balance, the weight of evidence points to command of procedure as having more importance than knowledge of policy in the process of lawyer selection. The significance of the former should not, however, be overestimated. As the following story illustrates, a lawyer's mastery of a particular area of the law can compensate for a lack of appellate litigation experience.

In my case, the client was represented by a fairly small firm, and after cert was granted they began considering who to bring in to handle the case. They considered three Washington-based firms. During this process, they noted that a Supreme Court preview of law professors and journalists at the University of Virginia was going to discuss the leading cases of the term, of which theirs was one. Two of the firm lawyers came to hear their case discussed, and the following Monday morning I got a call from the firm saying they wanted to discuss with me the possibility of arguing it. I said right off, "I've never argued in the Supreme Court; you've got the wrong person." She said, "We were very impressed with your remarks at the conference. Can you come up and talk to us?"

I was talking to a couple of my colleagues and said, "Why in the world would they hire me rather than —— [a former member of the solicitor general's office]? There's only one way to do this— I'm going to have to argue this case to them." So we tore into the library and did massive legislative history research, read dozens of cases, and figured out a much better way to argue the case than had been done before. I got the plane, met with the client and said, "Look, I want twenty minutes to argue this case to you." And I did it right on the spot, down to the details of the argument. They walked me to the elevator and said, "You're hired." Nobody else had discussed the details of the case with them. (CI)

An important lesson can be learned from this story: substantive expertise can be important in the selection of a lawyer. By mustering a compelling legal argument, this lawyer was able to offer something the prestigious Washington firms under consideration had not, a command of the substantive issues. To look at it another way, policy expertise was the wedge that allowed him to overcome his weakness, namely, his lack of experience in the Court itself—a resource in ample supply among the Washington firms. Beyond general appellate expertise, however, just how important is Supreme Court experience to those selecting counsel?

Supreme Court experience. A history of involvement in Supreme Court litigation in fact stands out as one of the most consistent reasons why a lawyer is chosen as counsel. Litigation seldom begins on the assumption that the case will eventually end up in the Supreme Court. Consequently, as has just been illustrated, Supreme Court veterans often enter the litigation after decisions have been handed down in the trial courts. This, of course, is not news to the Supreme Court lawyers themselves. Litigants frequently turn to them in the later stages of a case to tap their practical knowledge of the Court. One practitioner articulated this widely shared sentiment:

> I think one of the advantages of the publicity that has come about in the last five years of private practitioners specializing in Supreme Court practice is to enhance the consumer's view and interest. It is becoming much more common—for big corporations, certainly, when they have a case that's making its way up to the Court—to give serious thought to looking for somebody who has experience in the Court. (CI)

Another captured the situation in this way:

> We often have people come to us precisely because they know that we have Supreme Court experience. And it's clear that people go to former solicitors general like Rex Lee or Erwin Griswold because they are known and prominent as Supreme Court practitioners. (CI)

As this lawyer points out, the availability of lawyers from the elite inner circle of the Supreme Court bar has been fueled by simple attrition from the solicitor general's office—although some have characterized the phenomenon as more in the nature of an exodus (Caplan 1987). The list of alumni of that office who have moved into private practice is both extensive and distinguished: Erwin N. Griswold of Jones, Day, Reavis & Pogue; Rex E. Lee and Carter G. Phillips of Sidley & Austin; Andrew L. Frey, Kenneth S. Geller, Mark I. Levy, Kathryn A. Oberly, Stephen M. Shapiro, and Robert L. Stern, all of Mayer, Brown & Platt; H. Bartow Farr III and Richard Taranto of Klein, Farr, Smith & Taranto; and A. Raymond Randolph of Pepper, Hamilton & Scheetz, to name but a few. With few exceptions, these lawyers work in Washington and continue to have an ongoing Supreme Court practice.[6]

It is not solely these alumni, however, who are called on because of their Supreme Court expertise. A fair number of other private practitioners have also developed reputations as Supreme Court counsel.

One lawyer, also an established Court veteran, explained how attorneys with such reputations are identified:

> What I understand normally happens is that potential clients or their attorneys get together lists. The lists will normally have the same names on them, because there are so few who do this on a regular basis. Then they will call or come to see you, or make the choice by talking to other people. I knew of one instance where somebody was a very good friend with a Supreme Court justice who mentioned my name. So, you don't always know, but what usually happens is that you're selected from a list. (CI)

Generally, the lawyers on this shortlist are fairly few in number, "certainly less than a dozen," one lawyer suggested. Of course, parties may be swayed by a lawyer's reputation as Supreme Court counsel, even though he or she is not on the list. One way to test whether litigants take the reputation of lawyers as Supreme Court counsel into consideration is to examine statistically the effect of Supreme Court experience on the resulting decisions. If greater experience with the Court increases the chances of a lawyer being chosen on the basis of professional standing, then parties are probably looking for Supreme Court experience.[7]

The probabilities in table 5.9, calculated from probit estimates, confirm that, to the extent lawyers are selected because of their professional reputations, their Supreme Court experience makes a significant difference. Of the two types of Court work, experience at the merits stage counts more than experience with the Court's selection of cases. In part, this is because the justices control the number of arguments that can be made. That being so, it is "easier" to file petitions for certiorari and oppositions than it is to argue a case. Decisions on the merits are also more visible and attract more attention than does the granting and denying of review.

> If you've done it many times, people think you're proficient at it, and if someone is going around looking for a Supreme Court lawyer, they're more likely to pick you than someone who's never done it before. (CI)

In addition to corroborating these results, this lawyer also suggests why trying to utilize success rates to predict the selection of counsel is not very illuminating. Clients respond to the more straightforward

TABLE 5.9. Effect of Supreme Court experience on lawyer selection
on the basis of reputation

Agenda experience	
0	.15
25	.18
50	.21
75	.25
100	.28
Merits experience	
0	.16
5	.21
10	.28
15	.35
20	.43

Source: 1990 survey data.
Note: For the probit equations on which the probabilities are based, see Appendix 1.

indicator of participation, whereas success is more difficult to judge. Of course, some sophisticated players can make such a judgment (see Galanter and Palay 1991, 114). Chief Justice Rehnquist gives another reason: "[Mixed success] is generally the lot of the lawyer who has a reputation as a great advocate before the Supreme Court. . . . The reason [is] that frequently 'great advocates' are called in by one of the parties only when the legal situation is roughly equivalent to a baseball game in the last half of the ninth inning when there are two outs and the home team is down by a couple of runs. Even a great batter will hit less than .500, and even the greatest advocate will not win a majority of these cases" (1989, 5–6). There is some truth to the chief justice's statement: some Supreme Court specialists have only modest success on the merits (Wermiel 1989). I doubt, however, that they are considered any less attractive to clients for it.

Certainly, not all parties turn to the elite Supreme Court counsel. In fact, it would be unreasonable to expect every litigant to do so. Because of various constraints (institutional, financial, and so on), clients either cannot or do not seek veterans of practice in the Supreme Court. The data indicate, however, that a great many clients do consider experience in the Court to be relevant and thus select counsel on that basis.

On the decision to retain Mayer, Brown & Platt to handle its Supreme Court work, for instance, the chief counsel to one trade association put it simply: "We wanted the best" (Hayes 1989, 65). Many of the lawyers with whom I spoke felt that their experience in the Court helped to explain why they were sought in subsequent cases, and the survey data reinforce their perception.

Conclusion

There are strategic advantages to being represented by experienced counsel in the Court. The sooner after a trial decision that a veteran Supreme Court lawyer is involved, the better. If members of the inner circle, who possess the expertise that springs from regularized contact with the high court's litigation, are brought into the proceedings early on, they can mold a case in ways that might ultimately be attractive to the justices. Those who seek to influence the governmental process recognize the benefits of an early entrance in policy making, and legal action in the Supreme Court is no exception. Accordingly, the parties whose political instincts are the most developed will know when and how to seize the advantage by selecting one of the established members of the Supreme Court bar's inner circle.

But which litigants are perceptive enough to intuit a case's "Supreme Court potential"? Moreover, who knows which lawyers are among the active elite and which are not? Sophisticated litigants—large corporations, organizations, the wealthy, and the politically powerful—can evaluate the stakes in a given case. They know who the members of the inner circle are, or, at the very least, they know how to find them. In the Supreme Court, then, the legal elites are engaged by the political, social, and economic elites.

6

The Inner Circle at Work

Laurence Gold is the chief appellate litigator for the AFL-CIO. Working out of his Washington office, just north of the White House, this Harvard-educated practitioner is the primary representative of organized labor in the Supreme Court. In one six-year period, a handful of lawyers—scarcely a dozen—argued eight or more cases before the justices. All of them were lawyers for the federal government, except one: Laurence Gold. During the same period, Gold appeared as counsel on the merits in eleven other cases. Beyond this extraordinary participation, Gold has helped prepare as many as three hundred briefs during his tenure at the AFL-CIO. Counting the additional work that he devotes to preparing amicus curiae briefs, Gold estimates that a third of his time is dedicated to Supreme Court practice.[1]

Gold's dramatic involvement in so many facets of Supreme Court litigation vividly illustrates the ways in which the lawyers of the inner circle can use their skills to influence the judicial process. Arguments before the justices are the most visible portion of Supreme Court work, but they are only part of a broader range of activities. For every argument a lawyer has made in the Supreme Court, there are nearly twenty cases at the agenda stage in which he has served as counsel; for each amicus brief a lawyer has written on the merits, there are two others he has filed in support of petitions for review. Having noted the significance of the bar's stratification—its division into inner and outer circles—and the strategic importance of how the elite are mobilized in litigation, one can turn attention to the kinds of work, both formal and informal, that the Supreme Court lawyers perform. In what ways do these elite lawyers participate in cases before the Court, and why do they pursue those forms of participation over others? How, moreover, do those choices relate to the potential for securing access to the Court's agenda?

Visible and Invisible Participation

Scanning the pages of any volume of the *United States Reports,* one might begin to suspect that only a very few lawyers are active Supreme Court practitioners. After all, in any given term of the Court, only the lawyers in the solicitor general's office are conspicuous for their frequent appearances before the justices. Examining but a single avenue of influence, however—looking only at active participation on the merits—obscures the rich participation of lawyers in Supreme Court politics. If, for example, one considers petitions for certiorari, jurisdictional statements, briefs opposing review, and amicus curiae briefs, one discovers that a good many lawyers participate on a consistent basis. Even the number of arguments, when viewed across a longer period of time, would reflect patterns of frequent involvement by a variety of attorneys.

The participation of these lawyers in Supreme Court litigation can assume a great many forms. Some types of involvement, such as presenting oral arguments, are quite conspicuous. Others are less visible—almost invisible—and are thus apt to be disregarded or dismissed as unimportant. The fact of the matter, however, is that much of the behind-the-scenes work that takes place in Supreme Court litigation is vital to success in the Court, particularly at the agenda stage. No one has a more keen appreciation of this fact than the members of the inner circle.

Let us examine the range of activities of the Court's counsel. Perhaps the most obvious places to begin are the agenda and merits stages. After all, these lawyers are litigators, so their appearance in the Court—both on paper and in person—affords a useful denominator

TABLE 6.1. Lawyers with one or more previous cases at agenda and merits stages

Employment setting	Agenda stage (%)	Merits stage (%)	N
All lawyers	79.4	19.6	327
Solo practitioners	76.7	18.6	43
Law firm	75.6	15.9	201
State and local government	90.7	24.1	54

Source: 1990 survey data.

for comparing them. Since the lawyers in this study were drawn from a sample of the 1986 term, it is clear that each lawyer had, at minimum, one case at the Court's case selection stage. Was this the only case that lawyer handled, or was it but one of several?

The data in table 6.1 show the proportion of lawyers, overall and in the three largest employment settings, who had one or more cases in the Supreme Court, at either the agenda or the merits stage. No less than three-quarters of the Supreme Court bar, regardless of their employment setting, had handled previous cases, either seeking or opposing review of a lower court decision. At the merits stage, roughly one in five lawyers had argued one or more cases before the justices, the figure rising to one in four among attorneys who work in state and local government. Even among the ranks of the solo attorneys, there was a respectable showing of previous participation at the merits. In fact, firm attorneys and solo practitioners, while somewhat less likely to have argued in the Court before, come respectably close to rivaling state and local government lawyers at this stage.

As I have noted, however, appearing before the Court to argue a case is only one component of what these lawyers do (see, for example, Sorauf 1976, 159–64). Much of the work done by many Supreme Court practitioners—especially the experienced ones—takes place behind the scenes, as this veteran advocate explained.

> There are various roles in which people like us can help. We can take over a case, but we can also give advice to a lawyer, edit the stuff to make sure that it's presented in the right way to the Court, give moot courts to help the lawyer prepare for oral argument. (CI)

TABLE 6.2. Secondary activities of the Supreme Court bar in Supreme Court litigation (in percent)

Helped prepare an appeal or petition for certiorari	42.0
Helped prepare a brief on the merits	34.3
Helped prepare on oral argument	28.4
Served on a moot court	21.1
Filed an amicus brief supporting an appeal or certiorari	21.1
Filed an amicus brief at the merits	19.0
Filed an amicus brief opposing an appeal or certiorari	9.1

Source: 1990 survey data ($N = 327$).

Note: For these secondary forms of litigation involvement, I report the percentage of Supreme Court lawyers who indicated having served in those roles on one or more previous cases. These results reflect only the secondary activities of the lawyers who sought or opposed review in the Court's 1986–87 term. The results for lawyers who participated in Supreme Court litigation in other ways may be different.

The most frequent forms of such participation are listed in table 6.2. Even the most cautious assessment of these data permits the conclusion that Supreme Court lawyers engage in a considerable range of tasks. Of all the individual forms of participation, consultation on the preparation of petitions or oppositions at the agenda stage is the service Supreme Court lawyers most often provide, but, in the aggregate, the bulk of their effort appears to be targeted at preparing their colleagues to argue at the merits. Many of the experienced Supreme Court lawyers in Washington, for example, evaluate one another's oral preparations, criticize their briefs, and school less experienced counsel on what questions to expect from the justices (Greenya 1987). Prior to her fledgling effort before the Court, one nervous appellate practitioner allowed me to hear the first of her several moot court preparations in a case she was later to argue; among the "justices" were a former advocate for the ACLU and an alumnus of the solicitor general's office. (In fact, just after his first argument before the justices, another lawyer admitted that his appearance at the moot court had actually been more stressful.) Such activities are common.

Generally, when someone knows that I do quite a bit of Supreme Court work, he'll simply call and say, "I have my first Supreme

Court argument, and I'd like to sit down and talk," or "I'd like you to sit on a moot court," or something like that. (CI)

Far from being restricted to the private bar, similar practices take place among state government attorneys. Indeed, they have been institutionalized. The National Association of Attorneys General (NAAG), with the cooperation of the Justice Department, has implemented a program designed to prime state and local counsel for their appearances in the Court. The State and Local Legal Center has an analogous program (see Lempert 1982; Sylvester 1984). Even lawyers in the experienced public interest bar may provide assistance to outside counsel who are new to the Court. As one interest group litigator explained:

> Well, cases come to us in three different ways. Some of them are cases that are our own, that we've won or lost in the lower courts. That represents, in our case, by far the majority of them. Second, we read advance sheets and hear about cases and call people. It's less awkward for us to do that because we're not making any money. And indeed sometimes we make offers that people can't refuse—we take the case for nothing. And third, people come to us. We're basically trying to help people. So we get the word out to a lot of people as to what we're doing. (CI)

The exemplary organization in this regard is the Public Citizen Litigation Group, which, out of a concern for the lack of assistance for legal services counsel and small firm litigators, has instituted a program designed to help such lawyers with all phases of Supreme Court litigation.[2]

Providing assistance to colleagues is only part of the story. Lawyers may become active in Supreme Court cases even if they are not serving directly as counsel to one of the parties. Many Supreme Court attorneys are active as writers of amicus briefs, for instance, at both stages of the Court's decision making.[3] As table 6.2 shows, roughly one in five Supreme Court lawyers has filed amicus briefs supporting review. The same can also be said for amicus briefs at the merits. Such work might be done in conjunction with the lawyer who is formally handling a case, as this law professor illustrated:

> In one case I worked on, a person from another law school was actually arguing the case, and we got together with him and filed an amicus brief on behalf of the ACLU. (CI)

By now it should be clear that much of the work of the Supreme Court bar is dotted throughout the Court's discretionary and plenary dockets. Duties such as behind-the-scenes preparation and the secondary role of writing amicus briefs are not obvious at first glance. Nonetheless, a significant proportion of the Supreme Court bar carries out such tasks quite regularly. This raises the question of which Supreme Court lawyers are most likely to engage in these less visible activities. Once again, the evidence points to the inner circle as the principal suspect.

Quite apart from lawyers seeking the assistance of their peers, litigants may also turn to the experienced elite to perform these secondary roles. Many parties seek out the specialists specifically for the purpose of helping their inexperienced practitioners navigate the waters of the Supreme Court. Indeed, several Supreme Court experts saw this as a primary function of the Court's bar:

> Often the lawyer is not dumped when the case gets to the Supreme Court. A Supreme Court specialist will come in and work with whoever handled the case in the court of appeals. That's what we do—almost all the time. (CI)

> If I had only ten thousand dollars to spend, there are two things I would do. First, spend the money and get the people in there to help you write the petition or to write the opposition. It's not only in so much as the writing of it, as it is the strategizing and figuring out what to do. Second, at the merits, don't spend the money to have the expert come and argue the case. Spend it to have somebody read the brief. Not writing the arguments— any good lawyer can write the arguments—but thinking the thing through and doing a moot court. Use it on a consultative basis. (CI)

Another reason that the elite specialists end up serving as consultants is that arguing before the Court is a very attractive prospect for a lawyer, indeed, "a temptation few seem to be able to resist" (Wasby 1988, 147).

> I'll never forget the case where a young man lost in the Third Circuit, and he asked me to step in and file a petition for cert and argue the case in the Supreme Court. When I looked at it, I said, "Well, gee, before I do that, I ought to file a petition for reargu-

TABLE 6.3. Effect of Supreme Court experience on litigation roles in Supreme Court cases

	Argument	Petition	Merits brief	Moot court
Agenda experience				
0	.07	.19	.14	.05
25	.29	.44	.35	.20
50	.66	.72	.62	.49
75	.91	.90	.84	.78
100	.99	.98	.95	.94
Merits experience				
0	.20	.36	.27	.13
5	.54	.64	.55	.47
10	.85	.87	.81	.83
15	.98	.97	.95	.98
20	.99	.99	.99	.99

Source: 1990 survey data.
Note: For the probit equations on which the above probabilities are based, see Appendix 1.

ment in the Third Circuit," which I did, and we won it, 5–3. Then the government sought cert, and it was granted. So we wrote the brief, and then the day before the brief was filed, the young man came in and said, "Sir, I want to tell you that, but for you, we never would have gotten a reversal in the circuit. But my mother and father say, 'Look, this is the only case you'll probably ever have in the Supreme Court; you've just got to argue it.'" And so he said, "I'm sorry, you're not going to argue." So, we filed the brief, and he argued the case. He won it. (CI)

Lawyers, understandably reluctant to be displaced when given the chance to argue in the Court, wisely turn to the experienced elite for counsel and guidance.

Table 6.3 provides us with some empirical evidence for this judgment. Using probit analysis, I have used a lawyer's experience at the stage of case selection and on the merits to predict the probability of that lawyer's having served in each of the secondary roles. In every instance, the more experienced a member of the Supreme Court bar is, the more likely he or she will be at work providing assistance to lawyers formally serving in the litigation. Prior contact with the Court at the stage of case selection has an especially significant impact on secondary participation. Lawyers who have handled even a moderate number of petitions or oppositions are likely to have been consulted in another Supreme Court case.

If agenda experience is an important determinant of whether a lawyer will be asked to perform one of these alternative roles, having argued before the Court is even more significant. That a lawyer who has made more than five arguments before the justices will be called on to help a peer prepare at least one other case is almost a certainty. Such expertise is brought into play, for example, in the moot court program sponsored by the National Association of Attorneys General, where litigators such as former Solicitors General Robert Bork and Erwin Griswold, as well as the Washington community of Supreme Court specialists, routinely take part in preparing state counsel (see Marcotte 1986).

From an economic standpoint, tapping the resources of the elite in this way makes a good deal of sense. Reflecting on how experienced counsel are employed in an advisory capacity, one interest group lawyer with extensive experience litigating in the Court commented:

> If a client has a long-term relationship with a lawyer, and they've never had a case that's gone to the Supreme Court, and if the lawyer's won below, the client is going to be reluctant to quash the lawyer, if the lawyer is able at all. So the more sensible thing may be to get somebody else in to help you out a little bit. That will be undoubtedly much less expensive, and probably get about 90 percent of the benefits of the lawyer with experience, certainly, in terms of preparing for oral argument, reviewing the brief, thinking through a strategy. That's a lot less time-consuming and expensive than taking over the full representation. (CI)

While there are undoubtedly personal motivations that work against the notion of retaining experienced counsel (a lawyer's vanity, for example, or the thrill of arguing in the Court), market constraints can also preclude turning a case over completely to Supreme Court special-

TABLE 6.4. Effect of Supreme Court experience on the filing of amicus briefs

	Supporting review	Opposing review	On merits
Agenda experience			
0	.05	.04	.05
25	.20	.09	.18
50	.48	.19	.41
75	.77	.33	.68
100	.94	.50	.88
Merits experience			
0	.13	.07	.10
5	.47	.16	.46
10	.83	.31	.86
15	.98	.50	.99
20	.99	.69	.99

Source: 1990 survey data.
Note: For the probit equations on which the above probabilities are based, see Appendix 1.

ists: the experts are expensive. This leads to more behind-the-scenes roles for the inner circle. These lawyers are thus far more active than someone judging by visible participation alone might presume.

The role of the elite in the filing of amicus briefs is no less dramatic, as table 6.4 reveals. Amici are an important mechanism whereby the certworthiness of a case can be signaled to the justices (Caldeira and Wright 1988), as experienced Supreme Court litigators are well aware (Ennis 1984; Stern, Gressman, and Shapiro 1986, 394–97). It comes as no surprise, therefore, that those with expertise recognize the value of amici by their willingness to participate in such a capacity. Granted, experienced counsel are fairly likely to file amicus briefs opposing review, but they are considerably more apt to file amici supporting review. This is testament to the political savvy of at least some of the Supreme Court veterans, since briefs opposing review serve only to attract the justices' attention to a case (Caldeira and Wright 1988; see also Baker 1984).

Certain parties, such as interest groups and state governments, are frequent litigants before the Court. So one would expect their lawyers to perform a variety of tasks in Supreme Court litigation, including the writing of amicus briefs. Even these litigants, though, will sometimes seek out the Supreme Court specialists. One practitioner in a Washington firm, for example, told me that many organizations turn to him precisely for that reason. Perhaps, also, clients are prompted to seek a member of the inner circle to draft an amicus brief in the belief that the name of that specialist on the brief may carry some added weight. The elite bar is, in other words, sought as a means of cultivating access to the Court.

As it turns out, having the name of a specialist on your brief can prove no small advantage. On one of my visits to the Justice Department, a current member of the solicitor general's office told me that many amicus briefs are of decidedly questionable value to the Court: "I think a lot of the amicus filings are really trash." As he went on to point out, however, amici written by experienced Supreme Court counsel probably are of genuine worth to the bench:

> The justices really can't spend a lot of time closely scrutinizing all the amicus filings that are made. They look with some care at the briefs of the parties. I think they glance over the amicus filings much more lightly. But if they see that there's an amicus filing by a lawyer whose analysis they have found helpful in the past, they are more apt to take a closer look at it. (CI)

This opinion is shared by lawyers outside the solicitor general's office. In a perfect description of why parties would benefit from amici written by experienced Supreme Court litigators, one Court veteran said:

> Far too many of them are essentially "me too" briefs. I guess if you wanted your amicus brief read, it might be worth it to hire a Supreme Court practitioner. I think any of the recognized Supreme Court specialists would be unwilling to sign a "me too" brief. So, in that sense, if you've got a brief that you want somebody to read, it is worth it to get a specialist's name on it. (CI)

Another advocate, one who works in a large firm and has represented an environmental interest group in the Court, provided further validation by virtue of his disdain for the wanton filing of amicus briefs:

> "Me too" briefs I really discourage. We do not file them. Not only do we not file them, we don't join with sixteen other groups. If

we're going to get in, we're going to get in alone, solely on behalf of the client. (CI)

The Court itself has become increasingly less interested in hearing from amici whose substantive contributions to the litigation process are marginal (Mauro 1990b). Thus, the value of elite counsel as writers of and consultants on amicus briefs lies in the fact that their names assist the justices in separating the wheat from the chaff.

Experienced Supreme Court lawyers thus serve a great many functions, much of that work directed toward securing access to the justices' plenary agenda. Advising newcomers how to prepare petitions, for instance, or writing amicus briefs in support of review, as well as drafting petitions of their own, are common forms of involvement. The lawyers in the inner circle, however, do not choose these types of participation imprudently. Indeed, they are sophisticated players capable of deploying various strategies to gain access to the Court, depending on the circumstances. Let us explore why lawyers pursue some of those strategies and take a closer look at one particular tactic for securing entry to the Court.

Motives for Litigation

As cases make their way to the Supreme Court, lawyers are faced with choices: Should review be sought? Will review be sought, and if so how can the pleading be best supported? The answers to such questions will reflect the lawyer's perspective on the incentives and constraints of the case. Broadly speaking, a lawyer's approach to a case is a function of the interests he or she represents. As one scholar observes, "A good many of the differences in litigating strategies between major groups and the individual plaintiff or the ad hoc group grow from differences in the objectives they pursue" (Sorauf 1976, 92). In other words, inasmuch as the inner and outer circles represent different kinds of clients, they will choose distinctive paths when facing litigation before the Court.

At least since Casper's study of libertarian lawyers in the Warren Court (1972), scholars have recognized that there are systematic differences in how lawyers approach litigation in the Court. Some lawyers are concerned primarily with securing a legal victory on behalf of their clients. Their main interest turning on the immediate result of a case—

TABLE 6.5. Factors affecting the decision to seek Supreme Court review (in percent)

How important were these considerations?	Very	Somewhat	Not
Loss in a lower court	76.3	15.8	7.9
Desire of client to seek review	52.0	20.3	27.7
Need for a national standard	44.1	19.2	36.7
Resolution of previously unanswered issue	40.7	17.5	41.8
Conflict among courts	31.6	23.2	45.2

Source: 1990 survey data (*N* = 177).

did their client win or lose?—they have only incidental concern for the larger ramifications their cases may raise for public policy. Other attorneys may see their cases principally as vehicles for resolving important legal and social questions and thus be relatively less concerned with the fate of an individual client.

Although the application of these two basic orientations among counsel was made originally in the context of civil liberties cases (Casper 1972), there is no theoretical reason not to extend a similar classification to the bar as a whole. After all, policies can be economic, as well as social, but invite similar forms of legal involvement. A corporate lawyer, for instance, seeking only to protect a client's patent or secure an exemption from antitrust law, would presumably provide the traditional, results-oriented form of representation. Other lawyers may instead represent a particular long-term policy interest. Labor unions, for example, are among those clients whose basic political interests are economic. Thus, the differentiation between lawyers observed in cases pertaining to social policy may have broader applications.

How important are such considerations to the Supreme Court bar as a whole? Put another way, what motivates lawyers to take cases to the Supreme Court? One item in the survey asked those lawyers who had represented petitioners to note the relative weight of several considerations in their decision to seek review; table 6.5 summarizes their responses.

Losses in lower courts and client preferences stand out as the most common reasons for seeking review—and not surprisingly. Obviously, a lawyer would not petition the Court had his client not lost in a lower court and considered the case important enough to press on. At the same time, the importance of these two motivations demonstrates that many Supreme Court lawyers do simply serve as advocates on their clients' behalf. Corporate counsel, for instance, are fairly constrained by their clients (Heinz and Laumann 1982; Nelson 1988). Thus, when corporations decide to seek Supreme Court review, counsel probably have little to say in the matter, whether they be in-house lawyers or attorneys from a large law firm. Among the law firm counsel who petitioned the Court, for instance, nearly 60 percent reported that their clients' desire to seek Supreme Court review was a very important consideration. In short, many lawyers can, for the most part, do only what their clients will permit them to do. At best, their influence may be restricted to discouraging the client from seeking Supreme Court review, as this lawyer in a large Washington firm suggested:

> Certainly, if you are dealing with a longtime client, I think you will attempt to persuade the client to not file cert petitions in cases in which there is no realistic chance of the Court taking it and to limit his efforts to cases where there really is a chance. (CI)

Another lawyer, also from a large firm, saw the issue in a very similar light:

> Well, we're obviously constrained by the wishes of the client, but we can advise the client that it's not worth his money in the Supreme Court. But we're not out to change the law in a particular way like the ACLU is. We're just out to win particular cases. So we don't have any special interest in passing up a case and waiting for the next case because some case is not as good as we would like. (CI)

Similarly, solo practitioners generally do not have far-reaching social or political goals underlying their litigation strategies. Their interest in Supreme Court policy is incidental to the more immediate concern of a legal victory, as one can readily understand. The solo attorney does not have the stable client base that law firms enjoy; in fact, "[m]any of his clients come to him by chance" (Jacob 1984, 80). Moreover, these clients often have somewhat unsavory legal problems; they are being pursued by a collections agency, or there's a problem with landlord-tenant relations (Carlin 1962; Vago 1991, 260). Thus, not only does the volatile nature of solo practice perpetuate a short-term view of litigation outcomes but solo practitioners also fail to attract the kinds of clients who care about larger policy considerations. Accordingly, solo practitioners were the group least likely to report that policy considerations—the need for a national standard or the resolution of a novel issue—had motived them to seek review. Even when the solo practitioner does find himself representing a client whose case might raise important social or political issues, he is still likely to assume a short-term perspective.

> In the private bar, it's kind of hard to be selective. If you have somebody on death row and you think there's any chance of perhaps prevailing, you can't say, "Well, this case isn't consistent with what I would like." (CI)

In this respect, then, the Supreme Court bar is not an equal-opportunity employer. Not all of its members are permitted—or can afford—to pursue issue-oriented work with any regularity. Still, a fair number of private attorneys do seek review because of broader considerations, such as the need for a national standard on the concerns raised by a case, the need to resolve judicial ambiguity, or the presence of a novel issue which has gone unaddressed by the justices. Traditionally, though, it has fallen to counsel to organized interests to address such questions, and quite often their concern extends beyond the immediate outcome of litigation. Rather, they are interested in the degree to which their general public policy goals can be met via the judicial system (see also Casper 1972). Interest groups, such as the ACLU, NAACP, or the AFL-CIO, each have a special set of policy aims, many of which they attempt to achieve through litigation. Of course, interest group cases often arise under circumstances over which the group's attorney exercises little or no control (Wasby 1984). One former NAACP litigator pointed out that

> when we were involved with some of the civil rights cases, and those young kids were going to jail, we couldn't be selective and say, "Oh, this upsets our strategy." (CI)

Nonetheless, organized interests generally enjoy greater flexibility in their selection of cases than do other lawyers. As an alumnus of the ACLU's national office explained:

> We would select cases all the time. A lot of the ACLU cases raise similar issues, all around the country, and we did make judgment

calls about which one to push, which one to hold back on, which one to take up, which one not to take up. Fortunately, a lot of the clients that the ACLU represents are "public cause" type clients, and they understand if their case is not the best one to go up. (CI)

Such decisions are not always so easy. A lawyer may, for example, be very much concerned with responding to the wishes of the client but also see the case as an excellent opportunity to influence public policy. Among the lawyers in this study, 61 percent of those who sought Supreme Court review because it was very important to their clients *also* viewed the cases as potentially serving to develop a standard on some issue of national consequence. Similarly, 62 percent of the attorneys among whom losses in lower courts weighed heavily in the decision to petition the Court reported that their cases also raised new issues that merited the justices' attention. Thus, some lawyers may litigate with both short- and long-term goals in mind. Lawyers who represent corporations, for example, may apparently litigate with an eye only toward securing a legal victory. Yet corporations also have long-range interests, as well as reputations to consider, and they often mobilize the judicial system in an effort to protect both.[4] The issues that cluster around government regulation of the economy—the granting of patents, the setting of labor standards, regulations concerning industrial safety, rules concerning the transportation of hazardous materials in interstate commerce, to name but a few—tend to have a continued and sustained effect on corporate America. Thus, some lawyers may wind up representing a policy agenda that extends beyond the parameters of an individual case, even if that is not their ostensible purpose. What course of action will these lawyers follow in such cases?

Strategic Politics: The Case of Amici Curiae

At the level of the Supreme Court, one would not only expect lawyers to employ different strategies in their cases (see, for example, Casper 1972; Epstein 1985) but also suspect that the nature of the case determines the types of strategies they pursue. To put it another way, how do the variables operative in the decision to seek review influence what lawyers actually do in Supreme Court litigation? As an illustration, let us consider the question of whether lawyers solicit amicus support for their pleadings. After all, if an interest group lawyer is concerned with using a certain case to shape national policy, what better way to promote that goal than by demonstrating to the Court that the issues of the case are of serious concern to an outside set of public interests? By way of contrast, a solo practitioner seeking review solely to vindicate the rights of the client might not be aware that garnering external support for the case could be of considerable consequence. Furthermore, what about the lawyer who is guided both by client demand and the desire to promote a policy objective? Is that lawyer any more likely to seek the support of friends at the agenda stage?

It is instructive at this stage to consider the more basic issue of whether *any* Supreme Court lawyers encourage an endorsement from amici curiae. On balance, the answer is that the inner circle does, while the outer circle does not. Said one veteran of the Court:

> In the last five years, Supreme Court practitioners have started more conscientiously soliciting amicus support than they used to. I think now, the really sophisticated Supreme Court practitioners would think of that, right from the beginning. (CI)

As this observation reveals, seasoned Supreme Court advocates are more likely to engage in this practice than their less experienced colleagues. Moreover, most, if not all, experts on Court litigating would agree with this lawyer's interpretation. One alumnus of the solicitor general's office, now practicing in Washington, acknowledged that the practice

> is common, and it's entirely appropriate. At the cert stage, amicus support is particularly important. Many people don't realize this. Because the Court has to judge "How important is this issue?" it helps if other people come in and say, "Even though we don't have a stake in this litigation, we believe this legal issue is important, and you ought to hear it." (CI)

If many lawyers at the periphery of the bar have failed to grasp the significance of support from amici, it is common knowledge among both Supreme Court experts (see, for example, Baker 1984; Ennis 1984) and political scientists (Caldeira and Wright 1988; also O'Connor and Epstein 1982). In the survey, 25 percent of the lawyers petitioning the Court for review reported having sought amici on their behalf. Not coincidentally, these practitioners had, on average, served as counsel in at least ten other cases at the agenda stage—nearly three times as

TABLE 6.6. Effect of reasons for seeking review on decision to solicit amicus support

How important were these considerations?	Very	Somewhat	Not
Loss in a lower court	.02	.04	.07
Desire of client to seek review	.16	.14	.13
Need for a national standard	.39	.27	.18
Resolution of previously unanswered issue	.22	.18	.14
Conflict among courts	.14	.13	.12

Source: 1990 survey data ($N = 174$).
Note: For the probit equations on which the above probabilities are based, see Appendix 1.

many as had the lawyers who did not seek amici. Thus, although most petitioners do not seek amicus support, the active elite know that the justices will be more prone to give their cases serious attention when amici accompany their petitions. By the same token, only 8 percent of counsel in opposition sought to engage amicus participation. This suggests that lawyers are aware that amicus briefs opposing review serve only to make cases more viable candidates for certiorari (see Caldeira and Wright 1988).

If the elite practitioners actively seek amicus support, then, under precisely what conditions do they seek it? What can the factors that influence the decision to seek Supreme Court review tell us about whether and when lawyers try to find organized interests who will support their petitions? In general, the likelihood of encouraging amici appears to turn on the breadth of the perceived interests in the case. This applies to all kinds of litigation, economic as well as social. For example,

> I have sought amici. Particularly when representing a client in an industry where the industry is likely to be adversely affected by the outcome of a case, I have encouraged trade associations to file amicus briefs. (CI)

Table 6.6 sheds light on this issue. Using the importance of each of the considerations that might contribute to the decision to opt for review, I calculated the respective probabilities that a lawyer would seek amicus support.

Lawyers whose approach to Supreme Court litigation is dominated by client interests alone are, it turns out, relatively unconcerned with generating outside support for their cases. For instance, there is almost no interest in seeking amici among lawyers whose decision to seek review was motivated primarily by a loss in a lower court. Similarly, lawyers whose clients were anxious to take their cases to the Court do not appear especially eager to activate support from amici. Nor do lawyers typically solicit the assistance of organized interests in a case that has gone to the Supreme Court because of conflicting rulings in the lower courts. In contrast, it makes a great deal of difference whether the petitioner saw his or her case as a vehicle for setting a national policy or addressing a new legal question. In those instances, lawyers are much more likely to seek out amici to reinforce their claims. It is worth mentioning that, for the most part, the client-centered and policy-oriented considerations work independently of one another. For instance, when client concerns predominate (that is, when both lower court losses and client demand rate as very important), the probability of seeking amici is only .04. When broader social issues are significant (namely, when a new issue is coupled with a chance to set national policy), the probability of encouraging amicus support jumps to .56. Taken together, however, the collective effects of all five considerations generate a probability of .33—less than the maximum impact (.39) of the desire to set a national standard. One veteran litigator provided an excellent explanation of why one would expect to find precisely these results:

> It's my personal opinion that the cert stage is the place where amicus briefs are most important, especially if it's a case where cert is based not on conflict between circuits but is based on the nationwide importance of the question. If you've got nationwide organizations saying, "This case is important to us, not just to the parties," that's the most powerful argument you've got. So, if I've got a client who wants to have cert granted, I do encourage amicus briefs at the cert stage. (CI)

These findings suggest an informal yet strong impact on the part of the Supreme Court cognoscenti. Over half the lawyers who solicited amicus participation from outside interests indicated that briefs were filed in response to their encouragement. More important, nearly 80 percent of those lawyers who sought and received amicus support found that their petitions for review were accepted by the justices. On the face of it, then, the soliciting of amici support at the case selection stage offers a means to further a client's interests by mustering support for his or her position. At the same time, by effectively acting as a catalyst for interest group involvement, the Supreme Court counsel can influence the Court's decision whether to accept a case for plenary review (see chapter 8). This is not to diminish the important independent role of interest groups in Supreme Court litigation; organized interests are no doubt mobilized countless times without the prodding of a practitioner. Nonetheless, as gatekeepers to the Court, the inner circle of Supreme Court lawyers can facilitate access by alerting groups to potential amicus opportunities and letting them know that their voices would be a welcome addition to the pleading. As another Washington practitioner explained:

> Any good Supreme Court lawyer does whatever works in order to win a case. Whenever I have a case that's going up to the Supreme Court on certiorari, I look for amicus help. After it's granted, it's not as important. But [on certiorari] you want something that will flag the Court to the importance of your case. (CI)

Amicus solicitation at the merits stage is more common. Over 50 percent of the lawyers whose cases were granted review tried to engage organized interests in support of their clients. As the experienced Supreme Court bar will attest, however, once the Court has granted review, amici tend to make themselves known to counsel. One lawyer observed that, "At the merits, friends are coming out of the woodwork," while another veteran litigator of the Court commented:

> You don't have to do as much encouragement at the merits stage. When cert has been granted, generally amici seek *you* out. At the petition stage, nobody necessarily knows about your case. So you have to sort of inform them about your seeking cert. (CI)

Why, then, do so many lawyers try to establish interest group support at the merits? Lacking any specific clue, one might conjecture that lawyers simply view amici on the merits as the norm. For example, one of the Court's most eminent practitioners allowed that:

> We try to get amici because sometimes we're afraid that the absence of them might be noted. (CI)

In other words, lawyers may try to locate amici if only because they believe the Court expects amici to participate. Certainly, amicus briefs are present in the vast majority of cases that the Court decides on the merits (O'Connor and Epstein 1982), and scholars have long speculated on the impact of these briefs at the merits stage (Barker 1967). Indeed, evidence suggests that amici do figure prominently in judicial outcomes (see, for example, Ivers and O'Connor 1987).

I have used the example of amicus solicitation to characterize the strategic role that lawyers may play in getting a case through the doors of the Supreme Court, although other opportunities for lawyers to exercise an influence over Supreme Court politics do exist. By focusing on the mobilization of organized interests, though, one can begin to appreciate how lawyers articulate the importance of constitutional and statutory considerations to the justices as a means of securing access to the justices' agenda.

Conclusion

The elite members of the Supreme Court bar are very active in litigation. Of course, even the most experienced counsel are not signing every petition or arguing every case, but that does not mean they are uninvolved. Quite the contrary. The members of the inner circle are frequently engaged, both by litigants and by less experienced counsel, to provide assistance and advice. Their advisory role might be less significant were it not so extensive, but the roots of their activity run quite deep. At every turn, the seasoned advocates—the inner circle of specialized counsel—are likely to be almost constantly at work, soliciting amicus briefs in their own cases and writing them for others, as well as assisting the novice in the preparation of both briefs and arguments.

Naturally, there are constraints on what these lawyers can and cannot do, and those constraints are reflected in the motives for litigating in the Court. Some lawyers are bound by a relatively short tether to their clients, while short-term views of litigation outcomes—the desire or need simply to win the case—often narrow the scope of a lawyer's potential influence. Under other circumstances, however, lawyers have more flexibility, their range of strategic possibilities being the greatest when broad questions of public policy are at issue. The elite litigators know how to seize upon these opportunities, as is evident in their ability to muster the backing of organized interests to support their petitions for a position on the Court's agenda. Such behind-the-scenes strategies, though informal, are no less the influential for it.

In sum, there is depth and coherence to the practice of Supreme Court specialists and much of that practice is directed toward gaining access to the Court. Examining the inner circle at work in Supreme Court litigation reveals that the experienced elite are political as well as legal actors in the process of adjudication in the high court.

7

The Washington Community

and the Structure of Influence

Between 1977 and 1982, roughly four thousand lawyers participated in cases the Supreme Court decided on the merits. Some argued before the justices; others served as counsel on the briefs. A good many of these lawyers participated in more than one case. Naturally, those who served as Supreme Court counsel in multiple cases worked for a variety of clients—federal and state government, interest groups, corporations, and so on. But where is one most likely to find these experienced members of the Supreme Court bar? The plurality—nearly one third—are in private practice. Although many of these private practitioners hail from regions across the country, half of them work in a single geographic location: Washington, D.C.

In this chapter, I consider an issue implicit in much the discussion to this point—the degree to which the lawyers within the inner circle form a professional community. As we have noted, many of the experienced members of the bar are in close physical and social proximity to one another. But closely connected to the idea of the bar as a community of lawyers is the notion of the influences at work within that community. Why do some lawyers develop a reputation for skillful representation in the Supreme Court? Is it simply a function of the volume of their work in the Court, or do other factors—Supreme Court clerk-ships, experience in the solicitor general's office, or a Washington-based practice—have a bearing on a lawyer's status? To address this question, I have developed a predictive model to assess lawyer reputation as skillful Supreme Court counsel. In this model, I employ various lawyer characteristics to explain why some lawyers come to be viewed by their peers as expert Supreme Court counsel.

To aid in this inquiry, I have gathered additional data on a large group of experienced Court practitioners, specifically, the lawyers who participated in more than one Supreme Court case on the merits over a six-year period, from 1977 to 1982.[1] A six-year cross section, as opposed to a single term, is more likely to produce an accurate reflection of the extent of lawyers' activities, since in any given year a fair proportion of the active bar may not actually be involved in a case in the Court. At the same time, six years is also a short enough period to ensure that the experience of lawyers with the Court is both current and concentrated. Furthermore, lawyers who show only modest participation at the merits are nonetheless often involved in other cases—both formally and informally. Their frequent presence on the briefs or at oral argument over those six terms can thus be thought of as a plausible indication of other, less visible Supreme Court influence.

At the outset, I noted that the solicitor general would not be an explicit focus of this book, except insofar as he was relevant to the issues under consideration. Since I am discussing the experienced Supreme Court bar as an integrated community, it is important to include all of the active practitioners who are likely to interact with one another—including the lawyers in the solicitor general's office. Indeed, the desire to account for the full range of professional and social interactions that may take place among members of the inner circle compels us to consider these important actors within the Washington community.[2]

The Center of the Inner Circle

In what sense do the lawyers of the inner circle constitute a community of representatives? What, if anything, binds them together? For some time now, scholars have recognized the relevance of the concept of community for our understanding of the professions (Minar and Greer 1969). In the literature on social networks, the most consistent theme is that the greater the degree of shared backgrounds, attitudes, and norms, the greater the likelihood that interpersonal relationships will form (Laumann 1973, 5). In other words, any community, including a community of lawyers, will have certain defining characteristics. For the present purpose, I use the concept of community in a sociological sense: "persons in social interaction within a geographic area and having one or more additional common ties" (Hillery 1955, 111). The degree to which the Supreme Court bar can be thought of as a community can therefore be measured against these three closely related criteria—shared geography, common ties or bonds, and collegial interaction.

Geography

A host of political actors are constantly drawn to Washington, D.C., the center of governmental power in the United States. As a prominent national policy maker, the Supreme Court, too, attracts its fair share of political sophisticates. Not surprisingly, then, Washington stands out as one of the preferred locations for members of the Supreme Court bar, as we saw in chapters 2 and 3. What is true for the Supreme Court bar in general, however, is even more the case among its more experienced ranks. Table 7.1 presents the principal cities in which the experienced Supreme Court counsel practice; without question, the proportion of lawyers in the District of Columbia towers above that for every other locale. The same three cities from which the Supreme Court bar in general is most likely to hail—Washington, New York, and Chicago (see table 3.3)—contribute an even greater number to the experienced group of Supreme Court lawyers, the largest contribution, 43 percent, being made by Washington alone.

This large percentage is, at least in part, a function of the wealth of federal government attorneys who work in Washington and appear in the Court. Indeed, some 60 percent of the experienced Washington bar works for the federal government. The federal government counsel, however, do not tell us the whole story; a substantial proportion—roughly one third—of the Washington lawyers work in private practice. Taking private practitioners alone, one finds that the federal city is an even greater stronghold for the Supreme Court bar. In fact, these Washington lawyers make up nearly half of all the Court's experienced private practitioners. To put it another way, there is a fifty-fifty chance

TABLE 7.1. Experienced members of the Supreme Court bar practicing in selected cities

All lawyers	%	Lawyers in private practice	%
Washington	43.0	Washington	47.8
New York	9.4	New York	10.7
Chicago	5.4	Chicago	7.8
Los Angeles	3.2	Los Angeles	3.4
San Francisco	2.7	Phoenix	2.4
Austin	2.0	Philadelphia	2.0
Atlanta	1.7	San Francisco	2.0
Boston	1.6	Minneapolis / St. Paul	1.5
Phoenix	1.6	Houston	1.0
Minneapolis / St. Paul	1.3	Pittsburgh	1.0
	N = 709		N = 205

Source: Archival data 1977–82. These data were drawn from the *United States Reports, Briefs and Records of the United States Supreme Court,* and the *Martindale-Hubbell Law Directory.*

that any private lawyer who has had substantial experience in the Supreme Court will also practice in Washington.

This finding is congruent with a number of our previous observations about Supreme Court practice and about the capital. First, it reflects Washington's role as the nation's legal center. The District of Columbia has the largest per capita segment of the legal profession. Second, over the past decade, Washington has also been the city of choice when firms expand through branch offices. Much of this growth reflects the increased reliance upon Washington representation for governmental advocacy (see chapter 2). Third, many of the cases that end up in the Supreme Court are products of the Court of Appeals for the District of Columbia Circuit, as well as of the Federal Circuit. Many litigants no doubt turn to local counsel, retaining them for federal appellate representation and any subsequent work in the Supreme Court. Finally, and perhaps most obviously, the Court itself is in Washington. When clients have Supreme Court cases, they may want Supreme Court counsel and consequently choose to turn to firms that work in the Court's shadow.

The experienced Supreme Court lawyers themselves recognize that many, if not most, of them share a common geography. Said one public interest lawyer:

> There are a few outside of Washington, but most of the Supreme Court specialists tend to be here. (CI)

A lawyer in a large Washington firm echoed this observation:

> Most of the Supreme Court lawyers are here in Washington. Certainly, most of the people whose names would come up if you asked for an experienced Supreme Court lawyer are located here. (CI)

Although obviously not all Supreme Court counsel are located in Washington, as these lawyers attest, the most experienced litigators are found in the nation's capital. Nor should one lose sight of the concentration of experienced Court lawyers in that city relative to other cities. A skeptic might argue that, if 50 percent of the experienced circle of Supreme Court lawyers works in Washington, the other 50 percent does not. As the data in table 7.1 show, however, the other cities containing a statistically noteworthy number of Supreme Court lawyers, do not, even when taken together, begin to approach the lion's share that Washington commands. Clearly, the Supreme Court bar is concentrated in Washington. If not in Washington, its members are just as likely to hail from one city as the next (with a minor exception for New York and Chicago). That the elite bar locates in Washington in such substantial numbers can neither be ignored nor attributed to chance. These lawyers do share a common geography; namely, they work in close proximity to the Court itself.

Common Ties

The legal profession shares a number of common bonds. From their early training as law students to their professional memberships, many lawyers exhibit a certain similarity to one another (Heinz and Laumann 1982). How true is this for the Supreme Court lawyers? In this section, I consider two of the bonds that might unite Supreme Court practitioners—educational and organizational backgrounds.

Education.   One of the most frequent ties that elites share stems from their educational background (Mills 1956; see also Heinz and Laumann 1982; Carlin 1962). Accordingly, the experienced Supreme

TABLE 7.2. Legal education of experienced members of the Supreme Court bar (in percent)

Distinguished	53.3
Strong	18.8
Good	11.8
Average	9.0
Below average	7.2

Source: Archival data 1977–82 ($N = 670$).

Court bar evinces a good deal of homogeneity in its legal training, as the data in table 7.2 confirm. Over half of them are products of the nation's distinguished law schools, as opposed to about a third of the Supreme Court bar in general (see table 3.4), and an additional 20 percent were trained in the second tier of law schools. All told, then, nearly three-quarters of the experienced bar received their degrees from the most competitive and prestigious universities. At the other end of the spectrum, only 7 percent of the experienced Supreme Court lawyers attended a less than average law school, less than half the comparable percentage for Supreme Court lawyers nationally.

Table 7.3 provides a closer look at the legal training of the Supreme Court veterans. Among the most frequently attended law schools, Harvard makes the single largest contribution to the experienced bar, over twice that of the next two schools, Yale and Columbia, combined. Together, though, these three institutions produce a sizable proportion of the Supreme Court's elite litigators, the odds being about one in four that a veteran Court practitioner will have attended one of these three universities. More generally, the ten law schools most frequently attended by the experienced Supreme Court bar can be numbered among the nation's best. Only two of the ten are not distinguished schools, falling instead into the category of strong law schools. It is no accident that those two are located in Washington.

Narrowing the focus to Washington, one discovers an even greater similarity in educational background. A sizable majority—some 63 percent—of the private practitioners in Washington, for instance, graduated from a distinguished law school; the combined total for distinguished and strong law schools is nearly 90 percent. Thus, virtually all of the Supreme Court veterans engaged in private practice in the fed-

TABLE 7.3. Principal law schools attended by experienced members
of the Supreme Court bar (in percent)

Harvard University	14.9
Yale University	7.3
Columbia University	6.4
University of Chicago	3.6
University of Michigan	3.6
George Washington University	3.3
Georgetown University	3.3
University of Texas at Austin	2.8
University of California at Berkeley	2.7
New York University	2.4

Source: Archival data 1977–82 ($N = 670$).

eral city are products of the same law schools. If one cannot say for
certain whether the bonds of community among the experienced Supreme Court bar first form in law school, one can say that the educational background of the experienced Supreme Court lawyers is considerably more homogeneous than the legal training of the Court's bar
in general.

Organizational memberships.   Supreme Court lawyers have a number
of associational ties in common. The survey data, for instance, reveal
that 62 percent of all Supreme Court lawyers belong to the American
Bar Association. They are members of their respective state and local
bar associations in even greater proportion—85 percent and 73 percent, respectively.[3] In what sense might participation in professional
organizations serve as a common bond among the Supreme Court bar?
This private practitioner explained:

> I've been involved in the organized bar over the years. I've been
> chairman of the Tax Section of the ABA. I've been chairman of
> the American College of Tax Counsel, and I've also served in the
> House of Delegates of the ABA. So, by reason of that activity, I've
> become known to people who are leaders of the bar, and the
> leaders of the bar are likely to be people, who, everything else
> being equal, have the same qualities that make them likely candi-
> dates to argue cases in the Supreme Court. (CI)

By their very nature, then, certain organizational affiliations tend to bring Supreme Court lawyers together. After all, if the lawyers who constitute the experienced bar of the Court count among the profession's elite, then one would anticipate that they would be bound together by positions of leadership within the legal community.

Among these Supreme Court practitioners, one common characteristic is membership in the Supreme Court bar. At first glance, this might seem the most glaring organizational bond among Supreme Court counsel, but a lawyer's admission to practice in the Court is a very deceptive indicator. Why? Because admission to the bar of the United States Supreme Court is surprisingly easy to obtain. The Court's guidelines for admission specify that the applicant must have been admitted to practice in his or her highest state court for at least three years prior to seeking admission. The candidate must also be "of good moral and professional character." With the sponsorship of two current members of the Court's bar and a fee of $100, an attorney can become an official member of the Supreme Court bar.[4]

Admission to the bar has thus gone from being a formal event to a formality. In the Court's early years, lawyers would generally take the oath of office before the justices, an event of some importance, both to the Court and, quite obviously, to its newly admitted practitioners (see, for example, Garland 1983, 5). In 1970, however, under the leadership of Chief Justice Burger, the Court changed its rules to allow application and admission by mail, an increasingly popular option. All the same, that the Court did not suspend the personal appearance requirement for formal admission until 1970 suggests that, at least for most of the Court's history, the chief justices had deemed it significant, in spite of the increasing size of the Court's docket (see Stern, Gressman, and Shapiro 1986, 731–32, 738).

Although the Court requires that any legal documents submitted to it must carry the signature of a Supreme Court bar member, the reverse is not necessarily implied: the lawyer who seeks admission to the bar need not have any business before the justices. In fact, many lawyers seek admission to practice before the Court largely as a matter of prestige. In one recent case involving the question of whether lawyers should be allowed to advertise themselves as "certified civil trial specialists," Justice Stevens queried whether the attorneys who are members of the Supreme Court bar ought to be allowed to promote themselves on that basis. When the lawyer speaking in favor of advertising allowed that they should, Justice Stevens shot back, "Well, isn't that even more misleading than the claim here? It implies that they argue a lot of cases here and that we know them pretty well" (see Mauro 1990c).

As Justice Stevens points out, most official members of the Supreme Court bar do not appear regularly before the Court. Of course, there are lawyers who are relatively active before the Court and who are known to the justices, professionally and/or personally. But, by itself, formal membership in the Supreme Court bar will not tell us much about the degree to which the Supreme Court lawyers form a community.

The relative lack of community among the official Supreme Court bar stems in part from the absence of a set of formalized interactions such as one might find in other judicial settings. As one litigator suggested:

> All federal courts, through the judicial conferences of the circuits, have annual meetings where people socialize, exchange ideas and thoughts. States have that through their state bar association meetings. The Supreme Court doesn't have anything like that. So, you don't have that opportunity. (CI)

Thus, to the extent that there are common ties relevant to the Supreme Court bar, they will probably have less to do with formal bar membership and more to do with the activities and interactions of its members. Let us now consider a few possibilities.

Collegial interactions

Given that communities are essentially social in orientation (Hiller 1941), few considerations are more central to the nature of social structures than social interactions (Aiken and Mott 1970; Laumann, Siegel, and Hodge 1970). Occupations, moreover, figure prominently in delineating social strata (Laumann 1966), and the legal profession is particularly conducive to the analysis of contacts among colleagues. In their study of the Chicago bar, Heinz and Laumann (1982) demonstrate that interaction among lawyers is largely structured by the two hemispheres of the legal profession.

Among the Supreme Court lawyers specifically, collegiality manifests itself in several ways. As noted earlier, experienced lawyers often assume influential yet less visible roles in Supreme Court litigation. It should come as no surprise, therefore, that many Supreme Court lawyers have fairly extensive contact with one another. Naturally, much of their association is directly related to Supreme Court litigation, although their professional interactions are by no means limited to those deriving from the work of the Court. Furthermore, simple social friendships often exist among Supreme Court lawyers. Together, these various professional and social alliances promote a fair degree of integration within the Court's bar. It is, as one practitioner suggested, "a fairly collegial, close-knit group, most of whom are personal friends with one another" (CI). Let us begin, however, by exploring the relationships lawyers share that are specifically related to Supreme Court litigation.

Supreme Court contacts.   Two different levels of collegial association exist among Supreme Court lawyers. The first of these pertains to the professional relationships that can develop among experienced members of the Court's bar. The second relates to contacts between these lawyers and the Supreme Court bar in general.

An assessment of the social connections among the Court's specialists begins, appropriately, with the most obvious occasion for lawyer interaction: contact that occurs when counsel appear together or in opposition to one another in cases before the Court. Such contact takes place frequently and thus serves as a common mechanism for generating a sense of community within the group. As one Court veteran, a public interest lawyer, remarked:

> I know most of the Supreme Court specialists because they've been on the other side, or sometimes the same side, of cases with me. (CI)

A partner in one of Washington's largest firms further illustrated professional contact in the context of the Court:

> I find myself on the same side or on opposite sides with my competitors. And I've had that happen really quite often. It turned out, for example, in a case I had with —— [a large corporation] not long ago, Rex Lee and I were on the same side and worked together. I also recently argued a case in the court of appeals against Larry Tribe. So, you see each other that way. (CI)

Yet another attorney in a large Washington firm detailed some of his own interactions with his fellow Court specialists:

Professionally, we interact a fair amount, because we end up being on amicus briefs in cases together, or sometimes we're on the other side of cases together. At Onek, Klein & Farr, I'll probably talk to Joel Klein or Bartow Farr, you know, certainly once a month. Probably more often than that. For one reason or another, I've not had that much contact with Mayer, Brown. Although, even with them, we'll talk probably at least once a month in a lot of cases that come up. Barrett Prettyman, of late, I've had a number of cases with him. I haven't had any with Jones, Day, although it just turns out that way. I could envision those kinds of professional contacts. (CI)

The generally close relationship between Washington experts also stems in part from larger issues of representation in government. Much of the interest representation that takes place in Washington is done by lawyers (Nelson et al. 1988), and interest group alliances within particular policy domains often bring such representatives together (Salisbury et al. 1987). Thus, to the extent that Supreme Court experts represent similar interests, they will frequently find themselves working together in litigation, as this experienced practitioner revealed:

One of my clients is the American Medical Association. That's an amicus that a lot of people look to any time a case comes up. So I get a lot of contact from people asking whether the AMA would be interested in assisting them. Also, Joel Klein is counsel for the American Psychiatric Association. So we have a lot of cases in common, and we work together in that way. (CI)

Of course, professional interactions among the experienced bar are not restricted to Washington experts alone. Since the most experienced Court attorneys are likely to be tapped at the merits, there is consequently a greater chance that many cases—especially those involving large sums of money—will be argued by the most prolific members of the Supreme Court bar, regardless of where they practice law (see, for example, Lauter 1987). In *Northeast Bancorporation v. The Federal Reserve System,* a controversy over regional banking laws, for example, Stephen Shapiro, an alumnus of the solicitor general's office who now works in the Chicago office of Mayer, Brown & Platt, squared off against Solicitor General Rex Lee and Harvard's Laurence Tribe (see Denniston 1985). Furthermore, interactions among such lawyers need not be limited to direct participation in cases. As one Washington advocate indicated, the seasoned Supreme Court lawyers often seek guidance from their peers on a more informal basis:

> There are some of us who are close and often times help each other. If I have an argument, Barrett Prettyman or Alan Morrison or those guys would sit in on a dry run and do that for me. (CI)

Another good example of such collegial interaction comes to us from Alan Morrison, head of the Public Citizen Litigation Group, who describes his relationship with Laurence Tribe: "From time to time, [Larry] and I will sit down and talk about a case he's going to argue, before the argument, and I'll tell him what I think about what to do, and we'll discuss some ideas and some approaches" (Greenya 1987, 40).

The professional contacts among the experienced elite relevant to litigation in the Court are best characterized as lateral in nature. That is, the established members of the bar turn to their counterparts for advice. Within the Supreme Court bar as a whole, similar forces are at work. When it comes to the second level of lawyer contact, however—that is, interactions between veteran Supreme Court practitioners and the outer circle of the Supreme Court bar—the contact tends to be more hierarchically structured, with experienced lawyers providing assistance to the Court's relative newcomers. A former member of the solicitor general's staff, now in private practice, illustrated how this type of collegiality can come about:

> We had a case last year—it was a tax case that a colleague at another firm was arguing for a group of oil companies—and they retained my partner and myself to help him out. Not that he needs help; he's a very very able lawyer. Rather, it was just to give him the benefit of our thinking and work with him on the argument preparation. (CI)

Far from being surprising, this kind of interaction among Supreme Court lawyers is a logical consequence of the nature of legal representation in the Court. As was demonstrated in the previous chapter, the experienced Supreme Court lawyers participate in litigation in a broad variety of ways, including assisting others with filing petitions and briefs, evaluating arguments, and soliciting and writing amicus briefs. Furthermore, the reluctance on the part of many first-time advocates utterly to cede their position as Court counsel to the specialists only fuels such contacts, as these less experienced counsel are not similarly reluctant to seek the advice of the experts. In many respects, then, this brand of collegiality is built into the system of representation in the Court.

But if this hierarchical pattern of contact is a natural outgrowth of the dynamics of Court litigation, a question remains. Do less experienced practitioners who find themselves with a Supreme Court case consistently turn to the same group of expert counsel for assistance, or is contact among these lawyers relatively diffuse? This is an important issue because the extent to which lawyers seek contact with the same group of Court veterans has clear ramifications for our view of Supreme Court lawyers as a community. In the context of the Court's religion cases, Frank Sorauf has called attention to the pivotal role of Leo Pfeffer of the American Jewish Congress: "Pfeffer sat at the center of a network of legal information and communication. His own expertise and experience attracted queries and calls for help. His personal network . . . constituted the major informational network among attorneys working for separationist interests in these church-state cases" (1976, 161). Sorauf's comments suggest that at least some fields are dominated by legal experts who are routinely sought out by those in need of advice.

That relatively less experienced members of the Court's legal fraternity would turn consistently to the same experts for assistance considerably strengthens the status of the Supreme Court bar as a community. After all, if lawyers repeatedly seek advice and assistance from a discrete group of experts, this implies not only that they recognize who the Court's specialists are but also that a fair degree of social integration exists between the established Supreme Court lawyers and the Supreme Court bar in general. It is important to ascertain, then, how far the Leo Pfeffer example is typical.

Fortunately, the data permit us to determine the degree of contact between members of the Supreme Court bar generally and the experienced elite practitioners. In the survey of the 1986 term, the respondents were asked to name up to five lawyers they considered to be expert Supreme Court litigators, which yielded the names of some 166 different practitioners. In addition, the respondents were asked to name any experienced Supreme Court counsel from whom they sought advice in the preparation of their cases.[5] The survey was sent to a random sample of Supreme Court lawyers. It is thus conceivable that some of the respondents themselves numbered among the elite Court counsel, and doubtless the survey results could reflect elite peer—that is, lateral—contact. The extent of such contact among the survey respondents, however, is only marginal, given that there was no significant positive correlation between a lawyer's own experience in the Court and the likelihood of his or her seeking expert advice. Armed with this information, then, one can make a reasonably reliable assessment of the extent to which lawyers seek advice from a select group of skilled Court lawyers.

A comparison of the list of the 166 Supreme Court experts against the names of the lawyers who were sought for advice uncovers a fair amount of professional contact between the inner and outer circles of the Supreme Court bar. Nearly one quarter of the respondents volunteered that they had, at one time or another, contacted experienced Supreme Court counsel. More important, lawyers did seem prone to consult the same small group of experts over and over again. Some 28 percent of the expert lawyers were contacted more than once by lawyers seeking the perspective of seasoned Court talent. Moreover, the lawyers who were consulted more than once managed to generate nearly 40 percent of all the expert contacts. In other words, about a quarter of the recognized elite Court counsel were sought for assistance four times out of ten. Thus, even when evaluated with the requisite caution, these findings permit us to conclude that in a fair number of instances lawyers before the Supreme Court will seek out the same set of expert Court litigators. The relationship of such collegial contact to Supreme Court representation is especially important because, as we saw in chapter 6, the expert's secondary participation is such an integral component of the work that skilled practitioners are called upon to provide.

In short, regardless of their own experience, members of the Supreme Court bar recognize the existence of an elite group of experts, who are further viewed as natural candidates to dispense advice. It is scarcely surprising that most of the experts who were contacted more than once were among the most active Supreme Court litigators in the years prior to the 1986 term. On average, these experts each argued 2.3 cases and were involved in 7.2 briefs on the merits. These highly experienced lawyers are truly the Court's elite bar. They included Laurence Gold, chief counsel to the AFL-CIO; E. Barrett Prettyman, Jr., the prominent appellate litigator of Hogan & Hartson; Harvard's Laurence Tribe; Bruce J. Ennis, former counsel to the ACLU, now working for Chicago's Jenner & Block; and Michael Gottesman of Georgetown University's School of Law. Among them as well were a number of interest group litigators from the ACLU and the NAACP Legal Defense Fund.

Professional and social interactions.   A good many of the social contacts among Supreme Court lawyers take place outside the Court. Some stem from other sorts of professional interactions, but many result from personal friendships—friendships that may or may not arise from Supreme Court practice. It is important to consider both the professional and social contacts together, however, primarily because the lawyers themselves see these two types of contact as interrelated.

As in other professions, lawyers encounter their peers in a variety of work-related settings. Professional meetings, for example, are particularly important to experienced members of the Supreme Court bar, because their participation in such meetings is quite often a function of their distinction as Supreme Court experts. As one private practitioner explains:

> There are a lot of appellate advocacy panels, seminars, symposia, where you'll find a lot of Supreme Court lawyers. I've been on those, for example, with Rex Lee. In a few weeks, I'm going to be on one with Andy Frey. Those things go on regularly, and the same group tends to turn up. (CI)

At such meetings, Supreme Court lawyers not only interact with one another but also reinforce their role as leaders of the bar. Since many professional meetings are structured around appellate practice, these professional contacts provide opportunities to establish or cement social ties among the expert Court litigators as well as between the veteran and freshman Supreme Court counsel.

The work that many lawyers perform for the organizations that provide assistance to counsel for state and local government also encourages the growth of networks of association among various Supreme Court counsel (see Marcotte 1986). One former member of the solicitor general's staff described this collegiality:

> A fair number of Supreme Court lawyers are related to the State and Local Legal Center and participate in various kinds of functions which are both quasi-professional and quasi-social in na-

ture. I run into a number of folks in that connection. I also do a fair amount of work for the National Association of Attorneys General. (CI)

Another lawyer in a large Washington firm echoed this description:

There are various events at which you might see these lawyers. For instance, a lot of us do work for the State and Local Legal Center on a pro bono basis, you know, do amicus briefs for them. And they have a reception once a year for people. So you tend to encounter a certain group of people at these receptions that includes some of the Supreme Court practitioners. (CI)

As is evident from these comments, many Supreme Court lawyers see their opportunities for collegial contact as a mix of both professional and social activities. Once again, the importance of Washington as the center of such interaction looms large. The Supreme Court lawyers who work in the federal city frequently rub elbows with their peers, with members of the solicitor general's office, and even with the justices themselves. One partner in a major Washington firm testified to the fundamental importance of geography in this collegiality:

You tend to see each other at the same social events. That is, there'll be a reception given by the National Association of States' Attorneys General. There'll be some ceremony up at the Court, such as the issuing of the John Marshall stamp. There'll be some Justice Department function; they had one the other day on the hundredth anniversary of Taft becoming solicitor general. You know, at those things that are either directly or tangentially related to the Court in some way, you'll see a lot of the same people turning up. (CI)

Friendships can of course arise from Court-related work as well. Many Supreme Court lawyers, for example, become friends while in the solicitor general's office. They continue to have personal contact, even after having left the office, with fellow alumni as well as with the solicitor general's staff.

Many of my best lawyer friends are people whom I've worked with in the past in this [the solicitor general's] office who are no longer in the office and are now in private practice. And I do see some of them socially because we have a great fondness for each other. (CI)

I'm friendly with some of the people who've been getting a lot of Supreme Court cases in the private bar, and it's because I knew them working here [the solicitor general's office] or somewhere else. . . . We used to play softball or something like that. (CI)

Well, some are friends, some are acquaintances. The ones who are friends, I see socially, have lunch with, or [see] on other social occasions. (CI)

I bump into them at the same parties a lot, you know, and the same receptions. There is a group of people who really like the Supreme Court, follow it closely, litigate before it, write about it, live in Washington, go to parties at the Supreme Court. I wouldn't call it a Supreme Court bar. I guess it's too undignified to call them Supreme Court groupies, but it falls somewhere between the two. (CI)

Obviously, not all members of the Supreme Court bar have ongoing collegial relationships, but many do, especially those who are experienced and those who work in Washington. Said one practitioner:

Realistically, there are probably far more contacts among people in that group, however you want to define it, than in most other areas in private practice. But that's because it's a small group. (CI)

Beyond the banks of the Potomac River, however, collegiality tends to be less frequent among the Court's lawyers. One law professor—an alumnus of the solicitor general's office—when asked about the degree of social interaction among the Court's lawyers in general replied:

I guess I don't think that that exists very much, although maybe I just don't know about it. It seems to me that in particular places, in Washington, there are some people who are outside of government who do a fair amount of that. As far as the more generalized bar, I guess I just don't think there is much. (CI)

A decreased level of social interaction outside of Washington does not, however, indicate that Supreme Court lawyers do not form a professional community. To the contrary, it exemplifies the interconnection between geography and social interaction and the centrality of both to the notion of community. Once one moves beyond Washington—home of the Supreme Court itself—it is hard to think of a city with a concentration of Supreme Court lawyers sufficiently high to foster the development of a close-knit community.

Clearly, though, there is a fair amount of collegial interaction within the inner circle of lawyers, much of it a function of participation in the cases brought to the Court. Many litigators, especially the Court's expert counsel, join forces or oppose one another in the Court with considerable regularity. Furthermore, a sizable proportion of Supreme Court lawyers will seek contacts with the leaders of the Court's bar. Beyond that, social interactions are structured by a variety of professional activities—seminars, professional meetings, NAAG programs, and so on—that bring experienced Court attorneys into contact with one another and with the newcomers to the Court's bar who seek their counsel.

Undeniably, this collegiality finds its center in Washington. In some sense, the smaller physical distance between the lawyers in Washington tends to reduce their relative social distance, thereby increasing the likelihood of interpersonal ties. As the setting for the business of the Court, Washington draws a variety of Supreme Court counsel. Whether it is a matter of professional and social contacts among the experienced Court lawyers or interactions among Supreme Court lawyers in general, Washington serves as the hub around which much of the bar's collegiality revolves.

In sum, the concept of the Supreme Court bar as a community of lawyers has considerable utility. The elite circle of the bar, in particular, bears many of the marks of a professional community. Many of the Court's experienced lawyers share a common geography, mutual bonds, and collegial relationships. Of course, in several respects even the elite practitioners fall short of being a professional community. Many experienced lawyers practice outside of Washington; many have dissimilar backgrounds and no meaningful interactions with one another. Further, I have chosen to discuss only a handful of the many possible criteria by which lawyers might be compared.

Nonetheless, the idea of a community of lawyers is useful, particularly at the conceptual level. Viewing these advocates as a community—a stable and integrated center of lawyers who interact among themselves as well as with the outer circle of the Court's bar—enables us to pull together into a unified picture the different types of experienced Supreme Court counsel. Although the characterization is somewhat limited at the empirical level by the available data, the theoretical model of the Court's bar can help us come to grips with the structure of its influence.

Influence within the Community

As the last section illustrated, certain lawyers are viewed by their peers as unusually skillful Supreme Court advocates. Other lawyers recognize the effectiveness of these highly talented and knowledgeable few by seeking their help in Supreme Court litigation. Yet there is still no systematic explanation for how counsel develop this status.

For some time now, scholars have been intrigued by the issue of how one acquires influence within a community, and, given our characterization of the Supreme Court bar as a community, it is useful to approach our question in that light—albeit with one caveat. A lawyer's reputation for effectiveness in the Court is not a direct measure of influence per se. One might reasonably suspect that the lawyers seen as the most skillful would also be considered influential, but a correlation between skill and influence does not imply that the two are equivalent. Still, the use of reputations to measure influence enjoys a respectable tradition in the social sciences.

At the same time, scholars have debated the degree to which reputation can be used to judge political influence (see Knoke 1990, 119–48; Walton 1970). The principal point of contention concerns whether community influence is concentrated among political elites or distributed through a more pluralistic power structure. Floyd Hunter provided the earliest support for the elite thesis in a pioneering study of community power, for which he employed the reputational method (Hunter 1953; see also Knoke 1990, 119). Critics of the reputational approach argue, however, that it measures perceptions of power rather than power itself, presupposes the existence of a power structure, assumes power to be both general and stable in nature, and furthermore confuses status with power (Aiken and Mott 1970, 195–96; see also Dahl 1961; Polsby 1970; Wolfinger 1970). But as Aiken and Mott point out (1970, 196–97), notwithstanding such criticisms, the reputational method continues to serve as an important basis for examining the issue of influence. Rather than abandon this theoretical approach, then, I invoke it with the understanding of its limitations.

In their important study, Heinz and Laumann sought to uncover the social networks that exist among the Chicago bar and its elite lawyers as a means of elucidating the issue of influence within the community of legal practitioners.[6] In pursuing this goal, they asked their respondents whether they knew several of Chicago's most notable practitioners, which proved an effective method of characterizing the nature of interpersonal association among lawyers. Drawing upon their analysis, I have employed a similar strategy in my investigation of influence within the Supreme Court bar.

Who Are the Supreme Court Experts?

I asked members of the Supreme Court bar to identify fellow litigators whom they felt were especially skilled as Supreme Court practitioners. One of the common complaints about the reputational method, however, is that by asking respondents to make a selection from a list of presumably well-known community members, the researcher has already made certain assumptions about who has potential political influence. In order to avoid this difficulty, I did not offer these lawyers a preselected list of the Court's bar but rather asked them to nominate their own candidates. Thus, on the survey, I asked respondents to name up to five lawyers who deserved the reputation as a Supreme Court expert. As critics might charge, by limiting the list to a maximum of five, I made "an implicit assumption about the distribution of political power" (Wolfinger 1970, 246). That is, I decided at the outset that the universe of influential Supreme Court lawyers was relatively contained and hence eliminated the opportunity for lawyers to nominate more than five candidates. Fortunately, while 14.7 percent named but one lawyer and 32.7 percent named as many as three, only 4.6 percent nominated five Supreme Court notables. Clearly, five names was not too limiting a cutoff for the vast majority of survey respondents.

One might also wonder, though, how far the opinions of these lawyers constitute a indicator of community influence. That is, how competent is the Supreme Court bar to rank the relative effectiveness of its membership? The answer is that they are at least as qualified as any other set of people, such as individual or even corporate clients. This Washington advocate explained:

> There are a lot of clients who go with their trial lawyer in the Supreme Court. On the other hand, I think obviously from the

number of us who do argue there that there are a lot of clients who do think that our experience is valuable. Unfortunately, I think it's true that corporate clients sometimes believe that a big name, as opposed to an experienced name, makes a lot of difference, and I don't think that's true. . . . Many of the Court's lawyers are extraordinarily bright. I will not name names, but I will say that there are some on the list of "Supreme Court lawyers" who I do not believe to be that strong, including some with a lot of experience. I don't think they're that effective. (CI)

He was not the only lawyer to make this distinction. Indeed, it was plain from the interviews that it is the bench and bar that can most accurately gauge Supreme Court reputations. As one former member of the solicitor general's office cautioned:

You should not generalize about Supreme Court practitioners, because the Court's perception of them and the public's perception of them may be quite different. So some of them may have good reputations but may not actually be very good, and I think the Court knows that. (CI)

Lacking quantifiable data on the justices' perception of effective Supreme Court counsel, though, I am content to settle for the next best thing, the collective wisdom of the bar itself.

When Supreme Court counsel were asked to nominate their most distinctive peers, they generated a fairly lengthy list, totaling 166 different names, some 57 of which subsequently appeared in my 1977–82 data set on experienced lawyers. By confining the data set to lawyers with multiple participation at the merits during those years, I set a fairly rigorous threshold for lawyers to meet, although over a third were able to do so. Of course, lawyers who were named as experts but who had less than two cases during that period were eliminated in the data set.

Of those lawyers who were named as Supreme Court experts, some were nominated only once; others were mentioned several times. Below, I outline the professional backgrounds of the lawyers who were nominated four or more times.[7] By virtually any standard, these lawyers are luminaries within the bar nationally. More important, they are among the leading lights of the Supreme Court's insiders.

Anthony G. Amsterdam.   Anthony Amsterdam is a noted professor of law—he has taught at several of the nation's finest law schools—as well as a greatly respected appellate practitioner. A Philadelphia native, he received his law degree from the University of Pennsylvania, where he was editor-in-chief of the law review. Later that same year, he served as a law clerk in the chambers of Justice Felix Frankfurter. Following his clerkship, he worked as an assistant United States attorney but soon entered the ranks of the professoriate. He taught first at Penn before joining the law faculty at Stanford University. In 1981 he took a position at New York University, the law school at which he currently teaches. Throughout his career as an academic, Amsterdam has devoted a good deal of his time in the service of organized interests, including the American Civil Liberties Union, the NAACP Legal Defense Fund, and the Southern Poverty Law Center. A specialist in civil rights, as well as criminal and constitutional law, Amsterdam has garnered considerable professional distinction for his law reform practice.

William T. Coleman, Jr.   Few Supreme Court practitioners are more distinguished than William Coleman: a graduate of the University of Pennsylvania; editor of the law review at Harvard; law clerk to Justice Felix Frankfurter; noted corporate attorney; secretary of transportation under President Gerald Ford; member of the board of directors for the likes of Chase Manhattan Bank, IBM, and Pepsico; trustee of the Brookings Institution; senior partner in the Los Angeles-based megafirm, O'Melveny & Myers; and one of the most active Supreme Court practitioners. Coleman began his career in private practice with the firm of Paul, Weiss, Rifkind, Wharton & Garrison in New York but, after several years, returned to his native Philadelphia to join one of that city's most prominent firms. Coleman has also been at the forefront of desegregation cases. He was a protégé of Justice Thurgood Marshall in the 1950s when the two worked closely for the NAACP Legal Defense Fund, a group Coleman would later head. Coleman continues to represent clients in the Court in cases ranging from disputes over criminal and corporate law to charges of racial discrimination. His skills as an advocate—among them his noted poise and proficiency in oral argument—have earned him a reputation as one of the most deft counsel who appear before the justices.

Archibald Cox.   As an appellate litigator, Archibald Cox has truly impeccable credentials. Indeed, he is among the most active Supreme Court practitioners in history, having served for five years as the United States solicitor general in the early 1960s. Like many of his peers, Cox was educated at Harvard University, first as an undergraduate and then later as a law student. Cox also served as a clerk to the distinguished jurist Learned Hand. In 1938 he entered general practice with a firm in Boston and in 1941 began a brief stint as an attorney with the Justice Department in the Office of the Solicitor General. Soon thereafter, he became associate solicitor for the Department of Labor. In 1945, he returned to his alma mater and joined the faculty of the Harvard Law School, where he taught until 1961. That year, President Kennedy elevated him to the position of solicitor general. Following his tenure as the federal government's chief advocate, he assumed once again his professorship at the Harvard Law School, a position he continues to hold. As an academic, he has written extensively on labor law, civil rights, and the Supreme Court.

Bruce J. Ennis, Jr.   After his graduation from Dartmouth College in 1962, Bruce Ennis attended law school at the University of Chicago, where he was a member of the prestigious *Chicago Law Review*—a distinction that presaged his career as an outstanding practitioner. After law school and a clerkship on a federal district court, Ennis became a staff attorney for the New York Civil Liberties Union. After less than a decade in that position, he was named the National Legal Director of the American Civil Liberties Union, serving from 1977 to 1982. This work afforded Ennis a keen perspective on appellate litigation, as he was a frequent participant in cases before the Supreme Court. Ennis, who now works in the Washington office of Chicago's Jenner & Block, continues to maintain a high degree of visibility as an active advocate in the Court. In recent terms, for instance, he has successfully handled a number of cases dealing with punitive damages. He has published numerous professional articles that reflect his wide-ranging expertise, including writings on the process of litigation in the Supreme Court.

H. Bartow Farr III.   In some sense, the defining archetype of the modern Supreme Court practitioner is Bartow Farr. Well-educated, with the insider's perspective of a former Supreme Court clerk, he gained a good deal of appellate expertise as a member of the solicitor general's staff, and he put that experience to good use as an appellate litigator in his own firm in Washington. Farr graduated from Princeton University in 1966 and attended law school at Arizona State University, where he was editor of the law review. After graduating summa cum laude in 1973, he went to Washington as a law clerk to Justice William Rehnquist. Following his clerkship, he joined the Justice Department as an assistant to the solicitor general. Several years later, having left that office, he and two other former clerks formed Onek, Klein & Farr, a Washington boutique firm that emphasized, among other things, appellate practice in federal courts and agencies, as well as substantive specialties like antitrust, communications, health, and professional liability. In 1991 the firm dissolved, but Farr, together with several appellate specialists, went on to found Klein, Farr, Smith & Taranto, a firm specializing in "Supreme Court and Appellate Practice in all substantive areas, including Constitutional Law."

Laurence S. Gold.   Who represents organized labor in the United States Supreme Court? More often than not, the answer is Laurence Gold, general counsel to the AFL-CIO. As the chief spokesman for labor in the Court, Gold handles precisely the litigation he most enjoys. "The AFL-CIO," says Gold, "has always attempted to be the institutional representative of organized labor in Supreme Court cases, and that seemed to me to be a particularly interesting and challenging kind of work to do." Over the course of his legal career, Gold has cultivated a wealth of expertise in the field of labor law. Graduating from Princeton University in 1958, he attended the Harvard Law School. Following his legal education, he served as law clerk for the United States District Court in Houston. Then, in 1963, Gold headed for Washington to work in the general counsel's office of the National Labor Relations Board. After two years at the NLRB, he went into private practice, joining the Washington law firm of Woll & Mayer, where he worked for nearly ten years. In 1974 Gold became special counsel to the AFL-CIO and was elevated to the position of general counsel a decade later. In recent terms of the Court, Gold's participation in litigation has rivaled that of some lawyers in the solicitor general's office.

Michael H. Gottesman.   Most lawyers would be happy to argue on the winning side of a case in the Supreme Court. Michael Gottesman, however, has an extraordinary record: his appearances before the Court number in the double digits, and he has a near-perfect success rate on the merits. Educated at the University of Chicago and the Yale

University Law School, he worked for several years as a trial attorney in the Department of Justice's antitrust division. Labor law became Gottesman's specialty, an area which he emphasized in private practice with the firm of Bredhoff & Kaiser in Washington. In 1978 Gottesman began teaching as an adjunct faculty member of the Georgetown University Law Center, and in 1989 he joined that school's faculty on a full-time basis, remaining as "of counsel" to his firm.

Erwin N. Griswold.   Dean Griswold—so named for his lengthy service as head of the Harvard Law School—is unquestionably without peer among active Supreme Court practitioners. With over 125 appearances before the justices to his credit, Griswold has argued more cases in the Supreme Court than any living attorney. Indeed, only three other lawyers in history—John W. Davis, Walter Jones, and Daniel Webster—can contend with Griswold in terms of experience in the Court. Erwin Griswold's legal career, like his Supreme Court practice, is extraordinary. A native of Cleveland, he attended Oberlin College in the late 1920s and then received his legal training at Harvard University. After law school, he became special assistant to Solicitor General Charles Evans Hughes, Jr., a position he held until 1934, when he returned to Cambridge to join the faculty of the Harvard Law School. In 1946 he was elevated to the deanship and held that post until 1967, the year President Lyndon Johnson appointed him to the post of solicitor general. Griswold served as solicitor general until 1973, when he joined the Washington office of one of the world's largest law firms, Jones, Day, Reavis & Pogue. Dean Griswold's talents as a Supreme Court practitioner continue to be in high demand: between 1977 and 1982, Griswold argued more cases in the Court than any other lawyer in private practice.

Rex E. Lee.   There is no Supreme Court practitioner like the solicitor general of the United States. Drafting countless submissions favoring and opposing Supreme Court review, writing scores of briefs on the merits, submitting briefs amicus curiae, and, of course, arguing dozens of cases before the justices—all impart a degree of appellate expertise available to precious few litigators. It is no small wonder, therefore, that when Rex Lee left the Justice Department to join the Washington branch of Chicago's Sidley & Austin after having served as solicitor general from 1981 to 1985, he was one of the most highly sought after Supreme Court litigators, as evidenced by his six appearances before the justices in a single term. His rise to this position began not long after his graduation from the University of Chicago's law school in 1963. That year, he served as a clerk on the Supreme Court, working in Justice Byron R. White's chambers. Subsequently, he worked with the firm of Jennings, Strauss & Salmon before leaving in 1971 to become the founding dean of the law school at Brigham Young University, his undergraduate alma mater. He joined the Justice Department in 1975 as an assistant attorney general and in 1981 became the solicitor general. After his tenure in that office, he joined Sidley & Austin. Although he became president of Brigham Young in 1989, Lee remains as counsel to the firm, listing as his areas of concentration appellate and Supreme Court practice.

E. Barrett Prettyman, Jr.   If clerking for a justice of the United States Supreme Court heralds a renowned legal career, then one would have expected a rather extraordinary professional life for E. Barrett Prettyman, Jr.: he served as a law clerk to not one but three justices, a feat which only one lawyer in history has surpassed (Abraham 1986, 253n). As one of the Court's leading litigators, he has clearly met that expectation. Born in Washington, D.C., a son of a prominent judge, Prettyman was educated at Yale University and received his legal training at the University of Virginia. Following his clerkships at the Court, he joined the prestigious Washington law firm of Hogan & Hartson in 1955. During the early 1960s, Prettyman served as special assistant to the United States Attorney General and the White House. His subsequent work also included service as special counsel to a number of congressional committees. Today, Prettyman is a frequent Supreme Court practitioner, averaging, by his own estimate, "about a case per term or term and a half." An extremely capable appellate advocate, Prettyman has written a good deal about the Court and the process of litigating before it.

Laurence H. Tribe.   Not since Felix Frankfurter has a lawyer been elevated from academia to the Supreme Court. Many observers, however, speculate that, under a Democratic administration, Laurence Tribe might well be the next. As a professor of law at Harvard University, Tribe has been both a productive scholar and an active litigator in the Supreme Court. Admitted to Harvard at the age of sixteen, he graduated with a degree in math and then went on to attend the Harvard Law School. During the late 1960s, he clerked on the California

Supreme Court before heading to Washington to serve as a clerk to Justice Potter Stewart on the United States Supreme Court. In 1969 he joined the law faculty at Harvard, as a member of which he subsequently wrote an award-winning casebook, *American Constitutional Law*. Professionally, Tribe has continued to amass a considerable publication record, a recent book on abortion receiving a good deal of public attention. In the Supreme Court, he has represented a wide variety of clients—working on behalf of the American Civil Liberties Union as well as representing multibillion dollar corporations—reflecting his considerable breadth as an appellate practitioner.

What is perhaps most remarkable about this list of eleven lawyers is the degree of professional continuity among them. Four are alumni of the solicitor general's office; six served as clerks to Supreme Court justices; six are affiliated with large law firms, all in Washington; Washington is home to eight of them. Supreme Court lawyers are well aware of this social cohesion. As an alumnus of the solicitor general's office put it, "I think if you look at the folks who have a practice in front of the Supreme Court, they have fairly common backgrounds" (CI). The similarities shared by these notables provide some clues as to the general structure of community influence within the Supreme Court bar. Across the full range of experienced advocates, for example, former Supreme Court clerks and solicitor general alumni may be more apt to be seen by their peers as effective Supreme Court counsel.

One might use these personal professional attributes to develop a more systematic account of why lawyers acquire expert status. Table 7.4 provides an overview of the experienced lawyers with reputations as expert Supreme Court counsel. Given that geographic considerations are so important to the community of Supreme Court counsel, I have divided these lawyers into two categories: those based in Washington and those based elsewhere. Within those two groups, I report the proportion of specific kinds of lawyers who were named as Supreme Court experts. I also calculate the overall percentage of notables in and out of Washington.[8]

These data reveal stark contrasts in the distribution of Supreme Court experts. In fact, one must conclude that experience in the Supreme Court does not ensure that a lawyer will be ranked as an expert. Even among the Court's veteran litigators, a scarce few are seen by their peers as influential. This stands to reason; not everyone can be seen as influential. Still, some kinds of lawyers have considerably

TABLE 7.4. Reputation as Supreme Court experts for selected categories of experienced lawyers

	%	N
Experienced non-Washington counsel		
Academic lawyers	23	13
Interest group lawyers	13	55
Corporate counsel	8	13
Firm lawyers	7	107
State and local government lawyers	4	200
All lawyers	7	388
Experienced Washington counsel		
Alumni of solicitor general's office	50	10
Former Supreme Court clerks	30	46
Interest group lawyers	20	20
Lawyers in solicitor general's office	18	44
Firm lawyers	16	98
All lawyers	18	179

Source: Archival data 1977–82.

Note: The total number of experienced Washington counsel is less than the sum of the individual categories because some lawyers fall into more than one category. Many former clerks, for instance, are also in Washington law firms. There are, of course, academic lawyers in Washington, some of whom litigate in the Court. At the time this sample was taken, however, only one was in Washington. For the sake of convenience, then, I have classified this lawyer with the non-Washington attorneys. Not a single corporate lawyer with extensive Supreme Court experience practices in Washington.

enhanced reputations as influential members of the Supreme Court bar. Why?

Community Influence within the Non-Washington Bar

Among all the lawyers who work outside of Washington, only 7 percent are thought of as expert counsel. Looking at specific categories, one finds that the distribution of community notables is fairly restricted. Less than 10 percent of corporate counsel and firm lawyers were described as influential in the Court; among state and local government the figure drops to less than 5 percent. Clearly, leaders of the

Supreme Court bar do exist outside of Washington; in large measure, however, they are concentrated among two groups.

The experts: academic and interest group lawyers.   Outside of Washington, the lawyers most likely to be held in high esteem are law professors and attorneys for organized interests. A number of distinguished members of the legal professoriate practice in the Court, including Alan Dershowitz, Eugene Gressman, Laurence Tribe, and Charles Alan Wright—all of whom were named as expert Court litigators. In interviews, lawyers frequently volunteered their admiration for the work of these men. One law professor, also a Supreme Court practitioner, noted:

> In my course on the Supreme Court, I always play the tape of Charles Alan Wright's argument in *San Antonio v. Rodriguez* to my students. I think it's one of the best arguments I've ever heard. (CI)

This is high praise indeed, given that the position Wright argued in that case is at no small variance with this law professor's own liberal views. Another Supreme Court practitioner, employed in a Washington firm, offered this candid assessment of another academician:

> I heard Larry Tribe argue about a month ago. I knew he was going to argue that day, so I went up to hear him. And I came with a chip on my shoulder because in his casebook he devotes about ten pages to a case I won in the Supreme Court, and he tries to destroy the majority opinion. Of course, having read that and feeling a little proprietary about it because it was my argument, I was prepared to dislike Larry Tribe as a loudmouth anyway. So I got up there and found him to be just excellent. I really was impressed with him. And he gave the kind of performance I would have loved to have given. (CI)

Interest group counsel are held in similarly high regard. Laurence Gold of the AFL-CIO, Jack Greenberg and Julius Chambers of the NAACP Legal Defense Fund, and Burt Neuborne of the ACLU are among the more common nominees for notable Supreme Court practitioners. The reputations of interest group advocates in the Court are well known (see, for example, Epstein 1985; Kluger 1975; Provine 1980; Sorauf 1976).

The nonexperts: state and local government and corporate lawyers.   In contrast, lawyers who represent state governments and corporations are far less likely to be considered as community notables. Only 4 percent and 8 percent of their members, respectively, were singled out as influential counsel. These modest percentages probably reflect the relatively low visibility of these lawyers. More to the point, these figures confirm what many observers of the Court have long argued: state government and corporate attorneys simply are not effective as Supreme Court counsel. It would not be an exaggeration to characterize some of their Court work as wholly ineffective (but see Epstein and O'Connor 1988).

As we noted earlier, the driving force behind the creation of the National Association of Attorneys General program to help prepare state attorneys for the Supreme Court was the perceived lack of quality of state government representation (see Lempert 1982). As the result of this program, as well as the program at the State and Local Legal Center, state government work in the Court has improved. Nonetheless, state counsel still lag behind other lawyers in the calibre of their work. A current member of the solicitor general's office told me that:

> I think the quality of state representation has improved somewhat. Many times, the state is represented by someone who hasn't been selected for his office the way lawyers are selected for the Office of the Solicitor General. You don't get people with quite as much of a natural aptitude or much experience with the kind of work we do. We have a lot of former Supreme Court law clerks and other people who were academically stellar in their legal education. That tends to be much less true of the lawyers representing the states. (CI)

If anything, the Supreme Court work of corporate lawyers is even less praiseworthy. Tales of missteps by corporate counsel are legion. In 1988, for instance, Roger Kaplan, a corporate specialist in the New York office of Jackson, Lewis, Schnitzler & Krupman, argued that the Court should overturn one of its antidiscrimination decisions, *Runyon v. McCrary* (1976). According to one report of the oral argument, "Three times, Scalia asked Kaplan to offer . . . a single reason why the Court ought to single *Runyon* out amongst all its mistakes to reverse. Three times, a barely audible Kaplan offered the same, weak argument: that *Runyon* is so expansive that it 'intrudes' on the prerogatives of Congress in charting the course of civil-rights legislation. . . . Each time, Scalia showed increasing exasperation until he spat out his now-famous line, 'If that's all you have, Mr. Kaplan, I'm afraid it's nothing'" (Mauro 1988, 8).

In all fairness to corporate lawyers, the Supreme Court is simply not their venue, and, to their credit, most of them recognize this. That so few corporate counsel appear in the experienced lawyer data set suggests that corporations seek experienced Supreme Court counsel, rather than requesting their in-house lawyers to litigate. As we saw in the preceding chapter, rather than remain tied to a single firm or group of house attorneys, corporations tend to turn to different types of counsel, depending on the nature of their legal business (see Abel 1989; Galanter and Palay 1991). When corporations go to the Supreme Court, they wisely turn to the Court's experts for help. This explains why advocates like Tribe end up defending corporations like Pennzoil in the Supreme Court.

When corporations and corporate lawyers fail to recognize the importance of acquiescing before Supreme Court expertise, the results can be unpleasant, to say the least. In one of several important punitive damages cases decided by the Court in recent years, for instance, Pacific Mutual Life Insurance retained Bruce Beckman, a Los Angeles corporate lawyer, who by all accounts delivered a muddled, unpersuasive argument. In contrast, one of the bar's premiere litigators, Bruce J. Ennis, former ACLU advocate and a member of the Washington office of Chicago's Jenner & Block, appeared for the respondents in an argument that "carried the day with a masterful command of his arguments and the courtroom" (Mauro 1990c, 10).

> The Beckman debacle boiled down to another case of a lawyer who has carried the case from the early stages and is unwilling to let go of it when it gets to the big Court. Several moot courts on the West Coast and one in Washington—which apparently included a memorable scolding of Beckman by [Erwin] Griswold—left the corporate bar wishing Beckman would surrender the argument to someone like veteran Supreme Court advocate Andrew Frey of the D.C. office of Chicago's Mayer, Brown & Platt, who filed a brief in the case for the Business Roundtable. But Beckman wouldn't relinquish the case . . . and the corporate nightmare came true. There are times when an out-of-town law-

yer with passion about the case is more effective than a Washington heavyweight, but this wasn't one of them. (Mauro 1990c, 10)

Examples such as these aptly illustrate why corporate lawyers tend not to be seen as influential leaders within the community of Supreme Court counsel. Of course, the examples I have cited do not involve in-house corporate counsel but firm attorneys who specialize in corporate practice. Yet the argument is no less applicable: lawyers whose expertise lies with corporate representation—whether they work in firms or for corporations directly—simply do not provide the most effective representation in the Court.

The contrast between the corporate counsel from Los Angeles and the "Washington heavyweight" raises the question of influence among the Washington bar. The failure of substantial proportions of the non-Washington lawyers to win the praise of their peers would not be nearly so noteworthy if Washington counsel were generally held in similar esteem. Let us address this issue by turning our attention to the Washington lawyers.

Community Influence within the Washington Bar

Are the Supreme Court lawyers in Washington viewed as any more influential as community members than those who work elsewhere? Looking again at table 7.4, one sees the answer. By even the most conservative assessment, one cannot but conclude that Washington lawyers are far more routinely considered Supreme Court experts.

Private practitioners. The proportion of private practitioners in Washington who have reputations as effective counsel is twice as large as the percentage of the private bar in other cities. As I have noted, Washington is home to some of the most notable members of the community of Supreme Court lawyers, and many litigants respond by seeking out that expertise.

> In the cases that I've been involved in, the sense was that the local attorneys didn't really have—or at least perceived that they didn't have—the skills to handle the case, and therefore they sought out Washington counsel. (CI)

This is not to suggest, of course, that merely practicing in Washington will earn one a reputation as a notable Court litigator. At the very least, however, a private practitioner in Washington with a few Supreme

Court cases to his credit has a greater chance of being perceived as more closely connected to the daily workings of the Court. Notwithstanding that fact, if the perceptions of the Supreme Court bar are a valid indicator of community influence, then the private lawyers in Washington may well be deserving of their reputations, as we will shortly see.

Experience in the solicitor general's office.   Another set of Washington practitioners, members of the solicitor general's staff, have a reputation as effective Supreme Court litigators in roughly the same proportion as the attorneys in Washington law firms. The influence of the solicitor general has, of course, been thoroughly documented (see, for example, Caldeira and Wright 1988; Caplan 1987; Provine 1980; Segal and Reedy 1988); it is not necessary to justify either the solicitor general's successes or his reputation. But the percentage of lawyers on the solicitor general's staff who have earned reputations as expert Supreme Court counsel may strike the reader as low. Consider, however, that the reputation carried by that office is largely institutional in nature. Lawyers hold the office itself in very high esteem, yet they are hard-pressed to name individual members whom they consider to be distinctive Court practitioners. Among the survey respondents, for example, a fair number of lawyers listed "Lawyers in the solicitor general's office" as expert Supreme Court counsel but frequently volunteered that they did not know them by name. Even among members of the solicitor general's office itself, there is no consensus on individual reputations. In one interview, a former associate of that office and I were discussing those lawyers most frequently mentioned as notable experts. When I named one of his former colleagues, he made this observation:

> You know, it's interesting that you mention ——. The word was when I was in the solicitor general's office that he was not among the most effective advocates. The story was that apparently he was in a school play when he was in the third grade, and, when he went out on stage, he opened his mouth and no sound came out. I'm told that every time he went to the Court to argue a case, he was afraid that the same thing would happen. That tended to make him not quite as comfortable before the Court as some other lawyers might be. (CI)

This is certainly not to suggest that the lawyers who comprise the Office of the Solicitor General are not among the brightest legal minds who practice before the Court; quite the contrary. Most lawyers, however, simply do not know who they are.

Within the community of Supreme Court practitioners, the lawyers most likely to have earned reputations as influential members are those who have left the solicitor general's office and have subsequently used their extensive experience with the Court as a means of attracting potential Supreme Court clients.

> The most common reason lawyers develop a Supreme Court practice is my reason, which is that they've served in the solicitor general's office. They've acquired a lot of experience with the Court. They know how the Court works. They know what kind of arguments they make. They know how to write things that are likely to be persuasive to the Court. It therefore makes a lot of sense for clients with cases they care about to retain people like that. Unlike a lot of other areas, it's not as easy to become an experienced Supreme Court practitioner. There's sort of one place where you can really do it, and that's the solicitor general's office. (CI)

As I have already noted, one firm—Chicago's Mayer, Brown & Platt—has acquired a wealth of the solicitor general's talent and consequently has become a virtual magnet for actual or potential Supreme Court litigants, including Browning-Ferris Industries, the FMC Corporation, the General Motors Corporation, Price Waterhouse, and the Ford Motor Company (Hayes 1989, 65). If one were to use a lawyer's clients as a means of measuring community influence, then the alumni of the solicitor general's office who practice in this firm would obviously be among the notables.

One might question the appropriateness of including the former lawyers of the solicitor general's staff in the category of Washington counsel. The 1977–82 data convey vividly, however, that Washington is the city of choice for these advocates. Once they leave the office of solicitor general, they tend to remain in Washington to practice law. In only one instance in this sample did a former associate of the solicitor general practice law in a city other than Washington.[9]

Supreme Court clerks.   Clearly, Supreme Court clerks have spent at least some part of their legal careers in the District of Columbia. To a great degree, one is justified in considering them to be Washington

lawyers because so many of them end up practicing law there following their tenure with the Court. Nearly 80 percent of the former Supreme Court clerks who have considerable experience litigating before
the justices are Washington attorneys. Washington's closest competitors are San Francisco and Chicago, which draw but a paltry 7 percent
and 4 percent of the law clerks, respectively, into positions that lead to
Supreme Court litigation.

Why consider Supreme Court clerks in the context of the specialized
Supreme Court bar? The answer is that a Supreme Court clerkship
affords a young lawyer an insider's view of the machinations of the
Court, which will enhance that lawyer's ability to provide knowledgeable representation once he or she moves on to practice law. Having
screened petitions for review and acquired a sense for plausible arguments the Court will likely find appealing, clerks can often lend a critical eye to petitions they encounter in private practice. Not surprisingly,
the interviews are chock full of statements about the importance of
having served as a Supreme Court clerk. As one former clerk told me:

> Being a clerk is most helpful, I think, in the certiorari process—
> knowing how petitions are reviewed, what role law clerks play
> versus the justices, or knowing who's your audience and what are
> the constraints on your audience. I think that's a terribly im-
> portant piece of knowledge to have. If you know what it's like to
> try to go through a hundred cert petitions a week and make sense
> of them, if you understand that and think about what the reader
> is doing, it ought to significantly alter what you're trying to say
> to them.
>
> . . . It's kind of like the electronic sound bite. To a certain extent,
> what you do has to be designed in the same way, because the
> person you're writing for does not have the time to sit there and
> think great thoughts about what you're writing. He or she has to
> make a judgment almost immediately, and you're writing for that
> purpose. So I think that part helps. Having seen the other side of
> it and knowing which kinds of submissions were not helpful to
> me, I think, is a plus—a big plus. (CI)

In chapter 4 I argued that one of the defining characteristics of Supreme Court practice was the discretionary nature of Supreme Court
review. If this is indeed what separates the Court from other tribunals,
then those firms that hope to establish or maintain a Supreme Court

practice will want lawyers who understand the case selection process. Consequently, such firms will try to attract former clerks into the fold (see Kerlow 1990; also Wermiel 1989).

And attract these clerks they do. There can be little doubt that a clerk is a highly valued asset, as is evident from the willingness of many firms to offer lucrative signing bonuses, even in the face of a questionable economic future. In September of 1990, Andrew Frey, an alumnus of the solicitor general's office now working in the Washington office of Mayer, Brown & Platt, reported that their firm was offering a $35,000 signing bonus for former clerks. Sidley & Austin, the firm of former Solicitor General Rex Lee, was willing to contribute an additional $25,000 on top of a clerk's regular salary, while former Solicitor General Erwin Griswold's firm, Jones, Day, Reavis & Pogue, offered a "sweetener" in excess of $35,000, according to some lawyers. From the clerk's perspective, quite apart from the monetary benefits, the status of such firms is surely a drawing card.

Owing to such aggressive recruitment, a number of Washington firms have been able to build up a fairly extensive pool of ex-clerks. In large measure, the Court's expert litigators view them as useful when it comes to preparing the firm's cases. One Washington veteran, himself a former clerk, illustrated this point:

> We hire people here, some of whom have been Supreme Court clerks. Lance right next door was a law clerk to Justice Marshall. I think that gives him a different understanding. Craig was a law clerk to Justice Powell. Walter clerked, I think, for Justice Douglas. So we have about ten or twelve lawyers here who have been law clerks, and I do think that's a resource that does make a difference. (CI)

Accordingly, former clerks are highly valued as Supreme Court litigators. Their firsthand knowledge of the case selection process translates well into the preparation and evaluation of petitions upon entry into private practice. Said one Supreme Court advocate:

> I have conferred with former law clerks of the Court from time to time for that very reason. I think certainly they have an appreciation of what type of argument is likely to appease the Court, what the justices might be thinking. (CI)

The clerks themselves are well aware of their special perspective. When I asked one prominent Court litigator whether a clerkship was useful for the Supreme Court lawyer, his response was immediate and emphatic:

> Oh, God, yes! No question about it. Not so much in oral argument, but at the petition stage. When you read four or five hundred of those things a term, you get a perspective which there's no other way you could get. The only other way you could get it would be to go down to the Court and spend about a month just reading every cert petition you could get your hands on. And even then, it's not as good practice as when you have to write a memo on the case and when you see the justice's reaction to it. That's the telling point. (CI)

The evidence suggests that, because of their special experience with the Court, clerks have a strong chance of being recruited by a firm or organization engaged in Supreme Court litigation. This increases the odds of an ex-clerk becoming active and successful as a Supreme Court practitioner, which, in turn, may lead to a professional reputation as a skillful Court litigator.

Explaining Washington influence. An effective way to examine the relative contribution of the lawyer characteristics presented in table 7.4 to community influence in the Supreme Court bar is through the use of probit analysis. Since lawyers who work in Washington firms might also have served as Supreme Court clerks or in the solicitor general's office, it is particularly important to examine the influence of these three variables independently. These three characteristics can then be used to predict the likelihood that an experienced lawyer will be named as a notable. The estimated effects of the three variables are presented in table 7.5.

These data confirm that, when it comes to perceived effectiveness in the Supreme Court, firsthand knowledge of the Court is of singular importance, as a look at the impact of each variable in isolation reveals. Lawyers who have worked in the Office of the Solicitor General and have gone on to establish a subsequent Supreme Court practice are most likely to be named as experts; the probability is .34, well above the .04 baseline. But the other two characteristics also prove relevant. Former clerks, for instance, have nearly a 20 percent chance of being

TABLE 7.5. Effect of selected characteristics on reputation as notable Supreme Court counsel

Employment in a Washington firm	Former Supreme Court clerk	Alumnus of the solicitor general's office	Probability
no	no	no	.04
no	yes	no	.18
yes	no	no	.20
no	no	yes	.34
yes	yes	no	.50
no	yes	yes	.68
yes	no	yes	.71
yes	yes	yes	.92

Source: Archival data 1977–82 ($N = 709$).

Note: This model uses the ten lawyer characteristics presented in table 7.4 to predict whether an experienced lawyer was likely to be named as a notable. Estimates are based on probit coefficients with other lawyer characteristics set to their means. For the full model, see Appendix 1.

selected as Supreme Court experts, as do experienced lawyers who practice in the District of Columbia. When these two variables are combined, the probability increases sharply. A former clerk who remains in Washington to practice has a fifty-fifty chance of developing a reputation as effective Court counsel.

Not surprisingly, lawyers who possess all three characteristics are viewed as most effective by their peers. A former Supreme Court clerk with experience in the solicitor general's office who practices privately in Washington is, in a sense, the model Supreme Court litigator. Indeed, one Washington advocate argued that it is precisely these lawyers who are best equipped for the work of the Court:

> To my mind, the ideal Supreme Court lawyer is somebody who clerked on the Supreme Court, was in private practice for a time, and then went to the solicitor general's office where he rose to become a deputy solicitor general and has since been out for a relatively short period of time. All things being equal, that person ought to be a very good Supreme Court lawyer. (CI)

Such a comment makes perfect sense. After all, a Washington lawyer with the insider's perspective of a clerk and the litigation experience afforded by work in the solicitor general's office arguably should know, as well or better than anyone, what effective representation in the Court looks like.

These three attributes, by themselves or in combination, tell us a good deal about the structure of influence among Supreme Court lawyers. That these, and other, lawyer characteristics are so relevant to reputation, however, invites us to consider as well the importance of litigation experience. What can the extent and nature of this experience among the Washington lawyers tell us about the structure of influence within the Court's bar? Obviously, simply having served as a clerk to a Supreme Court justice does not qualify one as an expert on the Supreme Court, nor will a lawyer who practices in a Washington firm automatically be elevated to the status of a notable. As a former associate of the solicitor general's office, now an appellate litigator in a firm in Washington, put it:

> I think if you clerk for a justice, you have much more of a sense of how to litigate up there than someone who's never done that. But actually, in my experience, people who have clerked for a justice and done nothing else really don't know very much about practicing up there. Because they get such a different perspective on the whole process, they often are not in as good a position as someone who's practiced before the Court for a couple of years. Clerks know more about the inside workings of the Court, but I don't think they really appreciate how to get a case granted or how to argue a case successfully. (CI)

Doubtless, then, experience litigating before the justices increases a lawyer's chances of being selected as expert counsel. Indeed, expertise is a resource from which professional prestige often springs (Davis and Moore 1970, 127–28). Lawyers with relatively more Supreme Court cases to their credit should thus be natural candidates for the list of notable practitioners.

Table 7.6, which shows the average number of cases on the merits that the experienced lawyers handled from 1977 to 1982, reveals clear differences between Washington and non-Washington lawyers. As a group, the Washington advocates far exceed the merits experience of their peers who practice beyond the beltway. Ex-clerks and, in particular, former members of the solicitor general's office again appear as the most active Supreme Court practitioners. Or, to compare two catego-

TABLE 7.6. Average number of cases handled by experienced Supreme Court lawyers

	Arguments	Briefs	Total Cases
Experienced non-Washington counsel			
Academic lawyers	1.6	1.3	2.9
Interest group lawyers	.6	2.7	3.3
Corporate counsel	.2	2.4	2.6
Firm lawyers	1.0	1.3	2.3
State and local government lawyers	.7	2.5	3.2
All lawyers	.8	2.2	3.0
Experienced Washington counsel			
Alumni of solicitor general's office	2.0	2.5	4.5
Former Supreme Court clerks	2.0	5.2	7.2
Interest group lawyers	1.0	3.6	4.6
Lawyers in solicitor general's office	6.2	13.0	19.2
Firm lawyers	.8	1.8	2.6
All lawyers	2.2	5.0	7.2

Source: Archival data 1977–82.
Note: For Ns, see table 7.4.

ries directly: interest group lawyers who do not practice in Washington have fewer cases to their credit than their counterparts in the District of Columbia. In general, higher levels of experience in Supreme Court litigation are characteristic with those lawyers most likely to be held in high professional esteem by their peers—the Washington practitioners.

Let us take a closer look at the Washington bar and consider the role of experience within that context. To test the effect of Supreme Court experience on the nature of influence, one can examine the most visible form of Supreme Court representation—oral argument—in conjunction with various qualities of the experienced bar. By analyzing the characteristics of these lawyers in conjunction with the number of oral appearances made from 1977 to 1982, one can assess the relative impact of expertise on the likelihood that a lawyer will be chosen as notable Supreme Court counsel.[10]

Table 7.7 paints a clear picture, one which suggests that experience

TABLE 7.7.   Effect of oral arguments on reputation as notable Supreme Court counsel

Arguments	Washington firm	Other city firm	Washington interest group	Other city interest group	Supreme Court clerk	Solicitor general alumnus	State and local government
0	.05	.06	.06	.06	.06	.06	.05
1	.12	.09	.26	.12	.16	.19	.10
2	.23	.14	.61	.23	.33	.44	.16
3	.37	.21	.89	.37	.56	.71	.25
4	.54	.30	.99	.54	.77	.90	.37
5	.71	.40	.99	.70	.90	.98	.49

Source: Archival data 1977–82 (*N* = 709).

Note: Estimates are based on probit coefficients with other lawyer characteristics set to their means. For the full model, with all ten predictors interacted with the number of arguments, see Appendix 1.

for any advocate is the sine qua non to acquiring the reputation of an expert Court litigator. Among Supreme Court clerks and former members of the solicitor general's staff, for instance, the chances of being elevated to influential status march in lock step, increasing substantially with each additional argument. Since these data reflect lawyer activity over a six-year period, one could say that ex-clerks and solicitor general alumni who argue about one case each year are almost certain to be named by their peers as Supreme Court experts. The comparison between Washington and non-Washington private practitioners tells a similar tale. The firm attorney in Washington who argues regularly is nearly twice as likely to have a Supreme Court reputation as a firm lawyer in another city who has equal experience. Likewise, interest group counsel in the capital acquire expert status much more readily than their peers from places such as New York, Chicago, or San Francisco. State and local counsel, even those who have regular contact with the justices, cannot begin to compete with the prestige ranking of the Washington bar. Of course, any given lawyer who litigates before the Supreme Court has some chance of earning a reputation as an expert Court litigator. But those who find the Court most accessible—clerks, solicitor general alumni, and those who work in close proximity to the Court—have an enormous advantage.

Conclusion

In sum, the community of Supreme Court litigators and the structure of influence among its membership are fairly well defined. These lawyers share a good many common ties and significant collegial contacts; many experienced lawyers are products of the same legal training and the same work environment; they interact both in Supreme Court litigation specifically and in broader professional and social contexts. Importantly, it is in Washington where one finds a wealth of experienced Supreme Court talent, those lawyers who are intimately familiar with the Court. In short, the Washington community is the center of the bar's community. Elites normally "have a greater share than other people of the . . . experiences that are most highly valued" (Mills 1956, 278), and so it is with these lawyers. They have the lion's share of experiences such as Court clerkships, tenure in the solicitor general's office, and practice in the Washington law firms, combined with active involvement in the Court's docket. They constitute the core of the community of Supreme Court lawyers; within that community, they are elevated in the social hierarchy.

Critics may charge, of course, that simply delineating the sociometric structure within the community of the Court's bar fails to reveal whether any of the notables within that structure truly wield political influence. Status, as Wolfinger (1970) reminds us, does not necessarily imply power. Having mapped the contours of influence within the bar, I will now shift attention to the relationship between the bar and the Court itself in order to explore influence more directly. Stated another way, the Washington community is perceived as effective, but this perception should be tested against the facts. As with many representatives in the capital, the Washington lawyers within the inner circle are sought because of their abilities to secure access to the government's decision makers. Our account of their influence, therefore, must rest upon the degree to which these lawyers actually shape the actions of the justices as they select cases for plenary review.

8

The Political Impact
of the Inner Circle

What are the implications of expert representation in the Supreme Court? Can an experienced litigator more effectively gain access to the Court's agenda? Can the arguments of a sophisticated appellate practitioner shape the outcome of a case? Posing these questions to the lawyers themselves, of course, elicits a number of responses. If, however, there is one thing upon which all Supreme Court lawyers agree, it is that veteran litigators can play a crucial role in setting the Court's agenda. Lawyers consistently hold the view that experienced Supreme Court counsel can have a great impact at the stage of case selection—that their participation at the agenda stage might figure in the justices' selection of cases for plenary review. By contrast, there is a good deal of disagreement within the bar about the significance of Supreme Court experience for cases on the merits; some see experience as quite critical, while others remain skeptical.

At various points in American history, the bar of the Court has had a significant influence on the development of the law (see, for example, Irons 1982; Lawrence 1990; Twiss 1942; White 1988). Of course, lawyers have long speculated about their impact on the Supreme Court. In reference to Marshall's opinion in *Gibbons v. Ogden*, for instance, Daniel

Webster suggested that "the opinion of the court, as rendered by the chief justice, was little else than a recital of my argument" (White 1988, 285). Today, however, few lawyers would ascribe to themselves similar influence. Whether and to what degree these experienced Supreme Court lawyers do affect the choices the justices make is the subject of this chapter. For several reasons, the greatest scrutiny will be given to the process whereby the justices set the Court's agenda. From a theoretical perspective, scholars have applied far more systematic effort to analyzing the Court's selection of cases than its decisions on the merits. As a consequence, although there is a growing body of knowledge about decision making at the merits stage (see, for example, Ivers and O'Connor 1987; Segal 1984), a great deal more is known about the factors associated with the choices made in the case selection process. A good many competing explanations that might account for the Court's certiorari decisions can be distinguished; so greater confidence can be placed in conclusions regarding the effectiveness of counsel in agenda setting. Furthermore, many who have studied the Supreme Court's agenda setting have offered compelling reasons as to why and how experienced counsel might affect case selection. It is important, therefore, to test these explanations and their underlying assumptions. In addition, my interest in agenda setting is driven by the views of the lawyers I interviewed. The elite maintain that, to the extent the bar shapes the contours of judicial decision making, their influence is likely to be greater at the stage of case selection.

Access to the Agenda

Talk to an experienced Supreme Court practitioner about his or her role in the politics of the Court and the discussion inevitably will turn to the topic of case selection and that lawyer's potential to help secure access to the Court's plenary agenda. How does the Court's bar arrive at the conclusion that they possess such an ability? Their belief appears to be a function of two interrelated reasons: the quality of the petitions written by experienced counsel and the credibility of their submissions. Before one can assess the influence of experienced Supreme Court lawyers, it is therefore essential to consider why these two attributes are so meaningful in the eyes of the bar.

Quality of the Petition

Part of the reason why expert Supreme Court counsel may be more effective at securing review is that, by virtue of their experience, they have developed the skills necessary to make petitions attractive to the Court. Thirty-five years ago, in his study of the Supreme Court, John P. Frank pointed out that a fair number of the cases brought to the Court begin at a disadvantage because their authors lack a sense of how to construct compelling petitions. Many lawyers who are new to the Court hammer out briefs that are simply not up to the task of demonstrating that a case is worthy of review. "In hundreds of cases each year the private litigant is represented by a lawyer whose brief reveals that he has no notion at all of the requisites of Supreme Court litigation or of what is and what is not persuasive to the Court to which the brief is addressed. These are the cases that never get to argument because by its preliminary order the Court disposes of them" (Frank 1958, 95).

Today, the quality of a certiorari petition and its likelihood of persuading the justices to grant plenary review remain equally linked: cogent, logical briefs have a greater chance of succeeding than disorganized, implausible ones (see Rehnquist 1987, 264). Indeed, the Court's leading practitioners remind the counsel for the petitioners that

> what the Court said in 1917 in *Furness, Withy & Co. v. Yang-Tsze Insurance Assn.*, 242 U.S. 430, 434 (1917), remains highly relevant: We . . . necessarily rely in an especial way upon petitions, replies, and supporting briefs. Unless these are carefully prepared, contain appropriate references to the record, and present with *studied accuracy, brevity, and clearness* whatever is essential to ready and adequate understanding of points requiring our attention, the rights of interested parties may be prejudiced and the Court will be impeded in its efforts properly to dispose of the causes which constantly crowd its docket. (Stern, Gressman, and Shapiro 1986, 259–60)

Without question, some of the best briefs that the Court encounters are products of the solicitor general's office. It is thus natural to turn to the lawyers in that office for an assessment of the general quality of other pleadings. How do the solicitor general's lawyers view outside petitions for review? They are clearly aware of qualitative differences in the Court's submissions. Accordingly, they are quick to nominate the petitions produced by expert Supreme Court practitioners as exemplars of sound legal craftsmanship. In some instances, the quality of this work parallels that of petitions written by the solicitor general's lawyers, as this current associate of the solicitor general admits:

> To an extent, the two are comparable. You don't have the same institutional input and safeguards for nongovernment filings. These are lawyers who do work of a very high quality, and I'm sure the Court has found their filings to be very professional and very useful in its work. I've found them to be good. So, I think there is some comparison that can be made, but it's not quite the same. (CI)

When asked whether the quality of cert petitions filed by experienced Supreme Court counsel is generally superior to the average cert petition, another lawyer in the solicitor general's office volunteered without hesitation: "Absolutely. There's no comparison." On the issue of whether those superior briefs have a greater likelihood of success, he suggested that there is some advantage to having expert counsel at the petition stage:

> It gives them an edge, if they file a good brief. The way briefs are written makes a difference. I don't know that the Supreme Court has an area of expertise that is different from other courts, but it does require some expertise to be really good in the Court. That's something that's not always appreciated by outside counsel. (CI)

It stands to reason that the lawyer with experience in the Court is better equipped to draft a petition for review than the lawyer without any Court work to his credit. Such lawyers have the advantage of being what Galanter refers to as repeat players (1974, 114–19). Galanter argues that parties who litigate frequently have a variety of advantages over those who turn to the courts on an ad hoc basis. Moreover, since Supreme Court practice is so different from practice in other judicial settings, litigating before the Court is especially daunting to the novice counsel. This is not to suggest, of course, that inexperienced counsel will have every petition denied or that expert litigators can guarantee success. On balance, however, inexperienced lawyers must overcome the burdens of the unfamiliar, and thus the odds are against them.

Credibility of the Petition

Perhaps even more significant to the process of case selection are the reputations that the Court's notable advocates possess. When a lawyer who is known to the justices lends his or her name to a cert petition, the attorney conveys an implicit message to the Court: the arguments contained herein can be taken seriously and the issues raised are worthy of the your attention. Scholars of the Court have demonstrated, over and over again, that the justices give great weight to the arguments made by the institutional litigants who come before them at the stage of case selection and at the merits as well (see, for example, Caldeira and Wright 1988; Caplan 1987; Segal and Reedy 1988). By extension, as the justices come to know the experienced lawyers who practice before them, the seasoned advocates develop a similar credibility. Indeed, Galanter numbers credibility among the advantages that repeat players enjoy. The relationship of lawyer credibility to the process of case selection should thus be obvious: the petition bearing the name of an experienced member of the Supreme Court bar may be a harbinger of a potentially certworthy case.

As the Court's leading practitioners explain, the justices tend to view filings as extensions of the lawyers who write them: "[T]he member of the Bar must take responsibility for the document; he should therefore assure himself that it is accurate and in compliance with the Court's rules and that it satisfies his personal standards of quality" (Stern, Gressman, and Shapiro 1986, 733). By their own admission, the lawyers who litigate in the Court with any frequency need to guard their credibility and consequently are reluctant to advance unreasonable claims. As a Washington lawyer who has handled a number of the Court's more prominent cases explained:

> My partners and I don't like to put our names on a petition for cert if we don't think it's responsible. Of course, the odds against *any* private petition for cert are very high, but we don't think that you should just waste the Court's time. We value our own reputation in the Court. We don't want to put a silly petition up there. Now, we file a lot of them that aren't granted, but at least they're respectable. (CI)

Another practitioner in a large firm discussed how one of his partners—a former member of the solicitor general's office—works to protect his and his firm's reputation with the Court:

He doesn't put his name on a case to take an otherwise uncert-
worthy issue and create a Supreme Court case out of it. In fact,
I've seen him tell clients he won't put his name on a petition
because it's not a case that's worth going up there. Since he thinks
it has no realistic prospect of being granted, he just won't put his
name on the pleading. (CI)

Any lawyer who submits a petition for review obviously wants the
Court to take his case seriously, but the experts within the elite community of Supreme Court advocates have long-term interests at stake.
They want to maintain their practice in the Court, remain visible, attract future Supreme Court clients, and so on. None of these goals are
well served by alienating the justices or losing their trust. Spending all
of one's political capital on any given case simply does not outweigh
the broader interests associated with the reputation for effective appellate advocacy.[1]

It's a matter of credibility with the Court. The Court is accus-
tomed to you and is inclined to believe you. And if the Court
knows you're experienced from particular cases, it's always a
help. The core of good advocacy in that court is admitting the
weaknesses in your own case and not trying to dance around,
not trying to be just as positive about a weak point as a strong
point. That's what gets you credibility. (CI)

Another prominent Supreme Court litigator offered this view:

I would say that people like [Erwin] Griswold, Larry Tribe, I hope
myself, and certainly Rex Lee bring something special to the
Court. I guess the one thing is—particularly if you come out of
the solicitor general's practice—that the Court has confidence
that you will never overstate the case. And that is something important. (CI)

There is, of course, a great deal of difference between frivolity and
lack of certworthiness. As these lawyers have reminded us, they bring
many petitions to the Court that are denied review. The key to their
success with those petitions that are granted is their intellectual hon-
esty. By owning up to the frailties of one's case, as well as emphasizing
important questions, the expert earns the trust of the Court.[2] Thus, the
experienced elite serve as an index on which the justices and their

clerks can consistently rely because, much like those of the solicitor general, their submissions are bona fide plausible pleadings—in a sense, their cases are also "prescreened." The professional fortunes of these lawyers are not tied to any one case. Rather, these advocates see themselves in a long-term relationship with the Court—a long-term view of litigation being another attribute of Galanter's repeat player. One former associate of the solicitor general's office, now an appellate practitioner in a large firm, offered this perspective:

> I think that the Court probably consciously or subconsciously perceives that people like Larry Tribe or some other people just wouldn't file an insubstantial cert petition. Also, I think the Court has to be concerned that, if they grant a petition, it's adequately briefed. I think they know that if they grant a petition from someone like him or —— [that lawyer's firm], they'll get a good brief. (CI)

Are these assumptions sustained by the facts? To what extent can the notables within the community of Supreme Court lawyers affect the case selection process? Another Washington firm lawyer, with several years experience serving in the solicitor general's office, provided perhaps the best summary of our expectations:

> Fifty percent of the cert petitions filed have no chance of being granted. Anybody who read them before they were filed could have told the petitioner that. There are some marginal cases that may only have a 10 percent chance or a 5 percent chance but are worth trying. And I think that having our name on them probably subconsciously has an effect. For one thing, it'll get read a little more carefully. I'm sure of that. (CI)

We can expect the expert's arguments to be given greater weight. That their briefs will be held in higher regard by the justices, however, does not speak to the importance of the issues raised in those briefs. On the basis of interviews with members of the Court and dozens of former clerks, H. W. Perry, Jr., concludes: "Sometimes who counsel is, irrespective of the cause, is important for the justices. . . . [Some] attorneys are known by the Court as being particularly good. When the Court has an opportunity to pick among cases to resolve an issue, the case with good counsel will usually be chosen" (1991, 127). Thus, the influence of the experienced Supreme Court lawyers should be significant, though not necessarily deterministic. In other words, the appearance of the name of an experienced lawyer should increase a petition's chances for review, but that alone should not determine whether review is granted.

Quality and Credibility: Caveats

Those who do not subscribe to the idea that the Court responds to various signals of certworthiness could raise a number of reasonable concerns regarding the role of experienced lawyers. One might argue, for example, that the measured effectiveness of expert counsel is really only a manifestation of the selectivity exercised by these lawyers: they accept only cases they believe have a reasonable chance of succeeding. Although clearly lawyers can reject cases that they do not want, however, the power of the expert counsel extends no farther than the ability to dissuade the litigant from seeking review.[3] The reflections of this Washington notable are representative of the comments I encountered on this issue:

> Those of us in private practice will certainly advise clients if a case is not certworthy, and I'm always up front about that. In fact, many times, I will say, "Don't waste your money." On the other hand, if the client *wants* to waste his money and the question has been properly preserved and if it isn't a dead list case, I would normally go ahead and take it. I think the answer depends. As far as I'm concerned, I normally don't sit back and say, "Well, I won't take this because I don't think cert will be granted." (CI)

Another Washington lawyer, this one an alumnus of the solicitor general's office, suggests that, while many sophisticated clients seek experienced counsel, that may or may not reflect a sophisticated judgment about certworthiness. As he explained:

> Intelligent legal consumers don't spend what it costs to hire an expert Supreme Court practitioner unless they think they've got a good case. That's not always true. I spend a lot of my time trying to talk people out of filing cert petitions that I think aren't going to get anywhere. Everybody's instinct is, "I'll take it to the Supreme Court," and sometimes it's very hard to persuade them that they're wasting their money. It's also true that an experienced Supreme Court practitioner may be less likely to take on repre-

sentation for the purposes of filing an insubstantial cert petition. On the other hand, if you have a client, and the client says, "I want you to file a cert petition," and the cert petition is not frivolous, even though you know that chances are less than one in a thousand that it'll be granted, it's very hard to say, "Oh, I'm too good for your case. I'm not going to do it." Sometimes you file cert petitions that are real long shots just because your professional obligation to your client requires you to do it. (CI)

Although expert Supreme Court practitioners will want to ply their skills on cases that have reasonable chances of succeeding, one must remember that most members of the Court's bar are not free agents. The vast majority of Supreme Court lawyers are in private practice and ultimately must be attentive to the desires of those who call upon their services. Lawyers do not accept only the cases that they think will be granted cert, any more than the justices grant cert in order to hear from expert counsel.

The skeptic might also note that, with the retirement of Justice Brennan, no member of the Court examines all of the cert petitions that are submitted. Rather, the justices primarily examine memoranda prepared by clerks. How then can something like lawyer credibility ever enter into the calculation, especially when the clerks may not know who the elite Supreme Court lawyers are? I must confess my own initial wariness on this point. Fortunately, ex-clerks reassured me time and again that such ignorance was extremely improbable. As one former clerk, a professor of law at a prestigious university, put the matter:

> Remember, all these people have been in the big New York and Washington law firms, at least between their second and third years, sometimes between their first and second years. So, they've been in the big firm milieu. They've been clerks on the courts of appeals. They're from the very elite law schools, and they tend to know who the players are. They know who Barrett Prettyman is, and they know who Lloyd Cutler is. They certainly know Larry Tribe and Rex Lee. They know a lot about the reputation lawyers. They go to the Court and hear arguments in the summer. They're very sophisticated about this. (CI)

If clerks do have expectations about quality and credibility, then does that in any way affect how they handle the briefs? Said this former clerk:

> I think it helps. If you've got a hundred pieces of paper in front of you, seeing something that you know is likely to be good gives you a good feeling going into the pleading to begin with. (CI)

Offering another perspective on this issue, an active practitioner before the Court made this observation:

> I've often wondered whether lawyers make a difference. . . . Well, I'll put it this way: I can't imagine a brief signed by Rex Lee or Erwin Griswold or Larry Tribe that would ever make the dead list. I just think that they would say, "Wait a minute. We've got to look at it." (CI)

Again, this does not mean that clerks will recommend certiorari merely because an experienced Court advocate has signed the petition. It does suggest, however, that throughout the case selection process, actions may be guided by expectation. Thus, when clerks encounter the filings of active members of the community of Supreme Court lawyers, they are apt to give them greater attention, either because a lawyer's name carries some credibility or because a brief is well crafted. As this influential Washington lawyer—also a former clerk—revealed:

> I have had it reported to me by people who know law clerks, who have had lunches with them, or something like that, that when the clerks see certain names—including mine—on cert petitions, they do pay special attention to it, more than they do the petitions of Joe Schmoe. I think that's true. I still don't think they're going to recommend a grant just because my name is on it. All that means is that they're going to pay attention to make sure that they get it right. (CI)

Thus, the idea of influence within the Court's bar—the ability of the elite to gain access to the Court's agenda—appears to filter down through the Court itself. Indeed, even the law clerks have some notion of the importance of the bar's active membership and are willing to handle their petitions with greater care.

A Model of Case Selection

Are the lawyers of the inner circle truly gatekeepers? The influence of Supreme Court lawyers in the process of case selection can be measured by examining their participation in previous cases and testing the effect of that experience on the certiorari decisions made by the justices. If lawyers have the effect that they themselves claim, then the participation of lawyers who are known to the justices from previous cases should have an impact on their selection of subsequent cases for plenary review. Fortunately, our knowledge of the factors that affect the Court's agenda is extensive (see, for example, Armstrong and Johnson 1982; Brenner 1979; Caldeira and Wright 1988; Perry 1991; Provine 1980; Songer 1979; Tanenhaus et al. 1963; Teger and Kosinski 1980; Ulmer 1978, 1984). Given that we have such a clear picture of the impact of a number of predictors in the selection of cases, we can be that much more confident that any measured effectiveness of Supreme Court counsel is not a manifestation of some other set of influences.

The 1977–82 data on the lawyers active in multiple cases at the merits are ideally suited to the task at hand. Caldeira and Wright (1988) have examined the importance of amicus curiae briefs on the Court's case selection from the 1982 term. Using their data, their basic model can be reconstructed, but with the addition of several variables pertinent to the Supreme Court lawyers.[4]

Washington is a mecca for Supreme Court practitioners. Proportionately, it commands an extraordinary segment of the bar's active population, especially among its notable members. Assuming that one wishes to treat experienced Washington counsel as to some extent distinctive, one would want a measure of their participation to reflect both the breadth of their involvement as well as their status as influential members of the bar. Accordingly, I assess the effect of petitions brought by the named Washington notables with, on average, more than one case over the previous five terms. Similarly, for non-Washington counsel, I measure the effectiveness of lawyers who were involved in multiple cases in the five years preceding the 1982 term.

An overview. An initial examination of the data suggests that experienced lawyers play a central role in agenda setting. Included in the sample were 35 petitions brought by notable, experienced Washington counsel and 141 petitions brought by experts from outside the federal city. (Because two cases involved influential Washington experts as well as non-Washington veterans, the total number of cases is properly 174.) Of the cases brought by experienced counsel, 22 percent were granted review—as compared to 6 percent of those cases in which no veteran counsel were present. Among the Washington notables, the

TABLE 8.1. Probit model of the Supreme Court bar in case selection

Variable	Coefficient	*t*-score
Constant	−3.06	−13.45
Solicitor general	2.21	8.12
Disagreement among lower courts	.08	.58
Dissent in lower courts	.43	2.64
Alleged conflicts	.43	2.30
Actual conflicts	2.06	11.39
Civil liberties issue	−.11	−.73
Conservative decision in court below	−.68	−4.38
One or more amici supporting review	1.33	8.02
One or more amici opposing review	.65	2.22
Non-Washington expert counsel		
One to three prior merits cases	.53	2.14
More than three prior merits cases	.70	3.17
Notable Washington expert counsel		
One to three prior merits cases	1.09	2.26
More than three prior merits cases	1.18	2.71

Sources: Data collected as part of the "Project on Organized Interests in the United States Supreme Court," Gregory A. Caldeira and John R. Wright, principal investigators; archival data 1977–82 (*N* = 1757: 140 grants, 1617 denials).

Note: For further information on the model used to generate these data, see Appendix 1.

figure is even higher (26 percent); non-Washington experts also maintain a strong showing with 21 percent of their petitions being granted plenary review. Although encouraging, these results do not reflect careful control for other explanatory variables. Let us turn, then, to the multivariate probit model presented in table 8.1.

The results of this analysis are, statistically speaking, impressive.[5] Both the notables in Washington as well as the active bar from outside the District of Columbia have a strong impact on the Court's selection of cases. Thus, even when a host of variables that might also exercise some effect on certiorari are taken into account, experienced Supreme Court representation stands out as an important predictor. Presumably, the Court places greater trust in those judgments they know to be reliable.

From what I can tell—and this is anecdotal, what you hear from people—when the Court is deciding whether to exercise its discretion, the idea that they will have a known quantity in front of them, whom they can count on to make not necessarily winning arguments but to make good arguments, to do thorough re-search, and to help the Court as much as possible, consistent with their client's position, that's a plus in deciding whether to take a particular case or to take one case when there are two or three that present the same issue. (CI)

In short, if the justices had two cases that raised similar legal issues, they might give greater weight to the petition signed by the expert—especially if that expert was a familiar figure from the Washington bar.

Quality and credibility: The Washington community.   As I have argued, the two interrelated benefits of representation by the elite community of Supreme Court counsel are the quality of their work and the reliabil-ity that the Court can assign to their judgment. Nowhere is this better exemplified than among the notable members of the Washington bar: the experts who work in close proximity to the Court appear to have a strong impact on its proceedings. This connection between the Washington-based litigators and the Court's selection of cases comes as no surprise to the veteran Supreme Court bar. Their own perspective supports the notion that reputations for performing sound and solid work in the Court loom large in the process whereby the justices iden-tify potentially important cases. As one of the most frequently named Washington experts explained:

I think that if you are known to the Court as a Supreme Court practitioner—if you're thought of as competent and if they've learned over time that when you say, for instance, "It's a direct conflict," it *is* a direct conflict, that it's not strained—whether they agree with you or not, they know that what you say is going to be credible and supported by the record. They're not going to get embarrassed down the line and have to dismiss cert as improvi-dently granted because you were stretching on whether an issue was properly briefed and presented. I think that helps enor-mously at the cert stage in getting careful review. Enormously.

. . . I'm not trying to get you to retain me, so I can say this without sounding immodest about it: Hiring a lawyer at the cert stage who has a reputation at the Supreme Court for playing by

TABLE 8.2. Effect of experienced Supreme Court bar on case selection

No experienced lawyers	.01
Non-Washington expert counsel	
One to three prior merits cases	.05
More than three prior merits cases	.06
Notable Washington expert counsel	
One to three prior merits cases	.13
More than three prior merits cases	.15

Sources: Data collected as part of the "Project on Organized Interests in the United States Supreme Court," Gregory A. Caldeira and John R. Wright, principal investigators; archival data 1977–82.

Note: Probabilities are based on probit estimates in table 8.1 with other predictors set to their means.

the Court's rules is one of the most important things a client can do in terms of getting attention paid to his cert petition. (CI)

How much difference does the elite bar make? Table 8.2 shows the estimated effects of experienced lawyers on the probability of the Court granting certiorari. If non-Washington experts are associated with a case, the likelihood of review increases from the baseline of .01 to .05 or .06, depending on how many prior cases the lawyers have to their credit. The impact of the Washington notables is uniformly stronger, however, the probability of review rising as high as .15. Apparently, the expert counsel who work in the capital are better able to secure review than the experienced lawyers who practice outside of Washington. Why is the Washington litigator more effective? Perhaps the mere fact that he practices law in close proximity to the Court hones his abilities and sensitivities. A current member of the solicitor general's office commented:

As I have practiced before the Court over the years, I find that I am better able to anticipate what the justices are likely to be interested in about the case, what they may question me about, and so forth. I'm just a closer student of the Court in that way, because I have constant exposure. To a lesser extent, that's true of lawyers who practice more regularly before the Court but may work out of Chicago or Los Angeles or wherever they are. They don't really see the Court in action, but on rare occasions. (CI)

To illustrate this point: One morning during which I attended an argument at the Court, a member of the bar whom I was to interview later that afternoon turned up to hear the same case. He was not involved, directly or indirectly; he was just interested. Washington practitioners would often mention that they sit in on arguments to stay current with the justices, particularly before one of their own upcoming arguments. As one lawyer explained:

I always go down and just listen to arguments for a couple of days immediately preceding or in the week that the case that I'm arguing is going to be argued, just to kind of get the feel of the Court on a current basis. (CI)

Indeed, the experienced Supreme Court counsel specifically recommend this practice to the novice advocate (Shapiro 1984, 533). Naturally, the greater the distance from the Court, the higher the cost associated with attending arguments as a means of preparation. Logically, then, the Washington advocate is at an advantage. He can utilize the resources of the Court much more readily; he can sit in on arguments. Moreover, he has collegial interaction with other Court veterans in the city. In sum, the Washington lawyer is much more integrated into the environment of the Court.

Another Washington lawyer and former clerk corroborated these results. He suggested that, as they examine petitions for review, the justices and their clerks place greater trust in the filings of the experienced counsel:

You look at the cover and you say, "Well, this should be a decent brief. This guy should talk about the real issues and not bullshit me." So, it might get the brief read in circumstances where it wouldn't get read. (CI)

Since thousands of petitions land on the steps of the Court each year, the effect of experienced counsel is of no small consequence, as the data in table 8.2 indicate. Furthermore, I have controlled for most of the other criteria that affect case selection, so lawyers should only make an incremental difference. One lawyer, an alumnus of the solicitor general's office who practices in a large Washington firm, cited a cert success rate very close to the one reported in the table. Further, he saw his firm's success as a function of both credibility with the Court and the quality of the work that the firm provides its clients:

> For every ten cert petitions we file, I doubt that we get more than two of them granted. While that, compared to the outside world, is an incredible plus—it's a very high percentage—it is nevertheless overall a very low percentage, and we have to say that to clients: "You can hire us. You can use us, and we will provide you with both some name recognition and quality work product, but those combined don't guarantee the Supreme Court's going to hear your case." The problem is, you've got to have a question that's worthy of Supreme Court review. (CI)

The fit between the empirical results and the comments offered by the Court's bar is very reassuring. Both suggest that the estimated effectiveness of the elite community of lawyers is neither illogical nor overstated. Ultimately, the success or failure of any cert petition turns on the importance of the questions it raises. In a fair number of cases, however, the petitioner's lawyer is simply better at articulating these issues. One former member of the solicitor general's staff provided a useful summary of the process:

> When they open the brief and start reading it, I think it's more what's written on the page than who wrote it that's important. Although lawyers acquire reputations. There is an element of credibility, and if the Court feels from knowing you that you don't make arguments you don't believe in, they may give it a little more weight. In general, I think the most important thing is how to get the justices to pay attention to your brief. And my guess is that credibility does matter. Once they start to read the brief, it's the quality of the brief that largely is going to matter to them. (CI)

Undeniably, then, lawyers play an important role in the agenda process, although certain other factors may also be at work. A more conservative view of these results, for example, might see the effectiveness of the expert lawyers in tandem with the tendency for certain litigants to retain experienced Supreme Court counsel. As I have noted, those most likely to seek out expert counsel are the more sophisticated consumers of legal services—such as major corporations—many of whom

would be active Supreme Court litigants regardless of who their lawyers were. Thus, the changes in the probability of the Court granting
review would be a function of the presence of both lawyers and litigants who have experience in the Supreme Court. Furthermore, there
is surely a strong correlation between the willingness of experienced
Supreme Court counsel to take a case to the Court and a case's certworthiness. Even if the changes in the likelihood of review were only
partly attributable to experienced Supreme Court lawyers, however,
that by itself would still be important. Merely to establish a connection
between experienced counsel and the probability of the Court granting
certiorari is, at the very least, an important preliminary step in the
direction of assessing the role of lawyers in Supreme Court policy
making.

Winning and Losing

Once the Supreme Court decides to grant review in a case, what might
be the consequences of expert representation? Are experienced Supreme Court practitioners any more successful than counsel who appear in the Court for but a single case? The lawyers I interviewed generally held that, while it is of some help to have a veteran Supreme
Court practitioner as counsel, the benefits are marginal (see also Rehnquist 1987, 276–85). An experienced litigator, they suggest, can anticipate the behavior of the justices and knows how to respond to that
behavior. In short, they know what to expect from the Court and what
the Court expects from them. As a former associate of the solicitor
general's office who now practices before the Court as a member of a
Washington firm remarked:

> I think experience is a positive value in any area of the practice
> of law. Having been in the Supreme Court a few times, it makes
> it much easier the next time you show up. So I think there's no
> question that the comfort level and the ability to anticipate the
> kinds of problems that could arise is a major plus. I would recom-
> mend that any client that had a case in the Supreme Court give
> thought to finding someone who could, if not argue the case, at
> least assist whoever they want to argue it and give him the lay of
> the land. I think experience is a terribly important value. (CI)

Another lawyer in a Washington firm echoed this view:

> A lawyer who has done a lot of briefing in the Supreme Court or
> made a lot of oral arguments before the Supreme Court has been
> exposed to the practice and has had an opportunity to learn what
> type of approaches appeal to the Court, what type don't, what
> things please the Court or offend the Court. (CI)

Similarly, one of the Court's most active private practitioners offered
this assessment of experience and its relevance for effective advocacy
on the merits:

> Primarily it's knowing what to expect. I think it's normally a law-
> yer who's arguing his first case who will get totally thrown by the
> kinds of questions that the justices ask and who won't be properly
> prepared for what it's all about. So the experienced advocate,
> while he or she cannot always guess what the questions are, can
> come a lot closer than somebody who's not used to it. Also, I
> think having nine people come at you at once—particularly
> where they don't give you an opportunity to answer, where they
> interrupt each other, interrupt you, talk over you, and so forth—
> that can get to inexperienced people, and they get all discombob-
> ulated, and it can be a mess. Whereas those of us who have done
> it and know what's coming can know how to handle those ques-
> tions and how to get back on the track and where not to waste
> time. I think that's a very big item. (CI)

Of course, this experience may prove to be a double-edged sword, as
this veteran advocate explained:

> I think there are disadvantages as well. I've noticed in my own
> case, and I've noticed in the case of other Supreme Court prac-
> titioners, including some of the really best and brightest prac-
> titioners there are, that if the justices know that you're pretty
> good and pretty competent, they seem to feel freer to really probe
> and go after you in oral argument than they would if they
> thought you were some guy who was going to dissolve in a
> puddle of tears and fall apart if he were hit with some really
> tough questions. (CI)

Naturally, then, simply having experience in Supreme Court advocacy does not guarantee success; the Court is more interested in the

substantive issues raised by a case. It is important to bear in mind, though, that what was true of veteran counsel at the agenda stage also applies at the merits: as elite litigators, the insiders have earned the mark of credibility. The justices therefore need not make an additional intellectual investment in examining the reliability of counsel's claims, as this lawyer explained:

> There are ways to say things orally and in writing in the Supreme Court that you were not born knowing. And it helps to be known by the justices. If they know you, they can concentrate more on the merits of your case. They don't have to worry about whether what you're telling them is, strictly speaking, accurate or not. (CI)

It is interesting to note the relationship of credibility at the stage of case selection to decisions on the merits. After all, the justices are concerned ultimately with locating and resolving the most significant legal disputes. The more effective a lawyer can be in serving these basic goals in the present, the more likely it is the arguments of that lawyer will be given greater attention and respect in future cases. Thus, the experienced Supreme Court practitioners who develop reputations for straightforward, credible advocacy are, all other things being equal, likely to be afforded greater consideration by the Court. In contrast, those lawyers who are arguing an isolated case have less incentive to play the game conservatively. Consequently, they can advocate in a more lavish fashion, making extravagant claims about the significance of a case. The inexperienced lawyer who finds a petition granted on the strength of such arguments, however, may encounter problems at the merits.[6] As one former member of the solicitor general's office observed:

> Sometimes if you grant a petition that's not very well written, you're not going to get a very good merits brief, and you're going to have a hard time deciding what the right result should be. (CI)

Because of the credibility that experienced appellate practitioners can establish with the Court, these veterans have an advantage—at least in the abstract—over lawyers with no such reputation.

The idea that the Court is solicitous to these practitioners has been well illustrated by one lawyer active during the 1977–82 terms. H. W. Perry's interviews with justices and former clerks confirmed the common perception that attorneys for state governments are generally inef-

fective practitioners (Perry 1991, 127). The quality of state representation is not, however, uniform (see Epstein and O'Connor 1988), and
Perry's informants did single out one state representative whose appellate work, they felt, was of an exceptionally high quality: Slade Gorton
of Washington. Despite the frequency with which states appeared before the Court during the 1977–82 period, virtually none of the most
visible litigators in the Court was a state representative. In fact, among
the roughly forty lawyers who argued four or more cases during those
years, there was only one state attorney. Not surprisingly, that lawyer
was Slade Gorton, a generally successful litigator at both the petition
and merits stages.

As we have seen, experienced Supreme Court practitioners exercise
considerable influence at the agenda stage, but what role do they play
at the merits? Can an oral argument made by an accomplished appellate advocate, for instance, really alter the ultimate resolution of a case?
The answer I heard most consistently was that, while a good argument
cannot necessarily ensure victory, a bad argument can surely precipi-
tate a loss. For example, one Supreme Court practitioner and former
clerk commented:

> I think it's rare that a good argument wins a case, but a bad argu-
> ment can lose a case. In fact, it's not even so much that a bad
> argument loses the case. It's an inability to answer questions that
> have not been answered by the briefs. (CI)

A current member of the solicitor general's staff, however, painted a
somewhat different picture:

> The conventional wisdom is that a case can be lost at oral argu-
> ment more frequently than it can be won at oral argument. I think
> that either can happen. I do think the argument is a time when
> views are aired. The justices have a chance to think through the
> problems of the case and interchange with counsel. Sometimes
> counsel can say things that will be helpful, or an interchange be-
> tween counsel and one or two justices may have an effect on
> either one of them or one of the other justices. (CI)

Finally, though, the remarks of a Supreme Court practitioner who
works on behalf of a prominent interest group in Washington perhaps
sum up the situation best:

I think that cases are probably more often lost than won at oral argument, when a lawyer is unable to explain the ramifications of a position or is unable to draw a line between the position he's taken and one which is untenable or makes a concession that vaguely undercuts his position. Cases can be won at oral argument where the Court comes into the argument with an unclear understanding of what the case is about. In that case, the lawyer essentially spends the time clearing things up. Where the Court could think it was going to reach a decision which would have terrible ramifications, you're able to explain to the Court, "No, no, no, no. It's nothing like that." So, I don't think as between winning and losing you could say so much. I think the most important thing is that it's the last chance to avoid deciding the case based on a misunderstanding of something. (CI)

Testing such assertions across a broad range of cases is a difficult proposition. Even if one could demonstrate that experienced counsel prevailed more often than inexperienced counsel, one could not state—at least not with any great precision—whether the outcomes were a direct function of advocacy. A number of scholars have advanced the claim that certain litigants, such as governments, corporations, and organizations, are more likely to succeed than others, owing in part to their superior resources and their ability to command a higher calibre of legal talent (see Galanter 1974; also Atkins 1991; Songer and Sheehan 1992; Wheeler et al. 1987). What is the relationship between experience and success in the United States Supreme Court? To address this issue, I compared the relative amount of Supreme Court experience possessed by counsel with the outcomes of cases decided by the Court from 1977 to 1982. Armed with these data, I calculated the proportion of cases in which the party with the more experienced Supreme Court counsel won on the merits.[7]

Table 8.3 reveals that there is a good deal of variation in the outcomes of cases, depending upon which side has the more seasoned advocate. How much of a difference does this expert representation make? Quite a bit, it would seem. If the counsel for the petitioner has a more extensive track record in the Court than the respondent's lawyer, the petitioner is successful in nearly eight out of ten cases. This is noteworthy because that 75 percent success rate is well above the percentage of total cases in which the petitioner secures a favorable

TABLE 8.3. Success rate of Supreme Court bar for cases
on the merits

	Petitioner success rate	N
All cases	65.1	790
Counsel for petitioner has more experience	75.3	369
Neither counsel has more experience	57.5	160
Counsel for respondent has more experience	55.2	261

Sources: Archival data 1977–82 (because the identity of the lawyers and the nature
of their participation were sometimes unclear, several cases were omitted). Data
used in this analysis were also drawn from the *U.S. Supreme Court Judicial Data Base,*
Harold J. Spaeth, principal investigator.

outcome. When the two sides are evenly matched—regardless of
whether the advocates are two Supreme Court novices or a pair of
seasoned veterans—the outcome is roughly what one would anticipate, other things being equal. That is, across all cases, the party that
seeks review can be expected to win on the merits roughly 65 percent
of the time. In those cases in which there is no net advantage in representation, this is precisely the result. Alternatively, when the weight of
Supreme Court expertise is on the side of the respondent, the petitioner continues to enjoy success, but note that the level of his success
is lower by several percentage points. Thus, when there are disparities
in representation, the more experienced side wins more often and loses
less often. Why might this be?

One might begin by noting that a vote on certiorari often presages
a vote on the merits (Brenner 1979). My data are drawn from cases
decided during the years of the Burger Court, and a conservative
bench is more inclined to grant review to cases in order to reverse a
lower court outcome that it finds ideologically disagreeable (see
Songer 1979). Thus, it is possible that sophisticated Supreme Court
practitioners who lost conservative causes in the lower courts petitioned the Court with greater alacrity and consequently won more frequently. Even so, the outcomes still favor the party with greater Supreme Court expertise.[8] Furthermore, the benefits associated with
veteran counsel cannot, in this instance, be ascribed to the frequent
presence of the solicitor general. The solicitor general's appearances,

whether as petitioner or respondent, have been excluded from the data used to generate this table.[9]

Of course, more often than not, the Court accepts cases that it intends to reverse (Armstrong and Johnson 1982; Baum 1977), as is evident in the petitioner's overall success rate of some 65 percent. Still, the petitioner's ratio of wins jumps considerably—a 16 percent increase—when his advocate has spent more time before the justices than has the counsel for his opponent. To the extent that the outcomes of cases are a function of the relative experience of the lawyers involved, the difference may lie in the veteran's capacity to understand the needs and interests of the justices at oral argument. A former associate of the solicitor general's office, now a member of a large firm in Washington, provided an apt illustration:

> A good oral argument really helps the Court in focusing its ideas, as far as what kinds of theories to play out. If the lawyer who's in front of the bench can think through the problems with the justices, I think that that significantly aids them in terms of when they leave the bench and try to sort these problems out. If you have a lawyer who is barely competent to state his case—much less engage the justices in some kind of a serious dialogue—it doesn't do anything to assist the Court. (CI)

This is not to suggest that a lawyer with his or her first case before the Court is not capable of preparing and delivering a skillful argument. As any Supreme Court practitioner will tell you, some of the best arguments the Court has ever heard have been made by counsel making their first (and perhaps only) appearance before the justices. Rather, the suspicion is simply that lawyers who have been before the Court on previous occasions, who have acquired some measure of expertise, and who know what to expect are better placed to provide the kind of briefs and arguments that the justices find most valuable in their decision making. Another veteran Washington lawyer focused on an even more fundamental advantage:

> I suppose that, as anything else in life, if you know the people you're talking to, you may be able to communicate better. I have thought on occasion that my having some acquaintanceship with several of the justices and just simply having had the experience of a give-and-take in prior arguments is helpful. I have some ap-

preciation [of the justices], and maybe a justice knows how he can communicate with me because he's communicated with me before. (CI)

Similarly, another Washington practitioner, this one a former clerk, suggested:

> If you know the justices, you know what opinions they have written in an area. That's very, very important knowledge. Often that enables you to interpret a question. . . . Knowing where a particular justice stands on an issue in your case is quintessentially important. If you didn't have the keen appreciation, you might not do that kind of research. You know, you might read the case but not notice who wrote the opinions. I don't mean to suggest that you can pull the justices around by citing their opinions, but knowing exactly what they've said is important, because you can use it in responding to a question, or you can understand a question better, if it comes up, or you can understand the interplay between justices. (CI)

Here again, the veteran appellate practitioners have no monopoly on thoughtful preparation. With the benefit of experience, however, veterans of Supreme Court practice have, at minimum, a heightened sensitivity to certain of the dynamics that become operative in litigating before the justices. One might thus expect them to perform more ably and, logically enough, win more often.

Recognizing why the more experienced lawyers might enjoy an above-average success rate, though, is only part of the story. As I have noted, the lawyers I interviewed often suggested that, while experience might not win a case, inexperience might well lose it. A former litigator for an independent commission in the federal government, who had seen firsthand a good many cases before the Court, observed:

> I think a bad argument can certainly lose a potentially winning case. I think the real importance of oral argument is to let the justices ask questions. So often, I think, inexperienced advocates don't really foresee in their briefs everything that the justices may be concerned about, particularly with the implications of that decision on other areas of the law. So I think it's extremely important that the justices have a chance to ask questions. Obviously, if the

quality of the argument is not good, and if the justices get answers such as, "I don't know," it's not fulfilling its role. (CI)

Another active practitioner from a Washington firm had the additional vantage point of having litigated on behalf of the American Civil Liberties Union. He had this to say about the lack of practical experience in the Court as a determinant of case outcomes:

> It's my impression from the cases I've argued and from the many, many more cases I've seen argued that oral argument is rarely the key to success, but it is often the basis for loss. Not many cases are won because of a brilliant oral argument that would not have been won just based on the briefs. But I think several cases are lost because of a poor oral argument that might not have been lost just because of the briefs. The main reason is that attorneys, often when they're under the gun and under attack in Supreme Court arguments, make concessions that one or more justices seize upon as a way of slitting their throats. They don't understand the significance of the concession they've made. If they did, they wouldn't have made it. You can even see it in some opinions—"acknowledged at oral argument that . . . " or "in response to question, counselor admitted that . . . ," and BOOM!—they've got 'em. So, oral argument is very important. It's mainly important to try and focus the Court's attention on what is the Achilles' heel of the other side or what is the key point you have to persuade the Court on. (CI)

In one interview, an alumnus of the solicitor general's office, who still practices before the Court as a member of a large firm in Washington, offered some interesting speculations on the influence of veteran counsel on the merits. Specifically, he allowed that experienced Supreme Court practitioners might be most useful in cases in which the justices were sharply divided:

> In about two-thirds of the cases that come before the Court, representation probably doesn't make much difference. In about a third of the cases, however, I would say that the attorney may play a role. We were involved in a case last year against the state of Pennsylvania in which I'm convinced we could have won the case for the other side. It was a very narrow decision—the case was decided 5–4—and the state handled it very poorly. I'd like to

think that if we were representing the state, we could have just as easily won the case for them. (CI)

He raises an intriguing notion: perhaps the value of experience varies depending on the context of the case. I have explored this possibility, however, examining the frequency of lawyers' success for different marginal votes, and can find no systematic evidence to support his general view, although I do not deny that, in a close case, skilled counsel can tip the scales. While he may well have been correct in his assessment of that particular case, though, no patterns emerge across the plenary docket.

Overall, then, the variation in the relative litigating strength of Supreme Court practitioners is directly related to the outcomes of cases. The lawyers who practice before the Court have advanced some credible arguments about the circumstances under which one might expect their appellate expertise to affect the Court's decision making, notably, that lawyers with more experience have more credibility with the Court and a keener appreciation of the nuances of Court litigation. Still, as my respondents well knew, the justices are principally concerned with the issues in a case—the conflict between various courts of appeals, the interpretation of a statute, the meaning of the Constitution, the policy implications of a decision. This accounts for the prevailing opinion, namely, that the benefits of expert counsel can make a difference but that, in the greater scheme of things, that difference is probably marginal. Two former associates of the solicitor general's office who now practice in different firms in Washington offered good summaries of this position:

> Most arguments in the Supreme Court are not very good. On the other hand, the justices usually come to the argument with a fairly good idea of what they think about the case. They've read the briefs. They've discussed it with their law clerks. . . . I think it's very hard to measure in particular cases how the argument affects the Court, but I certainly think it's important. (CI)

> If you just show up for one argument, one brief, you're not really accustomed to what kinds of arguments make sense and don't make sense. You can say things in briefs that are incredibly stu-

pid, and once you've lost credibility with the Court, pretty much anything you do from there on out is a waste. The advantage [the inexperienced lawyer] gets is that the Court is smart. It could be that, even though your position is complete nonsense, the Court may still hold in your favor, because its concern is less with who wins and who loses the case. Rather, its concern is more in terms of making good law. (CI)

The data are consonant with their view. Litigants who retain Supreme Court lawyers with more experience than their opponents have an above-average success rate; notwithstanding the lawyer differential, a majority of cases are nonetheless decided in the petitioner's favor.

In short, lawyers play a role but by no means a decisive role. Moreover, the above results can be interpreted in a number of ways. The Court, for example, may simply be deciding cases in favor of sophisticated litigants who, as repeat players, retain expert appellate practitioners. Thus, representation may be but a very modest part of the explanation for their successes. Furthermore, outcomes alone do not tell us a great deal about the substantive decisions the justices embrace. An experienced lawyer could petition the Court and successfully secure a reversal for his client, but the Court's opinion might well have undesirable and unintended consequences for that client. Similarly, a veteran Supreme Court practitioner might sustain a loss, but the judgment announced may be much more moderate than it might otherwise have been. Be that as it may, this analysis was intended to address two issues. First, do the outcomes of cases depend on the nature of legal representation? And second, to the extent that those outcomes do seem a function of representation, what reasons can be advanced to explain this phenomenon? As this section has illustrated, there are indeed differences, and, when viewed through the eyes of the Court's insiders, they offer a useful perspective on the importance of lawyers in the Supreme Court's decision making.

Conclusion

The community of elite Supreme Court practitioners enjoys a distinctive relationship with the Court. By and large, the justices know that they can depend upon these litigators to provide competent legal analysis on a consistent basis. For this reason, many of the usual impediments to the Court's agenda are not present when these lawyers petition the Court on behalf of their clients. The justices are free to focus on the issues raised in the pleading, and, other things being equal, they are more disposed to grant review. This statement holds especially true for the experienced counsel within the Washington community—as is hardly surprising, given the strong concentration of elite lawyers within the capital city, their extraordinary experience with the Court, and their firsthand knowledge of the case selection process. Once the justices have decided to grant review, experienced representation continues to play a role, but, by the bar's own admission, that role is seldom pivotal. Retaining experienced Supreme Court counsel does appear to redound to the litigant's advantage, but so many factors come into play that only under special circumstances would one expect the outcome of a case to turn on the quality of advocacy alone.

On balance, specialized representation, while important at both stages of the justices' decision making, appears to be more significant at the petition stage. These expert lawyers often function much like the representatives who are invoked as advocates before the federal government more generally, that is, they are engaged as a means of gaining access. As a former associate of the solicitor general's office, now a professor of law, put it:

> There's a lot of work that goes on before the Court that's not arguing in oral arguments or even briefing on the merits. A lot of it is deciding whether to try to get Supreme Court review or opposing Supreme Court review—deciding how likely it is that the Supreme Court will grant review in a case and positioning yourself for that. That's an area where somebody who's had experience has a tremendous advantage in being able to assess the likelihood that review would be granted and writing a petition for cert in such a way as to maximize the chances for review. I think it's also true that experience is one of the things that tells you how to go about presenting the merits of the case in a way that is more likely to result in a favorable decision on the merits. If you're smart enough, you may be able to figure that out anyhow. (CI)

Still, the implication of an active and influential stratum of this community for the business of the Court itself should not be overestimated or dismissed, even if the exact nature of that influence is subject to interpretation. Regardless of how one views the above results, however, it is clear that the experienced elite within the Supreme Court bar are deeply engaged in many of the Court's most compelling cases and thus cannot but be agents of influence in the process of Supreme Court decision making.

9

Conclusions and Reflections

Reynold Colvin and Archibald Cox, the lawyers who appeared before the Supreme Court in *Regents of the University of California v. Bakke,* occupy the two ends of the broad spectrum of legal representation in the Court. On the one hand, there was Colvin, the private practitioner from outside of Washington, the trial lawyer whose case wound up in the Supreme Court, the advocate who, drawn by the chance to argue before the justices, simply was not prepared to address large issues of law and public policy despite his impressive credentials. On the other hand, there was Cox, the former solicitor general who went into private practice, the skilled appellate advocate and Washington player, the Supreme Court specialist whose expertise was valued by a sophisticated client. In many ways, these two lawyers personify the major themes of this analysis. Let us consider some of those fundamental findings.

The Nature and Role of the Supreme Court Bar

The foregoing analysis has revealed that the Supreme Court lawyers are not representative of the larger legal population. They are better educated, more liberal, and geographically more concentrated, especially in a few urban areas. When one considers where the Court's lawyers fall within the two hemispheres of the profession in comparison to lawyers generally, some similarities emerge—but so do some differences. As far as clients are concerned, Supreme Court lawyers operate in much the same fashion as other lawyers: corporate and organizational clients are clearly separated from individuals. But when it comes to the role of litigation, one discovers a marked difference between the Supreme Court bar and other American lawyers. For most of the American bar, it is the distinction between litigation and office work that is telling. Supreme Court lawyers, however, are overwhelmingly occupied with litigation. For them, the relevant divide runs between appellate and trial litigation.

Granted, to the extent that the Court's bar differs, it differs in ways that might be expected. After all, Supreme Court practice is different from other forms of practice. Many of the general differences noted above are a function of its unique character. Appellate litigators who work in the federal appellate courts, civil liberties and constitutional lawyers, and criminal defense attorneys, to name but a few, are the counsel most closely associated with Court litigation. In contrast, lawyers who represent small businesses counsel to the unemployed and to criminal defendants, and state trial lawyers seldom engage in Supreme Court work. The boundaries of the Supreme Court bar are thus well defined. Indeed, there is a small, stable, and elite community that handles Supreme Court litigation on a regular basis. Juxtaposed to this elite is a larger, more fluid group of lawyers who have only passing contact with the Court. These are the inner and outer circles.

Importantly, sophisticated clients—the wealthy and powerful litigants—recognize the importance of this stratification. They appreciate the skills that lawyers in the inner circle possess and use those skills to secure advantages in access to the Court's agenda. Although the activities of these elite practitioners might well go unnoticed, the inner circle is extensively involved with the Court's docket, helping less experienced counsel prepare arguments and briefs, soliciting amicus support, and even writing on behalf of amici. The mobilization of interest groups to gain the attention of the justices is evidence of the strategic activity undertaken by the inner circle of elite litigators.

This new Supreme Court bar bears many of the marks of a professional community, a modern analogue of the nineteenth century bar.

Admittedly, the characterization is a tenuous one, but at least at the conceptual level the experienced counsel are separated by relatively little social distance. Many have shared Supreme Court clerkships; others have served in the solicitor general's office. A fair number of lawyers have professional interactions, not the least of which are interactions in the Court. Of course, many of these bonds are cemented by the fact that so many of the Court's lawyers practice in Washington, D.C.

The community of experienced lawyers in Washington are held in the highest esteem by their peers, and in fact their reputations are deserved. The notable Washington lawyers specifically (and veteran litigators generally) play a central role in the case selection process, acting as gatekeepers to the Court. Of course, sorting out the precise nature of that role is difficult, but at this point it is abundantly clear that lawyers are closely tied to the case selection process. Our understanding of litigation in the Court can therefore only benefit from considering their potential influence.

Supreme Court Lawyers and Democratic Society

Americans have traditionally turned to the courts for fairness, equity, and an evenhanded distribution of justice. Regardless of one's social or economic standing within the community, one ought to be able to depend upon the Supreme Court to deliver "equal justice under law," as is engraved above the entrance to the Court itself. The development of specialized representation in government, however, has implications not only for administrative or congressional politics but for the Supreme Court as well. The emergence of an elite community of experienced Supreme Court lawyers—and their ability to gain access to the Court over and above a host of competing interests—might cause some to reconsider the Court's ability to serve its proper role. Given that high-priced legal talent remains beyond the reach of most parties to litigation, those who can afford to buy expertise are at an advantage, at least when it comes to ensuring that the justices will take notice of their cases and take their pleadings more seriously. One former member of the solicitor general's office illustrated this point:

> It's the sophisticated people—not Allan Bakke, who's never hired a lawyer before in his life—who know that they've got roughly

thirty million dollars riding on their case. I would think that they would not hesitate at all to spend the extra money to hire somebody and that they would know enough about that specialization to know that they're not Supreme Court specialists. (CI)

These veteran Supreme Court lawyers—especially the notable Washington advocates—share a special relationship with the Court, testimony to their credibility and professionalism, which, as one lawyer currently in the solicitor general's office believes, narrows the gap between institutional and private representation:

I think those lawyers can get pretty close—if not equal—to the kind of thing we have. I mean, the advantage the solicitor general's office has is familiarity with what the Court expects, and there's a certain trust level. The Court knows that it can depend on what the solicitor general says as being truthful, and I think the advocates that have been in the Court many times—private lawyers—can develop pretty much the same thing. Certainly the same comfort level and, I think, the same level of trust. Now there's still some difference, but I think the difference is small. (CI)

But these specialists don't come cheap. Even though they cannot guarantee success, they certainly fuel inequities in the nature of legal representation in the Court.

As this is being written, Supreme Court practice continues to develop as a unique (but narrow) area of emphasis for many lawyers. As former Deputy Solicitor General Kenneth Geller views it: "This is an age of specialization for lawyers. . . . If you're going to talk to the Supreme Court these days, you need specialists, as well" (Wermiel 1989, B3). Of course, the growth in Supreme Court practice as a specialty reflects broader changes in the legal profession—lawyers have become increasingly specialized in all areas of the law (Abel 1989)—as well as changes in pressure politics in general (Berry 1989; Schlozman and Tierney 1986). Viewed in those terms, it is puzzling, at least to this former lawyer of the solicitor general's office, that Supreme Court specialists have taken so long to appear:

I think basically what you have is some people trying to define and exploit a certain niche in the market. I'm certain that at one point there were no ERISA specialists or there were no specialists

in municipal bonds and so forth. At this point, you have a number of people who have decided that that's the spin, the focus
they want to put on what they're doing. In some ways, you might
pose the question the other way: Why didn't somebody do that
before? (CI)

This might also help explain why lawyers tend to hold the view that
there is no Supreme Court "bar" and yet have regular and continued
work in the Court. One lawyer, who denied the existence of an active
Supreme Court bar, argued no less than two cases before the justices
in less than a year after I interviewed him. Two lawyers in another
Washington firm, also skeptical of the existence of a Court bar, both
had copies of Stern, Gressman, and Shapiro's *Supreme Court Practice*
within an arm's length of their chairs.

One must be careful, however, not to make too much of the elite
community of experienced counsel and of Supreme Court practice as a
specialty. After all, Allan Bakke was admitted to the Cal-Davis medical
school. Moreover, the quality of representation in the Court has generally improved in recent years. The National Association of Attorneys
General, the State and Local Legal Center, and the Public Citizen Litigation Group, all of whom have programs designed to assist the novice
Supreme Court advocate, work to ensure that effective advocacy in the
Court need not be derailed by a lack of direct experience or insider's
expertise. Furthermore, as long as experts and novices pursue their
clients' interests in the Court, the Supreme Court bar will still mirror,
in some degree, the diversity of the legal profession. Although Supreme Court litigation does tend to attract certain kinds of counsel,
the doors of the Court are not wholly closed to most litigators.

Lawyers remain an inescapable part of the American political land-
scape. For good or ill, the bar of the Supreme Court plays a critical
role in this country's judicial system. As the primary intermediaries
between the nation's highest tribunal and disputes over competing al-
ternatives as expressed through legal conflicts, they help shape the
direction and scope of public policies. They deserve our attention, all
the more because "in the past five or six years, there's been an explo-
sion of this specialty, a Supreme Court bar" (CI). As the legal profession continues to divide its labor through specialization, the reliance
upon these legal elites—the inner circle of Supreme Court practitioners—may well serve only to increase their importance.

APPENDIXES

NOTES

BIBLIOGRAPHY

INDEX

Additional Information on Figures and Tables

Figures

Figure 4.1. These data are the results of the factor analysis of the clients, fields of specialization, and time spent in litigation settings for Supreme Court lawyers. The factor loadings used to create the dimensional diagram in figure 4.1 are presented below.

Factor Loadings for Supreme Court Lawyer Characteristics

Variable	Factor 1	Factor 2
Appellate litigation	.54	−.18
Civil rights and liberties	.29	.01
Constitutional law	.27	−.08
Criminal law	.47	.16
Labor law	.08	−.24
Patent law	−.16	−.18
Commercial law	−.16	.04
Environmental law	−.04	−.06
Municipal law	.04	−.03
Personal injury law	−.08	.38
Administrative law	.08	−.19
Major corporations	−.43	−.42
Blue-collar workers	.10	.51
Criminal defendants	.32	−.04
Sales and clerical workers	.01	.27
Small businesses	−.35	.03
Unemployed	.14	.18
Students	.24	.12
Political activists	.19	.01
Labor unions	.06	−.17
Professionals	.01	.19
Administrative proceedings	−.17	−.14
State trial courts	−.28	.61
State appellate courts	.39	.09

Variable	Factor 1	Factor 2
Federal trial courts	−.13	−.24
Federal appellate courts	.39	−.28
Eigenvalues	1.72	1.50

Tables

Several of the tables in chapters 5, 6, and 7 contain probabilities that were calculated from probit equations. Below are the full results of those models from which the probabilities were generated.

Probit Equations for tables 5.4 and 5.5.

Dependent variable: lawyer involved at trial stage.

Independent variable	Intercept	b	t	r-squared	N
Agenda experience	1.13	−.34	−3.17	.05	321
Agenda success	.60	−.04	−.97	.01	319
Merits experience	1.05	−.48	−3.45	.06	325
Merits success	.74	−.19	−3.40	.05	325

Dependent variable: lawyer involved at appeals stage.

Independent variable	Intercept	b	t	r-squared	N
Agenda experience	−1.11	.20	1.85	.02	321
Agenda success	−.86	.05	.98	.01	319
Merits experience	−.78	.05	.36	.01	325
Merits success	−.84	.08	1.37	.01	325

Dependent variable: lawyer involved at Supreme Court agenda stage.

Independent variable	Intercept	b	t	r-squared	N
Agenda experience	−1.80	.16	1.15	.01	321
Agenda success	−1.41	−.03	−.40	.01	319
Merits experience	−2.26	.55	3.55	.08	325
Merits success	−1.89	.22	3.26	.07	325

Dependent variable: lawyer involved at Supreme Court merits stage.

Independent variable	Intercept	b	t	r-squared	N
Agenda experience	−3.29	.50	2.91	.11	321
Agenda success	−3.25	.28	1.72	.18	319
Merits experience	−2.87	.53	2.70	.08	325
Merits success	−2.30	.12	1.19	.02	325

Probit equations for table 5.8.

Dependent variable: lawyer selected for professional reputation.

	b	t
Intercept	.98	−8.25
Appellate litigation	.20	.99
Administrative law	−.19	−.60
Criminal law	.04	.19
Civil rights and liberties	.03	.10
Labor law	−.45	−1.56

$N = 294$; 83.6% correctly classified; −2LogL = 4.07 with 5 df; r-squared = .04

Dependent variable: lawyer involved by peer referral.

	b	t
Intercept	−1.20	−9.26
Appellate litigation	.35	1.67
Administrative law	−.23	−.67
Criminal law	.10	.42
Civil rights and liberties	.04	.14
Labor law	−.46	−1.44

$N = 294$; 87.0% correctly classified; −2LogL = 6.26 with 5 df; r-squared = .06

Dependent variable: lawyer selected for professional reputation.

	b	t
Intercept	−1.16	−4.54
Administrative courts	−.46	−.79
State trial courts	.45	1.22
State appellate courts	−.23	−.45
Federal trial courts	−.09	−.21
Federal appellate courts	1.39	2.46

$N = 294$; 83.6% correctly classified; $-2LogL = 8.36$ with 5 df; r-squared $= .06$

Dependent variable: lawyer involved by peer referral.

	b	t
Intercept	−.87	−3.61
Administrative courts	−2.18	−2.27
State trial courts	.10	.28
State appellate courts	−.38	−.74
Federal trial courts	−.57	−1.31
Federal appellate courts	.30	.50

$N = 294$; 87.0% correctly classified; $-2LogL = 9.84$ with 5 df; r-squared $= .15$

Probit equations for table 5.9.

Dependent variable: lawyer selected for professional reputation.

Independent variable	Intercept	b	t	r-squared	N
Agenda experience	−1.17	.12	.98	.01	321
Merits experience	−1.22	.21	1.50	.01	325

Probit equations for table 6.3.

Dependent variable: lawyer helped prepare an argument.

Independent variable	Intercept	b	t	r-squared	N
Agenda experience	−2.47	.97	5.61	.31	321
Merits experience	−1.77	.94	5.79	.21	325

Dependent variable: lawyer helped prepare a petition for review.

Independent variable	Intercept	b	t	r-squared	N
Agenda experience	−1.61	.73	5.15	.21	321
Merits experience	−1.11	.74	4.62	.14	325

Dependent variable: lawyer helped prepare a merits brief.

Independent variable	Intercept	b	t	r-squared	N
Agenda experience	−1.77	.69	5.11	.19	321
Merits experience	−1.35	.74	4.83	.14	325

Dependent variable: lawyer served on a moot court.

Independent variable	Intercept	b	t	r-squared	N
Agenda experience	−2.46	.81	5.48	.24	321
Merits experience	−2.18	1.05	6.35	.25	325

Probit equations for table 6.4.

Dependent variable: lawyer filed amicus brief supporting review.

Independent variable	Intercept	b	t	r-squared	N
Agenda experience	−2.41	.79	5.45	.24	321
Merits experience	−2.18	1.05	6.35	.25	325

Dependent variable: lawyer filed amicus brief opposing review.

Independent variable	Intercept	b	t	r-squared	N
Agenda experience	−2.24	.45	3.62	.09	321
Merits experience	−2.00	.50	3.37	.07	325

Dependent variable: lawyer filed amicus brief on the merits.

Independent variable	Intercept	b	t	r-squared	N
Agenda experience	−2.32	.70	5.22	.19	321
Merits experience	−2.42	1.16	6.78	.28	325

Probit equation for table 6.6.

Dependent variable: lawyer for petitioner encouraged amici at cert stage.

	b	t
Intercept	−1.22	−1.89
Loss in a lower court	−.26	−1.48
Desire of client to seek review	.07	.57
Need for a national standard	.31	2.28
Resolution of previously unanswered issue	.15	1.18
Conflict among courts	.04	.27

$N = 174$; 77.0% correctly classified; $-2\text{LogL} = 13.27$ with 5 df; r-squared $= .13$

Probit equation for table 7.5.

Dependent variable: reputation as notable Supreme Court lawyer.

	b	t
Intercept	−2.32	−8.33
Alumnus of solicitor general's office	1.38	3.16
Supreme Court clerk	.84	3.59
Solicitor general's office	1.22	3.38
Washington firm lawyer	.95	2.90
Washington interest group lawyer	1.40	3.26
Academic lawyer	1.23	2.48
Non-Washington firm lawyer	.80	2.39
Non-Washington interest group lawyer	1.16	3.30
Corporate counsel	.89	1.53
State and local government lawyer	.56	1.75

$N = 709$; 92.2% correctly classified; $-2\text{LogL} = 59.47$ with 10 df; r-squared $= .22$

Probit equation for table 7.7.

Dependent variable: reputation as notable Supreme Court lawyer.

	b	*t*
Intercept	−1.87	−8.33
Alumnus of solicitor general's office	.67	1.92
Supreme Court clerk	.26	2.20
Solicitor general's office	.11	3.70
Washington firm lawyer	.54	3.79
Washington interest group lawyer	.94	2.90
Academic lawyer	.42	1.58
Non-Washington firm lawyer	.29	3.79
Non-Washington interest group lawyer	.43	1.95
Corporate counsel	—	—
State and local government lawyer	.32	2.92

$N = 709$; 92.9% correctly classified; $-2\text{LogL} = 83.29$ with 9 df; r-squared $= .34$. This equation contains lawyer variables interacted with the number of arguments made from 1977 to 1982. The corporate counsel variable will not compute in the probit routine because no corporate lawyer who made an argument during that period was named as a notable.

Note on table 8.1.

The data for the case selection model were collected and analyzed by Caldeira and Wright (1988) in their study of the role of organized interests in the Supreme Court's decision to grant the writ of certiorari. $N = 1757$ (140 grants, 1617 denials); 95.4% correctly classified; $-2\text{LogL} = 560.18$ with 13 df; pseudo r-squared $= .55$. Given that, with regard to the present analysis, our substantive interest in this equation lies in the addition of the lawyer variables to Caldeira and Wright's model, it is not necessary to dwell upon the other predictors (but see Caldeira and Wright 1988, 1117). I did, however, make some slight modifications to their model. I introduced a variable to account for the presence or absence of dissent in the lower courts (1 if dissent was present in the appellate court, 0 otherwise). I also produced a simplified version of their three amicus curiae predictors by collapsing them into a single variable, the presence or absence of any amici supporting certiorari.

As it turned out, the addition of the lawyer predictors produced no meaningful change in the original estimates. Finally, because the role of experience for those lawyers who are *not* members of the solicitor general's office was of particular interest in this study, I set the variables for Washington's expert counsel to 0 when the solicitor general variable equaled 1. The following description and coding of variables has been adapted from the probit equation used by Caldeira and Wright.

Solicitor general—1 if the federal government is the petitioning party, 0 otherwise

Disagreement among lower courts—1 if the appellate court reversed a lower court decision, 0 otherwise

Alleged conflict—1 if conflict was *alleged* by the petitioning attorney in one or more of the following situations:
a. conflict between two state supreme courts
b. conflicts between two federal circuit courts
c. conflict with U.S. Supreme Court precedent
d. conflict between a state court and a federal court, 0 if no alleged conflict or more than one alleged conflict

Actual conflicts—1 if *real* or *square* conflict occurred in one or more of situations a-d above, 0 otherwise

Civil liberties issue—1 if the case concerned civil liberties, 0 otherwise

Conservative decision in court below—1 if the court's decision immediately below was ideologically conservative, 0 if the lower court decided liberally

One or more amici supporting review—1 if one or more amicus briefs were filed in support of certiorari, 0 if no briefs were filed

One or more amici opposing review—1 if one or more amicus curiae briefs were filed in *opposition* to certiorari, 0 otherwise

Non-Washington expert counsel, from one to three merits cases—1 if petitioning counsel did not practice in Washington and had, on average, from one to three cases on the merits from 1977 to 1981, 0 otherwise

Non-Washington expert counsel, more than three merits

cases—1 if petitioning counsel did not practice in Washington and had, on average, more than three cases on the merits from 1977 to 1981, 0 otherwise

Notable Washington expert counsel, from one to three merits cases—1 if one or more of petitioning counsel were named as notable lawyer(s) practicing in Washington and had, on average, from one to three cases on the merits from 1977 to 1981, 0 otherwise

Notable Washington expert counsel with more than three merits cases—1 if one or more of petitioning counsel were named as notable lawyer(s) practicing in Washington and had, on average, more than three cases on the merits from 1977 to 1981, 0 otherwise

APPENDIX 2

Survey Instrument

Project on United States Supreme Court Bar

Part I. Supreme Court Experience

1. In the 1986–87 term of the Supreme Court, a case in which you were the attorney of record was on the Court's docket. How did you become involved in this case? (Check as many as appropriate. If you participated in more than one case, please refer to the latest case.)
____ Previously represented the client
____ Referral by another lawyer
____ Referral by a group in which you are a member
____ Selected because of professional reputation
____ Request by a friend
____ Other (please specify): _____
_____

2. At what stage in the litigation did you become involved in the case?
____ Administrative proceeding
____ Trial
____ Appeal
____ Supreme Court certiorari/appeal
____ Supreme Court merits

3. What was your role in this case?
____ Lead counsel
____ Co-counsel

4. In your case from the 1986–87 term, were you representing the party seeking review from the Supreme Court?
____ Yes ____ No

If yes, how important was each of the following considerations in the decision to seek review?

Very	Some-what	Not	
_____	_____	_____	Lost in the lower court
_____	_____	_____	Conflict existed among courts
_____	_____	_____	Sensed the need for a national standard
_____	_____	_____	To resolve a previously unanswered issue
_____	_____	_____	Client wanted to seek review
_____	_____	_____	Other (please specify): _____

5. At the certiorari/jurisdictional stage, were you the primary author of the brief?

____ Yes   ____ No

If your case was reviewed by the Supreme Court, were you the primary author of the brief on the merits?

____ Yes   ____ No

6. In your case from the 1986–87 term, did you encourage other parties or organized interests to file amicus briefs in support of your case?

____ Yes   ____ No

If so, at what stage?
____ Appeal/Certiorari
____ Merits

If so, what kinds of organizations were invited to participate as amici?

_____

_____

_____

Were amicus briefs filed as a result of your encouragement?

____ Yes   ____ No

If requested amicus briefs were not filed, on what basis did they choose not to participate? (Check as many as appropriate.)

____ Lack of time and resources
____ Felt the case was not in their best interest
____ Deterred by the facts or issues of the case
____ Unwilling to litigate in a secondary role
____ Other (please specify): _____

7. Some lawyers say that in preparing briefs or oral argument for the Supreme Court, it is useful to speak with other lawyers who have had the same experience. In preparing your case, did you ever seek such advice?
        ____ Yes   ____ No

If yes, please list up to five (5) of these lawyers and the cities in which they practice law.

	Name	City
1)		
2)		
3)		
4)		
5)		

8. Some lawyers say that in preparing briefs or oral argument for the Supreme Court, it is useful to consult a number of other resources for assistance. In preparing your case, did you have occasion to use any of the following resources?
____ Stern, Gressman, and Shapiro's *Supreme Court Practice*
____ Supreme Court rules
____ Reprints of prior petitions or briefs
____ Law review articles on Supreme Court advocacy
____ Law school faculty
____ Other (please specify): _____

9. Are there any lawyers who have appeared before the Supreme Court whom you consider to be particularly experienced or skilled in Supreme Court practice?
        ____ Yes   ____ No

If yes, please list up to five (5) of these lawyers and the cities in which they practice law.

	Name	City
1)	_____	_____
2)	_____	_____
3)	_____	_____
4)	_____	_____
5)	_____	_____

10. Other than in the 1986–87 term, have you ever sought or opposed review of a lower court decision by the Supreme Court?
_____ Yes   _____ No

If so, about how many times have you served as:
_____ Attorney for the appellant/petitioner
_____ Attorney for the appellee/respondent

If so, about how many times were you successful:
_____ Gaining review
_____ Opposing review

11. Other than in the 1986–87 term, have you ever made an oral argument before the Supreme Court?
_____ Yes   _____ No

If so, about how many times have you argued as:
_____ Attorney for the appellant/petitioner
_____ Attorney for the appellee/respondent

If so, about how many times were you successful:
_____ Reversing the decision of the lower court
_____ Affirming the decision of the lower court

12. Have you ever had any other involvement in Supreme Court litigation?
_____ Yes   _____ No
If so, about how many times were you involved in each of the following ways?
_____ Helped prepare an oral argument
_____ Helped prepare an appeal or petition for certiorari
_____ Helped prepare a brief on the merits

____ Filed an amicus brief supporting an appeal or certiorari
____ Filed an amicus brief opposing an appeal or certiorari
____ Filed an amicus brief on a case to be decided on the merits
____ Served on a moot court
____ Evaluated a mock argument
____ Other (please specify): _____

Part II. Professional Experience

1. At present, in which of the following settings do you work?
____ Solo practice
____ Law firm
____ Federal government
____ State government
____ Municipal/county government
____ Corporation house counsel
____ Interest group house counsel
____ Law school
____ Other (please specify): _____

2. Prior to your current position, have you ever been employed in any of the following settings since becoming an attorney? (Check as many as appropriate.)
____ Solo practice
____ Law firm
____ Federal government
____ State government
____ Municipal/county government
____ Corporation house counsel
____ Interest group house counsel
____ Law school
____ Clerk for a U.S. supreme court justice
____ Clerk for a state or federal judge
____ Other (please specify): _____

3. In what year were you admitted to the bar? _____

4. In what year did you begin your current job? _____

5. What is your present job title? _____

_____

6. Do you regard yourself as a specialist in any particular area(s) of the law?

_____ Yes   _____ No

If yes, in what area(s)? (Check as many as appropriate.)

___ Administrative law	___ Commercial law	___ Municipal law
___ Admiralty	___ Consumer law	___ Patents/Trademarks
___ Antitrust	___ Corporate law	___ Personal injury
___ Appellate practice	___ Criminal law	___ Probate
___ Banking	___ Environmental law	___ Real estate
___ Civil liberties	___ Family practice	___ Securities
___ Civil litigation	___ Labor law	___ Tax law

___ Other (please specify): _____

7. In thinking about the clients you have represented over the last twelve months, what proportion of those clients fall into these categories?

_____ % Major corporations
_____ % Small businesses
_____ % Professional, technical, or managerial personnel
_____ % Sales and clerical personnel
_____ % Blue-collar workers
_____ % Unemployed
_____ % Students
_____ % Political activists
_____ % Other (please specify): _____

8. In the course of your practice, during the last twelve months, what proportion of your time was spent preparing for and appearing in:

_____ % Administrative proceedings
_____ % State trial courts
_____ % State appellate courts

____ % Federal trial courts
____ % Federal appellate courts
____ % Other courts (please specify): _____

9. In addition to direct involvement in litigation, many lawyers often are involved in other activities which affect the governmental process. What about you? In the past five years, about how often have you represented clients in the following settings?

		Not at	
A lot	Some	all	
_____	_____	_____	Before U.S. Congress
_____	_____	_____	Before independent agencies
_____	_____	_____	Before executive branch departments

10. Have you ever held an appointed or elected government office?
____ Yes ____ No

If so, please specify which positions:
_____
_____

11. Are you a member of the ABA? ____Yes ____No

12. Are you a member of your city bar association?
____ Yes ____ No

13. Are you a member of your state bar association?
____ Yes ____ No

Part III. Education

1. Undergraduate college:
   Institution: _____
   Degree granted: _____ Year: ____

2. Law school:
   Institution: _____
   Degree granted: _____ Year: ____

3. Graduate education (e.g., LLM, LLD, MA, MPA, PhD):
   Institution: _____
   Degree granted: _____ Year: _____

Part IV. Background Characteristics

1. In what year were you born? _____
2. Where were you born? _____
3. What is your race?
____ Caucasian
____ African American
____ Hispanic
____ American Indian
____ Asian, Pacific Islander
____ Other (please specify): _____

4. What is your religious preference?
____ Roman Catholic
____ Protestant (please specify): _____
____ Jewish
____ Other (please specify): _____
____ None

5. Here is a scale on which the attachment to political parties might
be arranged. Where would you place yourself on this scale?
____ Strong Republican
____ Moderate Republican
____ Independent, but leaning toward the Republican party
____ Independent
____ Independent, but leaning toward the Democratic party
____ Moderate Democrat
____ Strong Democrat
____ Other (please specify): _____

6. Here is a scale on which the political views that one might hold
are arranged from extremely liberal to extremely conservative.
Where would you place yourself on this scale?
____ Extremely liberal
____ Liberal

____ Slightly liberal
____ Moderate
____ Slightly conservative
____ Conservative
____ Extremely conservative

Your contribution to this study is greatly appreciated. If you would like a summary of results, please print your name and address on the back of the return envelope (NOT on this questionnaire). We will see that you get it.

NOTES

1. Introduction

1. The following discussion of *Regents of the University of California v. Bakke* 438 U.S. 265 (1978) is based primarily on *The Complete Oral Arguments of the Supreme Court of the United States, 1969–1979 Terms* 1982, 44–58, and on Dreyfuss and Lawrence 1979.

2. The quotations from Supreme Court lawyers used throughout the book are drawn from a series of personal interviews conducted with various lawyers who have practiced in the Court. Because these interviews were confidential, I have sometimes found it necessary to alter names or other identifying references. None of the changes I have made, however, bear on the substance of these lawyers' remarks.

3. Apparently, Colvin did not even seek the assistance of an experienced Supreme Court lawyer. Rather, "Colvin was assisted . . . by Robert Links, so fresh out of UCLA Law School that he did not have the three years experience in private practice required to appear before the Supreme Court" (O'Neill 1985, 25). Together, they prepared both the brief in opposition to certiorari and the brief on the merits.

4. In fact, then, neither attorney carried the day in the historic decision on reverse discrimination, although, from Colvin's perspective, he was the victorious attorney, in that the Court ordered that Bakke be admitted to the Davis medical school. Some have noted, moreover, that it was Colvin's conscious strategy to assume the role of the "outsider" and to avoid the larger question of equity in affirmative action by focusing exclusively on the facts in Bakke's case (Dreyfuss and Lawrence 1979). By the same token, however, Colvin illustrates the limitations of one kind of advocacy in the Court. Lawyers who are highly oriented toward results are apt to encounter difficulties when faced with the broad policy discussion of an oral argument in the Supreme Court.

5. I have coded the employment setting of the sample based upon the list of addresses. The results are as follows: private practice, 78.4 percent; state and local government, 15.4 percent; interest group 3.5 percent; academic 1.2 percent; legal aid / public defender, 1.0 percent; corporate counsel, 0.6 percent. A comparison of these percentages to those of the respondents in table 3.1 shows that the maximum difference between categories of lawyers is only 2.4 percent.

2.   The Supreme Court Lawyer in Historical Perspective

1. Edmund Quincy, quoted in Warren 1939, 254. A letter written in 1815 by a lawyer from Massachusetts to his wife expands on the same theme: "My anticipations were almost infinitely short of the reality, and I can truly say that the first appearance of this seat of the National Government has produced in me nothing but absolute loathing and disgust. . . . From Washington to Baltimore we went in the first day. There we took passage in a packet for French-Town, in the Chesapeake Bay, and were delayed by a dead calm, so that we were twenty-four hours performing a passage usually completed in six. On Wednesday, we left our packet and went overland to Newcastle. There we again took a packet, and arrived in Philadelphia late in the evening. On Thursday, we remained in that city, the stage being too full to receive us that day. . . . This morning we left it at two o'clock, and ought to have arrived in New York this evening. But the excessive badness of the roads has arrested our progress at a distance of about forty miles from it. I shall make no stay in New York, but shall press my journey with all the rapidity in my power, and shall be with you, my dear Harriette, I hope, by the Friday stage" (Warren 1939, 254–55n).

2. In the following discussion, I quote liberally from Charles Warren's *A History of the American Bar* (1939)—and with good reason. It is a meticulous study that carefully documents the transformation of the early bar of the Supreme Court, its prominent members, and their role in litigation. I enthusiastically recommend this volume to any reader who seeks further information on the federal bar of the nineteenth century.

3. The first solicitor general, Benjamin H. Bristow, assumed office in the fall on 1870 (Caplan 1987, ix). The solicitor general now handles virtually all of the federal government's appearances in the Court. For a discussion of Wirt's career as a Supreme Court practitioner, see White 1988, 254–67.

4. For a discussion of the legal careers of Taney, Key, and Pinkney, see Lewis 1965, Delaplaine 1937, and Ireland 1986, respectively.

5. See Baxter 1966 for a list of cases argued by Webster, who is widely regarded as the most active Court practitioner. The authors of the authoritative volume on Supreme Court litigation, however, single out another early member of the bar. "The all-time record," they suggest, "was established by a now-unknown advocate, Walter Jones, who argued 317 cases between 1801 and 1850" (Stern, Gressman, and Shapiro 1986, 732n). Jones, a member of the Washington bar, participated in many notable cases, representing, among others, the state of Maryland in *McCulloch v. Maryland* (Warren 1939, 379). He was appointed United States attorney for the District of Potomac in 1802 and attorney for the District of Columbia two years later (see *Who Was Who in America* 1963, 285).

6. Today, the *United States Reports* will from time to time evince some signs of similar meetings; such meetings, however, are only artifacts. "On some occasions,

the Solicitor General acts as spokesman or head of the Bar of the Supreme Court. Thus, following the death of a Justice, the Solicitor General traditionally presents to the Court the resolutions memorializing the late Justice adopted by an *ad hoc* group of 'members of the Bar of the Supreme Court'" (Stern, Gressman, and Shapiro 1986, 732n).

7. See 43 U.S. xi–xiv (1843).

8. The significance of these living arrangements for political life in Washington is well known. Young's 1966 study of the Washington community of the early nineteenth century shows the important role these boardinghouses played in establishing common bonds among legislators, bonds that were manifested in roll call voting in the Congress. In the context of state legislators, see Caldeira and Patterson 1987.

9. A copy of both letters, as well as the names of the attorneys who signed the letter to Nelson, can be found in 81 U.S. (14 Wallace) viii–x.

10. Warren notes that "[t]he impress of the War of 1812 on legal history is markedly seen . . . in necessitating the development of internal means of communication—the coasting trade being ruined by the British blockade—and thus promoting the construction of canals, multiplying turnpikes, and preparing the people to demand the swifter means of transportation by steam railroads" (1939, 276).

11. These ratios are estimated from United States census figures, 1830 to 1860, and from Washington populations reported by White 1988, 202.

12. These data reflect the proportion of nongovernmental petitions for review in the Supreme Court filed by law firms in Chicago, New York, and Washington between 1940 and 1985. A systematic random sample of cases ($N = 4,964$) was taken—at five-year intervals—from various editions of *United States Law Week*, noting the geographic location of the lawyers who filed petitions for certiorari or jurisdictional statements. Naturally, there are other ways of examining the geographic distribution of the bar across time. One could, for instance, study only the lawyers who argued cases on the merits. Indeed, in later chapters, I explore the importance of lawyers at both the agenda and merits stages. For now, I prefer to focus broadly on the lawyers who bring cases to the Court because it provides us with a larger, more diverse set of counsel.

13. The *Legal Times*, July 29, 1991, p. 8. The background information on these lawyers to follow was taken primarily from the *Martindale-Hubbell Law Directory*.

3. An Elite Set of Litigators

1. The data used in this section are based on the results of the mail survey of a random sample of lawyers who participated at the agenda stage of the 1986–87 Supreme Court term. The text of the survey instrument can be found in Appendix 2.

2. These figures can be found in *United States Law Week*, Aug. 11 1987, p. 3102.

The Supreme Court's workload is also summarized annually in the November edition of the *Harvard Law Review*.

3. It is not difficult for an attorney to become a member of the Supreme Court bar. A discussion of the admission qualifications and procedures, as well as the active versus the inactive members, can be found in chap. 7.

4. The working environment is an important criterion for assessing an attorney's practice. Some scholars have chosen to study lawyers within specific employment settings (Nelson 1988; S. Olson 1984; Smigel 1964). Such attention has been extremely useful in making comparisons between groups of attorneys, as Heinz and Laumann's intensive study of differences within the Chicago bar clearly attests (1982; see also Erlanger 1978).

5. Sadly, because of their small numbers, it is difficult to draw reliable conclusions about interest group counsel on the basis of the survey data. For this reason my discussion of interest group lawyers is undergirded primarily by the interview material.

6. It is worth noting that Tribe's opposition, appearing on behalf of the cigarette industry, was the Washington practitioner H. Bartow Farr III, whose career and firm were discussed briefly in chap. 2. Farr's father, Henry Bartow Farr, Jr., is counsel to R. J. Reynolds (see *Who's Who in American Law* 1990).

7. See the *Martindale-Hubbell Law Directory* 1982, U.S. Government section.

8. As even the most casual perusal of the *Martindale-Hubbell Law Directory* bears out, it is quite common for law firms to operate several branches in addition to their principal offices. Moreover, the number of branch offices increased by 205 percent between 1978 and 1988. The city that leads all others in offices is, not surprisingly, Washington, with a total of 165 (Bellows 1988–89, S13).

9. Another way to reinforce the centrality of the District of Columbia vis-à-vis Supreme Court lawyers is to consider the proportion of the United States population that resides in these cities. For instance, three of the top four cities in table 3.3 are also the most populous cities: New York is first, Los Angeles is second, and Chicago is third. Washington, in contrast, is seventeenth in population ranking (*Statistical Abstract of the United States* 1990). Even so, Washington eclipses virtually every other city in terms of its proportion of Supreme Court lawyers.

10. The regression results are: percentage difference $= .63 - .0004$ (distance from Washington) $+ e$; $t = -1.53$ for distance coefficient, $N = 22$, r-squared $= .11$. Data on distance of cities from Washington were obtained from the geographical software package PC-USA.

11. These rankings were taken from *The Gourman Report* (Gourman 1987). For over a decade, this publication has rated the strengths of professional education programs. It has also been subject to considerable criticism. Other, more widely accepted rankings of law schools, however, tend to consider only the top ten or twenty institutions, giving little mention to other schools. *The Gourman Report*, in contrast, provides a quantitative ranking of all accredited American law schools

and, is thus well suited to our purpose of examining the educational background of all lawyers, as opposed simply to those who are products of a handful of elite schools. Without getting into a discussion of specific institutions, I should at least point out that those that rank among the top ten law schools on other lists likewise appear in the highest category in *The Gourman Report*. I should also note that Gourman uses the terms "acceptable plus" and "adequate" in place of "average" and "below average." I modified this terminology in order better to convey what is, in my opinion, the substance of the continuum. For an explanation of the method of evaluation used to arrive at these ratings, see Gourman 1987, 1–3.

12. For a discussion of the "repeat player," see Galanter 1974.

4. The Boundaries of the Bar: Law Practice and Supreme Court Practice

1. The Judiciary Act of Feb. 13, 1925, ch. 229, sec.1, 43 stat. 936.

2. For example, in 1988 Congress passed the Act to Improve the Administration of Justice, which gave the Court almost absolute discretion over writs of appeal (Pub. L. no. 100-352, 102 stat. 662, 1988).

3. On the importance of opposing review in the Supreme Court, see Frey, Geller, and Harris 1987.

4. For a discussion of oral argument in the Supreme Court, see, for example, Davis 1940; Jackson 1951; Prettyman 1953; Prettyman 1978; Stern 1981, 358–442; Stern, Gressman, and Shapiro 1986, 577–613; Wiener 1967.

5. The issue of aggressive questioning has been particularly troublesome in recent years, causing consternation for lawyers as well as the less inquisitive members of the Court (see Mauro 1990a). Further, although the conventional wisdom is that lawyers ought not to suggest to the Court, "Wait till I get to it," the skilled Supreme Court advocate may have some latitude here (see O'Brien 1990, 271).

6. According to Chief Justice Rehnquist, the "present rules for oral argument are about right.... A good lawyer should be able to make his necessary points ... in one half hour" (Rehnquist 1987, 274). As others note, however, "Longer argument time can still be obtained, of course, for those cases that are shown to be so complex or important as to justify it" (Stern, Gressman, and Shapiro 1986, 580). *Dames & Moore v. Regan* (1981), which dealt with President Carter's handling of Iranian assets in the wake of the hostage crisis, is exemplary in that regard (see O'Brien 1990, 267).

7. For good discussions of case selection in the Supreme Court, see Perry 1991; Provine 1980.

8. For an excellent discussion of this literature, see Abel 1989, 202–7.

9. These figures are taken from Abel 1989, 307, who calculates the distribution of work by the percentage of receipts from various clients. The following comparison of the two groups is therefore necessarily rather rough. Nonetheless, the rela-

tive differences do reveal, in a broad way, that the American and Supreme Court private bars serve a somewhat different client base.

10. Factor analysis assumes that the observed correlations between variables—in this case the observed similarities between certain lawyers—are a function of some unobserved factor(s). In other words, the characteristics of lawyers are dependent variables, and the factor(s) are the independent variables. A useful discussion of the appropriateness of factor analysis for this sort of task can be found in Kim and Mueller 1978.

In any form of multidimensional scaling, moreover, a "spatial analogy is intrinsic. . . . A geometric model is used to represent certain of the relations among variables, with selected features of a geometric space being used to represent specific features of the observed data" (Weisberg 1974, 358). "Suppose," for example, "you are given a map showing the locations of several cities in the United States, and are asked to construct a table of distances between these cities. . . . It is a simple matter to fill in any entry in the table by measuring the distance between the cities with a ruler, and converting the ruler distance into the real distance by using the scale of the map. . . . Now consider the reverse problem, where you are given the table of distances between the cities, and are asked to produce the map. . . . [C]onsiderably more effort would be required. In essence, multidimensional scaling . . . is a method for solving this reverse problem" (Kruskal and Wish 1978, 7). Here, we face a similar problem and are simply providing a geometric representation of the Supreme Court bar. To extend the map analogy, we take data on the "distances" between different lawyers—that is, the correlations between various characteristics of members of the bar—and, by using factor analysis, "draw the map" that best fits these data.

One of the issues with which one must grapple in a factor analysis is the appropriate number of underlying factors. Here, initial factor solutions consistently pointed to a two-dimensional solution. Of the several forms of factor rotation, I employed what is probably the most standard, the varimax rotation. This assumes an orthogonal solution, namely, that the factors are uncorrelated. In other words, one can assume that the factors are perpendicular to one another (see figure 4.1). The factor loadings for the individual variables are given in Appendix 1.

11. There is a fair amount of similarity between this figure and the scalogram presented by Heinz and Laumann 1982, 75. They find a U-shaped pattern similar to the one in figure 4.1, although there the U-shape is inverted relative to this diagram. Of course, there is some variation between the diagrams, but in light of the differences in scaling procedures, data sets, and variables—to say nothing of the different lawyer populations—even a general resemblance is worth noting.

12. A partial correlation, with a range of −1.0 to 1.0, is analogous to a multiple regression model, where coefficients are estimated to show the relative effect of some variable X on some dependent variable Y while controlling for the explanatory effects of other predictors (see Blalock 1979, 455–62). In this case, the correla-

tions have been calculated between the practice characteristics and the log of the number of cases lawyers have had in the Court, as opposed to the number of cases themselves. The reason for this has to do with the distribution of the number of petitions and oppositions filed, as well as the number of arguments made. Most Supreme Court lawyers, for instance, have handled but a handful of previous cases at the agenda stage. That number increases slowly but then begins to increase ever faster. Such a distribution does not conform well to estimates of linear relationships (for example, correlations or least-squares solutions in regression analysis). Estimates of such relationships, however, are appropriate for these data if some functional form of the variable—such as its log—enjoys a linear relationship with other variables. Although there is no formal way to distinguish which method is more appropriate, it is useful to compare residual variances from one regression equation to the next (see Hanushek and Jackson 1977, 96–101). In the interests of conserving space, I do not report the regression equations that used the practice characteristics to predict the volume of agenda and merits cases. The comparison of residual variances, however, suggested that the functional form approach was the preferable alternative.

13. This conclusion may seem to run counter to the data in table 4.1, which suggest that there are more appellate than there are trial lawyers in the Supreme Court bar. Bear in mind, however, that the survey results derive from only a single term of the Court. In a given term, one might encounter more appellate lawyers, but across time this group remains stable (they are a smaller, consistent group who handle more Supreme Court cases per lawyer) while the trial group is more variable (they are a larger group whose membership fluctuates and who thus handle fewer Supreme Court cases per lawyer).

14. For example, the *Harvard Law Review* summary of the Court's 1987 term indicates that the justices reviewed the actions of a number of administrative agencies, including the Federal Communications Commission, the Federal Energy Regulatory Commission, and the National Labor Relations Board (1988, 355).

15. The correlation between the amount of time a lawyer spends working for corporations and the prestige ranking of his or her law school is .19; in contrast, the correlation of the law school ranking with the amount of time a lawyer spends working for the unemployed is −.15. Both coefficients are significant at the .01 level.

5. Activating the Elite

1. The perspicacious reader may notice a slight variation in the number of counsel in the various categories between table 5.2 and tables in previous chapters. The reason is that a few of the lawyers changed employment settings between the 1986–87 term and the time of the survey. Thus, I do not know, for instance, whether a lawyer who reports having worked in a law firm since 1989 held a similar position

at the time his or her case was before the Court. Because employment setting is especially important to several of the issues addressed in this chapter, I have, in the appropriate tables, excluded those counsel whose employment settings changed since the 1986–87 term. Practically speaking, however, this turns out to be of little consequence, as the percentages remain virtually unchanged in most instances.

2. As one scholar of the Court notes, "Lawyers handling federal criminal appeals are now quite likely to enter cases at the appellate level because the Criminal Justice Act of 1964 provides appointed appellate counsel for those who cannot afford to retain their own attorney" (Wasby 1988, 147). On the government's side, of course, the United States divides these functions, not only in the solicitor general's office but also in the federal agencies and departments.

3. As anyone who has spent any time examining Supreme Court briefs will attest, the great majority of state cases on the Court's docket will bear the name of the state attorney general and perhaps a handful of his or her lieutenants; state trial court lawyers, in contrast, appear much less frequently, if at all. In their study of state governments as Supreme Court litigants, Epstein and O'Connor found that over 60 percent of the states maintain specialized litigation offices to handle their Supreme Court work (1988, 665). Those states with centralized operations were significantly more likely to prevail in the Court.

4. It is worth noting that, although bound up most closely with business and industry, administrative law is, strictly speaking, content-neutral. As Black defines it, administrative law is the "[b]ody of law created by administrative agencies in the form of rules, regulations, orders, and decisions" (1979, 43). A specialization in administrative law is thus in some ways analogous to a specialization in appellate litigation. As was noted in chap. 4, few lawyers are purely procedural specialists. Rather, their procedural expertise permits them to concentrate on a range of issues. In the dimensional analysis in chap. 4, administrative law is accordingly located in close proximity to labor and environmental law.

5. For a good introduction to probit analysis and the calculation of such probabilities, see Aldrich and Nelson 1984. Here, for the success rates, I have pooled the number of petitions and oppositions to serve as the denominator and divided it into the number of cases in which a lawyer reported success in either gaining or opposing review at the case selection stage. Similarly, the success rate on the merits is the proportion of all arguments made by a lawyer in which he or she was victorious (won by affirmance or reversal). For simplicity, I have collapsed the experience and success data into categories: 0, 1–25, 26–50, 51–75, and 76–100. This approach is particularly helpful for the experience data in that it helps control for the confounding effects of extreme values, a problem encountered in some of the analyses presented in the previous chapter. Alternatively, one could compute the logs of the experience data and use those as predictors. The categorical data are, however, a bit more straightforward and readily interpretable. In addition, because they perform

similar functions, I have grouped those lawyers who were involved first at the administrative stage with those in the trial stage category.

6. Levy, Shapiro, and Stern work in the Chicago office of Mayer, Brown & Platt. Although now the president of Brigham Young University, Lee still maintains his practice through the Washington office of Sidley & Austin (see Wermiel 1989).

7. One might, at this point, wonder whether the causal arrow runs in the other direction. Do experienced counsel actively seek involvement in Supreme Court cases? Of course, there may be lawyers who actually solicit Supreme Court business, but, in my experience, this is neither extensive nor systematic. First, virtually all of the lawyers with whom I spoke suggested that cases had come to them. Those who did mention the possibility of lawyers actively seeking cases did so only pejoratively ("I've never done that. Personally, I think that goes a bit too far"). Second, to the extent that lawyers do pursue cases, the habit of so doing appears to be restricted to a handful of advocates. Lawyers consistently volunteered the name of only one Supreme Court specialist who seeks out Supreme Court work ("The Court granted cert in my case at ten o'clock, and by eleven o'clock —— was on the phone").

6. The Inner Circle at Work

1. See Greenya 1987, 40. I assembled the data on Gold's arguments and merits briefs for the years 1977 to 1982 from the *United States Reports*, vols. 434–63.

2. For a description of this program, see *Clearinghouse Review*, July 1988, p. 295.

3. For a discussion of the preparation of amicus briefs, written by one of the Court's most active members of the bar, see Ennis 1984.

4. See, e.g., Galanter's 1974 discussion of the repeat player in the corporate context.

7. The Washington Community and the Structure of Influence

1. For each lawyer ($N = 709$), I have collected background information relating to their work as well as the extent of their activity in the Court during that time period.

2. In the discussion to follow, when I speak of the Supreme Court bar "in general," I do so to the exclusion of the solicitor general's office, primarily because the survey data with which we have been concerned to this point did not include lawyers from that office. The data I have assembled on the so-called elite or experienced members of the Supreme Court bar—those with two or more cases on the merits between 1977 and 1982—do, however, include lawyers who represent the federal government. Thus, one must be careful about comparing the Supreme Court bar with the "subset" of its experienced lawyers, since the elite bar as I have operationalized it in this context is not in fact a subset of the lawyers in the survey

data. Moreover, the number of lawyers in the elite "subset" is twice as large as the number in the general Supreme Court bar sample. Rather, the main purpose of the foregoing analysis was to characterize the nature of nonfederal government Supreme Court representation.

3. Although most of this chapter focuses on the experienced Supreme Court lawyers as opposed to the Court's bar in general, unfortunately I do not have comparable figures for the experienced lawyers in particular. Martindale-Hubbell used to note membership in the American Bar Association but in recent years has dropped this information.

4. Of course, some lawyers are admitted to the bar *pro hac vice*, that is, for a particular case only (Black 1979, 1091), but if a lawyer makes more than one appearance on the merits, then by definition he or she should be a formal member of the Court's bar (see Stern, Gressman, and Shapiro 1986, 746–47). For a more detailed description of the procedures involved in seeking admission to the Court's bar, see Stern, Gressman, and Shapiro 1986, 731–44.

5. In their study of the Chicago bar, Heinz and Laumann undertook a similar analysis by asking respondents whether they had social contact with any lawyers from a list of "notable" Chicago practitioners (1982, 274–80). Whereas Heinz and Laumann developed their list independently of the respondents, I permitted the respondents to nominate their own notables.

6. Heinz and Laumann 1982; see especially chap. 9, "The Constituencies of 'Notable' Chicago Lawyers."

7. The information on the careers of these eleven practitioners is adapted from a variety of sources: Caplan 1987; Greenya 1987; Jenkins 1983; Kerlow 1991; Kluger 1975; Mauro 1990c; O'Brien 1990; B. Olson 1984; and Reuben 1989. I also drew on *Who's Who in American Law* and various editions of the *Martindale-Hubbell Law Directory*.

8. One might also calculate these proportions as percentages of the total number of experienced Supreme Court lawyers overall ($N = 709$). When computed in this fashion, the figures range from less than 1 percent to slightly more than 2 percent.

9. The alumni of the solicitor general's office who currently work in the Chicago office of Mayer, Brown do not show up in the 1977–82 data set. Many were still in the solicitor general's office during this period. That they went on to practice in Chicago does not detract from the larger point, namely that alumni of the solicitor general's office vastly prefer Washington.

10. Here, as elsewhere, it is important to note the time span between the 1977–82 data and the surveys and interviews in 1990. Some of the lawyers recognized as experts may not appear in the 1977–82 data, since a fair number of notables may have developed their reputations subsequent to 1982. Furthermore, those who were active during that six-year period may well have been involved in even more cases

in the intervening years. Thus, if anything, the analysis may underestimate the relationship between experience and skill.

8. The Political Impact of the Inner Circle

1. In a book I much admire, *Deciding to Decide* (1991), H. W. Perry, Jr., makes a very similar argument (see chap. 5, "Indices and Signals"). Likewise, John Mark Hansen begins his analysis of interest representation in the legislative branch along comparable lines: "Members of Congress establish close working relationships with policy advocates; those advocates thereby gain access. Their good fortune contrasts with the plight of those denied access. The policy views of advocates with access receive consistent, serious consideration from lawmakers. The policy views of advocates without access do not receive consistent, serious consideration" (1991, 11).

2. As Provine notes in her study of Supreme Court case selection, "[P]rivate lawyers who handle numerous petitions can anticipate many of the weaknesses in their cases that might otherwise prevent review. They have also learned how to marshal their arguments to touch upon the Court's concerns and interests. . . . [T]he litigants who project an image of competence and expertise cannot but benefit. Theirs will be the arguments read first and relied upon without hesitation" (1980, 45).

3. Even in the context of interest group litigation, the notion of case selectivity has perhaps been somewhat overstated (see Wasby 1984).

4. The issue of measuring lawyer participation requires some explanation. On any given cert petition, lawyers appear in various numbers. Some petitions carry the names of only one or two lawyers; others might be submitted by a dozen or more. For each petition, I coded the number of cases on the merits in which each lawyer participated from 1977 to 1981. (Obviously, their merits cases from the 1982 term need to be excluded, given that the analysis is predicting case selection for that year.) Most petitions were submitted by lawyers with no prior involvement as counsel. For those petitions that did have prior participation (roughly 10 percent), I simply took the average number of cases for the five most active lawyers on the petition. For example, a case with three lawyers having 3, 1, and 1 previous cases, respectively, would have an average lawyer experience value of 1.67. To test for the independent effects of Washington-based counsel in the Supreme Court bar, I coded these lawyers separately but, in like fashion, took the average number of cases per participating Washington lawyer. Of course, one might conceive of other means of calculating lawyer experience; my choice is one of several reasonable methods. My interest in this model lies in the importance of experience for those lawyers outside of the solicitor general's office. Accordingly, I have created non–solicitor general participation variables only.

Thus, although cases brought by the solicitor general would doubtless fall into the category of petitions brought by lawyers who averaged at least one case per term, I do not consider them as such in the model. I am interested in the role of experienced non–solicitor general litigators in the process of case selection. The lawyer variables for notable Washington experts consequently equal o when the solicitor general is the petitioning counsel.

5. The overall chi-square value is significant, and, with 95.4 percent of the cases correctly classified, the model reflects a 43 percent reduction in error.

6. Assuming, that is, the case makes it to the merits stage; on closer inspection, the justices may dismiss the case as improvidently granted (see Perry 1991, 106–12).

7. Calculating these percentages requires some explanation. I used a lawyer's total number of cases during the 1977–82 period as a means of characterizing his or her experience in the Supreme Court for any given case. Thus, irrespective of whether a case was decided in, say, 1979 or 1982, the value of counsel's experience is equal to the total number of cases on the merits across all six years. This approach, of course, has some drawbacks. In cases heard earlier during the period, for instance, lawyers with multiple appearances are treated as having more experience than they actually had at the time. In addition, this method takes no account of the improving ability of lawyers as a result of experience. The alternative, however—keeping a running tally of each lawyer's record and applying it in each case—encounters a far greater difficulty: it assumes that 1977 is the starting point for all lawyers appearing before the Court. For example, given this method, one would assign a value of o previous cases to the solicitor general's first case in 1977 and a value in excess of one hundred for his last case in 1982—hardly a sound statistical strategy. Instead, I chose to aggregate experience and assume, quite plausibly, that those six years were indicative of a continuing pattern of participation. Another methodological note: Often, several lawyers represent a single party in a case. To characterize the degree of prior Supreme Court practice, I simply chose the lawyer with the greatest number of cases on the merits and assigned that value as the party's level of Supreme Court experience.

8. If, for instance, one divides the sample by the ideological direction of the lower court and recomputes the percentages in table 8.3, the success rates for the bar remain virtually unchanged, regardless of whether the lower court's decision was liberal or conservative.

9. As it happens, including the solicitor general's cases in the calculation of these percentages makes virtually no difference.

BIBLIOGRAPHY

Abel, Richard L. 1989. *American Lawyers.* New York: Oxford Univ. Press.

Abraham, Henry J. 1986. *The Judicial Process.* New York: Oxford Univ. Press.

Aiken, Michael, and Paul E. Mott, eds. 1970. *The Structure of Community Power.* New York: Random House.

Alba, Richard A., and Gwen Moore. 1982. "Ethnicity and the American Elite." *American Sociological Review* 47:373–83.

Aldrich, John H., and Forrest D. Nelson. 1984. *Linear Probability, Logit and Probit Models.* Beverly Hills, Calif.: Sage.

Alexander, Holmes Moss. 1958. *The Famous Five.* New York: Bookmailer.

American Bar Association Journal. 1983. "LawPoll."

Armstrong, Virginia C., and Charles A. Johnson. 1982. "Certiorari Decisions by the Warren and Burger Courts: Is Cue Theory Time Bound?" *Polity* 15:141–50.

Atkins, Burton A. 1991. "Party Capability Theory as an Explanation for Intervention Behavior in the English Court of Appeal." *American Journal of Political Science* 35:881–903.

Auerbach, Carl A. 1984. "Legal Education and Its Discontents." *Journal of Legal Education* 34:73–76.

Baker, Stewart A. 1984. "A Practical Guide to Certiorari." *Catholic University Law Review* 33:611–32.

Barker, Lucius J. 1967. "Third Parties in Litigation: A Systemic View of the Judicial Function." *Journal of Politics* 29:41–69.

Baum, Lawrence. 1977. "Policy Goals in Judicial Gatekeeping: A Proximity Model of Discretionary Jurisdiction." *American Journal of Political Science* 21:13–36.

———. 1986. *American Courts: Policy and Process.* Boston: Houghton Mifflin.

———. 1987. "Explaining the Burger Court's Support for Civil Liberties." *PS* 20:21–28.

———. 1989. *The Supreme Court.* 3d ed. Washington, D.C.: CQ Press.

Baxter, Maurice G. 1966. *Daniel Webster and the Supreme Court.* Amherst: Univ. of Massachusetts Press.

Bellows, Paul F. 1988–89. "Branches: Key to Growth." *The National Law Journal*, Dec. 26–Jan. 2.

Berry, Jeffrey M. 1989. *The Interest Group Society.* Boston: Little, Brown.

Black, Henry Campbell. 1979. *Black's Law Dictionary.* St. Paul: West.

Blalock, Hubert M. 1979. *Social Statistics.* Rev. 2d ed. New York: McGraw-Hill.

Bowers v. Hardwick. 1986. 478 U.S. 186.

Brenner, Saul. 1979. "The New Certiorari Game." *Journal of Politics* 41:649–55.

Brigance, William Norwood. 1934. *Jeremiah Sullivan Black: A Defender of the Constitution and the Ten Commandments.* Philadelphia: Univ. of Pennsylvania Press.

Butler, Charles Henry. 1942. *A Century at the Bar of the Supreme Court of the United States.* New York: G. P. Putnam's Sons.

Caldeira, Gregory A., and Samuel C. Patterson. 1987. "Political Friendship in the Legislature." *Journal of Politics* 49:953–75.

Caldeira, Gregory A., and John R. Wright. 1988. "Organized Interests and Agenda Setting in the U.S. Supreme Court." *American Political Science Review* 82:1109–27.

——. 1990a. "Amici Curiae before the Supreme Court: Who Participates, When, and How Much?" *Journal of Politics* 52:782–806.

——. 1990b. "The Discuss List: Agenda Building in the Supreme Court." *Law and Society Review* 24:807–36.

Caplan, Lincoln. 1987. *The Tenth Justice.* New York: Alfred A. Knopf.

Carlin, Jerome E. 1962. *Lawyers on Their Own: A Study of Individual Practitioners in Chicago.* New Brunswick, N.J.: Rutgers Univ. Press.

Casper, Jonathan D. 1972. *Lawyers before the Warren Court: Civil Liberties and Civil Rights, 1957–1966.* Urbana: Univ. of Illinois Press.

Cipollone v. Liggett Group, Inc. 1992. 60 L.W. 3027.

The Complete Oral Arguments of the Supreme Court of the United States, 1969–1979 Terms. 1982. Frederick, Md.: University Publications of America.

Craig, Barbara Hinkson. 1988. *Chadha: The Story of an Epic Constitutional Struggle.* New York: Oxford Univ. Press.

Curran, Barbara A. 1986. "American Lawyers in the 1980s: A Profession in Transition." *Law and Society Review* 20:19–52.

Curran, Barbara A., Katherine J. Rosich, Clara N. Carson, and Mark C. Puccetti. 1985. *The Lawyer Statistical Report: A Statistical Profile of the U.S. Legal Profession in the 1980s.* Chicago: American Bar Foundation.

——. 1986. *Supplement to the Lawyer Statistical Report: The U.S. Legal Profession in 1985.* Chicago: American Bar Foundation.

Dahl, Robert. 1961. *Who Governs? Democracy and Power in an American City.* New Haven: Yale Univ. Press.

Dames & Moore v. Regan. 1981. 453 U.S. 654.

Dartmouth College v. Woodward. 1819. 4 Wheat 517.

Davis, John W. 1940. "The Argument of an Appeal." *American Bar Association Journal* 26:895–99.

Davis, Kingsley, and Wilbert E. Moore. 1970. "Some Principles of Stratification." In *The Logic of Social Hierarchies,* ed. Edward O. Laumann, Paul M. Siegel, and Robert W. Hodge. Chicago: Markham.

Delaplaine, Edward S. 1937. *Francis Scott Key: Life and Times.* New York: Biography Press.

Denniston, Lyle. 1985. "No Questions Asked: Three Pros Wow the Court." *The American Lawyer,* July / August: 108.

Douglas, William O. 1949. "Stare Decisis." Eighth Annual Benjamin N. Cardozo Lecture delivered before the Association of the Bar of the City of New York. In *Courts, Judges, and Politics: An Introduction to the Judicial Process,* ed. Walter F. Murphy and C. Hermann Pritchett. New York: Random House, 1979.

Dreyfuss, Joel, and Charles Lawrence III. 1979. *The Bakke Case: The Politics of Inequality.* New York: Harcourt Brace Jovanovich.

Dye, Thomas R. 1990. *Who's Running America? The Bush Era.* Englewood Cliffs, N.J.: Prentice-Hall.

Ennis, Bruce J. 1984. "Effective Amicus Briefs." *Catholic University Law Review* 33:603–9.

Epstein, Lee. 1985. *Conservatives in Court.* Knoxville: Univ. of Tennessee Press.

Epstein, Lee, and Karen O'Connor. 1988. "States and the U.S. Supreme Court: An Examination of Litigation Outcomes." *Social Science Quarterly* 68:660–74.

Erlanger, Howard S. 1978. "Lawyers and Neighborhood Legal Service: Social Background and the Impetus for Reform." *Law and Society Review* 12:253–74.

Fisk, Margaret Cronin. 1990. "Winning: Successful Strategies from 10 of the Nation's Top Litigators." *National Law Journal,* Feb. 12:S1–S15.

Frank, John Paul. 1958. *Marble Palace: The Supreme Court in American Life.* New York: Alfred A. Knopf.

Frey, Andrew L., Kenneth S. Geller, and Daniel Harris. 1987. "Opposing Review: The Art of Finding 'Uncertworthiness.'" *Inside Litigation* 1:27–30.

Galanter, Marc. 1974. "Why the 'Haves' Come Out Ahead: Speculations on the Limits of Legal Change." *Law and Society Review* 9:95–160.

Galanter, Marc, and Thomas Palay. 1991. *Tournament of Lawyers: The Transformation of the Big Law Firm.* Chicago: Univ. of Chicago Press.

Garland, Augustus Hill. 1983. *Experience in the Supreme Court of the United States.* Littleton, Colo: Fred B. Rothman.

Gibbons v. Ogden. 1824. 9 Wheat. 1.

Gideon v. Wainwright. 1962. 372 U.S. 335.

Goulden, Joseph C. 1972. *The Superlawyers.* New York: Weybright and Talley.

Gourman, Jack. 1987. *The Gourman Report: A Rating of Graduate and Professional Programs in American and International Universities.* 4th ed. Los Angeles: National Education Standards.

Greenya, John. 1987. "Supreme Lawyers." *The Washington Lawyer,* May / June.

Handler, Joel. 1967. *The Lawyer and His Community.* Madison: Univ. of Wisconsin Press.

Hansen, John Mark. 1991. *Gaining Access.* Chicago: Univ. of Chicago Press.

Hanushek, Eric A., and John E. Jackson. 1977. *Statistical Methods for Social Scientists.* Orlando, Fla.: Academic Press, Inc.

Hayes, Arthur S. 1989. "Supreme Court Specialty: Does It Work?" *The American Lawyer*, June.

Heinz, John P., and Edward O. Laumann. 1982. *Chicago Lawyers: The Social Structure of the Bar*. New York: Russell Sage Foundation.

Hiller, E. T. 1941. "The Community as a Social Group." *American Sociological Review* 6:189–202.

Hillery, George A., Jr. 1955. "Definitions of Community: Areas of Agreement." *Rural Sociology* 20:111–23.

Hunter, Floyd. 1953. *Community Power Structure: A Study of Decision Makers*. Chapel Hill: Univ. of North Carolina Press.

INS v. Chadha. 1983. 462 U.S. 919.

Ireland, Robert M. 1986. *The Legal Career of William Pinkney: 1764–1822*. New York: Garland.

Irons, Peter H. 1982. *The New Deal Lawyers*. Princeton: Princeton University Press.

——. 1990. *The Courage of Their Convictions*. New York: Penguin Books.

Ivers, Gregg, and Karen O'Connor. 1987. "Friends as Foes: The Amicus Curiae Participation and Effectiveness of the American Civil Liberties Union and the Americans for Effective Law Enforcement in Criminal Cases, 1969–1982." *Law and Policy* 9:161–78.

Jackson, Robert H. 1951. "Advocacy before the Supreme Court: Suggestions for Effective Case Presentations." *American Bar Association Journal* 37:801–4.

Jacob, Herbert. 1984. *Justice in America*. 4th ed. Boston: Little, Brown.

Jenkins, John A. 1983. "The Solicitor General's Winning Ways." *American Bar Association Journal* 69:734–38.

Kerlow, Eleanor. 1990. "Supreme Payoff for Clerks: $35,000 Bonus." *Legal Times of Washington* September 17.

——. 1991. "Onek, Klein's Demise Signals Closing of Era." *Legal Times of Washington*, May 27.

Kim, Jae-On, and Charles W. Mueller. 1978. *Introduction to Factor Analysis*. Beverly Hills, Calif.: Sage.

Kluger, Richard. 1975. *Simple Justice: The History of Brown v. Board of Education and Black America's Struggle for Equality*. New York: Alfred A. Knopf.

Knoke, David. 1990. *Political Networks: The Structural Perspective*. New York: Cambridge Univ. Press.

Krislov, Samuel. 1965. *The Supreme Court in the Political Process*. New York: Macmillan.

Kruskal, Joseph B., and Myron Wish. 1978. *Multidimensional Scaling*. Beverly Hills, Calif.: Sage.

Landon, Donald D. 1985. "Clients, Colleagues, and Community: The Shaping of Zealous Advocacy in Country Law Practice." *American Bar Foundation Research Journal*, Winter: 81–111.

Laumann, Edward O. 1966. *Prestige and Association in an Urban Community.* Indianapolis: Bobbs-Merrill.

———. 1973. *Bonds of Pluralism: The Forms and Substance of Urban Social Networks.* New York: Wiley.

Laumann, Edward O., Paul M. Siegel, and Robert W. Hodge. 1970. *The Logic of Social Hierarchies.* Chicago: Markham.

Lauter, David. 1987. "The Best Argument That Money Can Buy?" *The National Law Journal,* Jan. 26.

Lawrence, Susan E. 1990. *The Poor in Court: The Legal Services Program and Supreme Court Decision Making.* Princeton, N.J.: Princeton Univ. Press.

Lempert, Larry. 1982. "DOJ Loans Lawyer to NAAG to Follow High Court." *Legal Times of Washington,* Aug. 30.

Lewis, Walker. 1965. *Without Fear or Favor.* Boston: Houghton Mifflin.

McCloskey, Robert G. 1960. *The American Supreme Court.* Chicago: Univ. of Chicago Press.

McCulloch v. Maryland. 1819. 4 Wheat. 315.

Marcotte, Paul. 1986. "Dress Rehearsal." *American Bar Association Journal* 72:26.

Margolick, David. 1992. "Abortion-Rights Team Leaves A.C.L.U." *New York Times,* May 21.

Martineau, Robert J. 1983. *Modern Appellate Practice: Federal and State Civil Appeals.* Rochester, N.Y.: Lawyers Co-Operative.

Mauro, Tony. 1988. "Corporate Lawyer 'Quayles' Before Court." *Legal Times of Washington,* Oct. 24.

———. 1989a. "Drama, Subtleties at Abortion Argument." *Legal Times of Washington,* Dec. 4.

———. 1989b. "Rehnquist Rumbles as Marshall Stumbles." *Legal Times of Washington,* Nov. 6.

———. 1990a. "What's Wrong with Oral Argument?" *Legal Times of Washington,* Apr. 16.

———. 1990b. "Court Gets a Tad Less Friendly to Amici." *Legal Times of Washington,* Feb. 19.

———. 1990c. "Damaging the Anti-Punitive Crusade." *Legal Times of Washington,* Oct. 8.

———. 1990d. "How Advocates Pay for Shrinking Docket." *Legal Times of Washington,* Jan. 22.

Michigan State Police v. Sitz. 1990. 110 S.Ct. 2481.

Mills, C. Wright. 1956. "The Higher Circles." In *The Logic of Social Hierarchies,* ed. Edward O. Laumann, Paul M. Siegel, and Robert W. Hodge. Chicago: Markham, 1970.

Minar, David W., and Scott Greer. 1969. *The Concept of Community.* Chicago: Aldine.

Missouri v. Jenkins. 1990. 110 S.Ct. 1651.

Nelson, Robert L. 1981. "Practice and Privilege: Social Change and the Structure of Large Law Firms." *American Bar Foundation Research Journal,* Winter: 95–140.

——. 1988. *Partners with Power.* Berkeley: Univ. of California Press.

Nelson, Robert L., John P. Heinz, Edward O. Laumann, and Robert H. Salisbury. 1988. "Lawyers and the Structure of Influence in Washington." *Law and Society Review* 22:235–300.

Neubauer, David W. 1991. *Judicial Process: Law, Courts, and Politics in the United States.* Pacific Grove, Calif.: Brooks / Cole.

Nie, Norman H., Sidney Verba, and John R. Petrocik. 1979. *The Changing American Voter.* Cambridge: Harvard Univ. Press.

Northeast Bancorporation v. The Federal Reserve System. 1984. 472 U.S. 159.

O'Brien, David M. 1990. *Storm Center: The Supreme Court in American Politics.* New York: W. W. Norton.

O'Connor, Karen, and Lee Epstein. 1982. "Amicus Curiae Participation in the U.S. Supreme Court: An Appraisal of Hakman's Folklore." *Law and Society Review* 16:311–20.

——. 1989. *Public Interest Law Groups: Institutional Profiles.* Westport, Conn.: Greenwood Press.

The Official Guide to U.S. Law Schools 1990–91. 1990. Newtown, Pa.: Law School Admission Services.

Ogden v. Saunders. 1827. 12 Wheat. 212.

Olson, Betsy G. 1984. "Veteran Advocates Unfazed by High Court's Rigor." *Legal Times of Washington,* Apr. 30.

Olson, Susan M. 1984. *Clients and Lawyers: Securing the Rights of Disabled Persons.* Westport, Conn.: Greenwood Press.

O'Neill, Timothy J. 1985. *Bakke and the Politics of Equality: Friends and Foes in the Classroom of Litigation.* Middletown, Conn: Wesleyan Univ. Press.

Pennzoil v. Texaco. 1986. 481 U.S. 1.

Perry, H. W., Jr. 1991. *Deciding to Decide.* Cambridge: Harvard Univ. Press.

Polsby, Nelson W. 1970. "How to Study Community Power: The Pluralist Alternative." In *The Structure of Community Power,* ed. Michael Aiken and Paul E. Mott. New York: Random House.

Prettyman, E. Barrett. 1953. "Some Observations Concerning Appellate Advocacy." *Virginia Law Review* 39:285–302.

Prettyman, E. Barrett, Jr. 1978. "Supreme Court Advocacy: Random Thoughts in a Day of Time Restrictions." *Litigation* 4:16–20.

——. 1984. "The Supreme Court's Use of Hypothetical Questions at Oral Argument." *Catholic University Law Review* 33:555–91.

Provine, D. Marie. 1980. *Case Selection in the United States Supreme Court.* Chicago: Univ. of Chicago Press.

Regents of the University of California v. Bakke. 1978. 438 U.S. 265.

Rehnquist, William H. 1987. *The Supreme Court: How It Was, How It Is.* New York: William Morrow.

———. 1989. Speech delivered at the Daniel Webster Symposium, Dartmouth College, Hanover, N.H., May 12.

Reuben, Richard. 1989. "Tribe Record Establishes Him as One of Premier Supreme Court Advocates." *Chicago Daily Law Bulletin,* Nov. 2.

Runyon v. McCrary. 1976. 427 U.S. 160.

Salisbury, Robert H., John P. Heinz, Edward O. Laumann, and Robert L. Nelson. 1987. "Who Works with Whom? Interest Group Alliances and Opposition." *American Political Science Review* 81:1217–34.

San Antonio Independent School District v. Rodriguez. 1973. 411 U.S. 1.

Sarat, Austin, and William L. F. Felstiner. 1986. "Law and Strategy in the Divorce Lawyer's Office." *Law and Society Review* 20:93–134.

Schlozman, Kay L., and John T. Tierney. 1986. *Organized Interests and American Democracy.* New York: Harper and Row.

Segal, Jeffrey A. 1984. "Predicting Supreme Court Cases Probabilistically: The Search and Seizure Cases, 1962–1981." *American Political Science Review* 78:891–900.

Segal, Jeffrey A., and Cheryl D. Reedy. 1988. "The Supreme Court and Sex Discrimination: The Role of the Solicitor General." *Western Political Quarterly* 41:553–68.

Shapiro, Stephen M. 1984. "Oral Argument in the Supreme Court of the United States." *Catholic University Law Review* 33:529–53.

———. 1987. "William Pinkney—The Supreme Court's Greatest Advocate." *Litigation* 13:63–67.

Smigel, E. O. 1964. *The Wall Street Lawyer: Professional Organization Man?* New York: Free Press.

Songer, Donald R. 1979. "Concern for Policy Outputs as a Cue for Supreme Court Decisions on Certiorari." *Journal of Politics* 41:1185–94.

Songer, Donald R., and Reginald S. Sheehan. 1992. "Who Wins on Appeal? Upperdogs and Underdogs in the United States Courts of Appeals." *American Journal of Political Science* 36:235–58.

Sorauf, Frank J. 1976. *The Wall of Separation: The Constitutional Politics of Church and State.* Princeton, N.J.: Princeton Univ. Press.

Stanley, Harold W., and Richard G. Niemi. 1990. *Vital Statistics on American Politics.* Washington, D.C.: CQ Press.

Statistical Abstract of the United States. 1990. Washington, D.C.: U.S. Bureau of the Census.

———. 1991. Washington, D.C.: U.S. Bureau of the Census.

Stern, Robert H. 1981. *Appellate Practice in the United States.* Washington, D.C.: Bureau of National Affairs.

Stern, Robert H., Eugene Gressman, and Stephen M. Shapiro. 1986. *Supreme Court Practice*. 6th ed. Washington, D.C.: Bureau of National Affairs.

Stover, Robert V. 1981–82. "The Importance of Economic Supply in Determining the Size and Quality of the Public Interest Bar." *Law and Society Review* 16:455–80.

Sylvester, Kathleen. 1984. "Getting Ready for the Supreme Court." *The National Law Journal*, Mar. 5.

Tanenhaus, Joseph, Marvin Schick, Matthew Muraskin, and Daniel Rosen. 1963. "The Supreme Court's Certiorari Jurisdiction: Cue Theory." In *Judicial Decision-Making*, ed. Glendon Schubert. New York: Free Press.

Teger, Stuart H., and Douglas Kosinski. 1980. "The Cue Theory of Supreme Court Certiorari Jurisdiction: A Reconsideration." *Journal of Politics* 42:834–46.

Tigar, Michael E. 1987. *Federal Appeals: Jurisdiction and Practice*. Colorado Springs, Colo.: Shepard's / McGraw-Hill.

Twiss, Benjamin R. 1942. *Lawyers and the Constitution*. Princeton, N.J.: Princeton Univ. Press.

Ulmer, S. Sidney. 1978. "Selecting Cases for Supreme Court Review: An Underdog Model." *American Political Science Review* 72:902–10.

———. 1984. "The Supreme Court's Certiorari Decisions: Conflict as a Predictive Variable." *American Political Science Review* 78:901–11.

Vago, Steven. 1991. *Law and Society*. Englewood Cliffs, N.J.: Prentice-Hall.

Walker, Jack L. 1983. "The Origins and Maintenance of Interest Groups in America." *American Political Science Review* 77:390–406.

Walton, John. 1970. "A Systematic Survey of Community Power Research." In *The Structure of Community Power*, ed. Michael Aiken and Paul E. Mott. New York: Random House.

Warren, Charles. 1926. *The Supreme Court in United States History*. Boston: Little, Brown.

———. 1939. *A History of the American Bar*. New York: Howard Fertig.

Wasby, Stephen L. 1984. "How Planned is 'Planned' Litigation?" *American Bar Foundation Research Journal* Winter: 83–138.

———. 1988. *The Supreme Court in the Federal Judicial System*. Chicago: Nelson-Hall.

Weisberg, Herbert F. 1974. "Dimensionland: An Excursion into Spaces." In *Theory-Building and Data Analysis in the Social Sciences*, ed. Herbert B. Asher, Herbert F. Weisberg, John H. Kessel, and W. Phillips Shively. Knoxville: Univ. of Tennessee, 1984.

Wermiel, Stephen. 1989. "More Litigants Turn to Appeals Specialists." *Wall Street Journal*, July 5.

Wheeler, Stanton, Bliss Cartwright, Robert A. Kagan, and Lawrence M. Friedman. 1987. "Do the 'Haves' Come Out Ahead? Winning and Losing in State Supreme Courts, 1870–1970." *Law and Society Review* 21:403–45.

White, G. Edward. 1988. *The Marshall Court and Cultural Change, 1815–35*, vols. 3 and 4 of *History of the Supreme Court of the United States*. New York: Macmillan.

Who Was Who in America. 1963. Historical Volume 1607–1896. Chicago: A. N. Marquis.

Wice, Paul. 1991. *Judges and Lawyers: The Human Side of Justice.* New York: Harper Collins.

Wiener, Frederick Bernays. 1967. *Briefing and Arguing Federal Appeals.* Washington, D.C.: Bureau of National Affairs.

Wolfinger, Raymond E. 1970. "Reputation and Reality in the Study of 'Community Power.'" In *The Structure of Community Power,* ed. Michael Aiken and Paul E. Mott. New York: Random House.

Young, James Sterling. 1966. *The Washington Community 1800–1828.* New York: Harcourt, Brace, and World.